EARNINGS MAGIC AND THE UNBALANCE SHEET

EARNINGS MAGIC AND THE UNBALANCE SHEET

THE SEARCH FOR FINANCIAL REALITY

GARY GIROUX

WILEY

JOHN WILEY & SONS, INC.

Library of Congress Cataloging-in-Publication Data:

ISBN-13 978-0-471-76855-5
ISBN-10 0-471-76855-3

Printed in the United States of America

10 9 8 7 6 5 4 3 2 1

ABOUT THE AUTHOR

Gary Giroux is Shelton Professor of Accounting at Texas A&M University. He received his Ph.D. from Texas Tech University and has been at Texas A&M for over two and a half decades. He teaches financial analysis and other financial and governmental courses in the undergraduate program. He also teaches research methods in the Ph.D. program.

Dr. Giroux has published over 50 articles, including publications in *Accounting Review; Journal of Accounting Research; Accounting Organizations and Society; Journal of Accounting and Public Policy,* and numerous other journals. He is the author of five earlier books, including *Financial Analysis: A User Approach, Detecting Earnings Management,* and *Dollars & Scholars, Scribes & Bribes: The Story of Accounting.* His primary research areas are governmental and financial accounting. He also is interested in accounting and business history.

CONTENTS

PREFACE

After the swell Y2K party, the twenty-first century quickly saw a stock market collapse, recession, and one corporate scandal after another. For me, Enron and the Houston office of Arthur Andersen were nearby, unlike Wall Street. Since I teach financial statement analysis at Texas A&M (about 90 miles north of Houston), I should have understood what happened at Enron. But I did not. It took the 2001 Enron earnings restatements, the Powers Report on the scandal, and research on special-purpose entities to start to figure it out. Not very useful after Enron declared bankruptcy and frustrating given that a major purpose of financial analysis is to predict both success and failure.

I wrote a short financial analysis textbook, which had its share of content and analysis—but was short on predicting scandals. My frustration led, in part, to writing a textbook, *Detecting Earnings Management,* specifically to evaluate the viability of financial disclosures. The basic lesson of that book was that there exist signals of potential financial corruption and misstated earnings. Equally important is the difficulty of measuring financial reality for a complex corporation—one measure of transparency (i.e., complete and accurate reporting) and earnings quality. This is partly based on manipulation but also based on the complexities of financial reporting and accounting standards. Considerable information is disclosed, but it is not necessarily easy to interpret. Extensive disclosures also may be incomplete or deceptive. The process of measuring economic reality is not impossible, but it is difficult.

There have been big changes since Enron, WorldCom, and the other financial fiascos. Eliot Spitzer became a household name prosecuting major Wall Street firms, insurers, mutual fund companies, and other corporate bad guys. Congressional hearings led to the Sarbanes-Oxley Act of 2002, a major overhaul of financial regulation and expanded oversight of the key players. The theory is that this should vastly improve relevant oversight and regulation and make earnings magic (at least the really blatant stuff) difficult, if not impossible. There are reasons to be optimistic—key factors are in place for effective oversight. However, it still pays to be skeptical. Earnings magic is alive and well, and corporate scandals still happen.

Experts exist on any aspect of economic and legal complexity, but it is not clear to what extent detailed financial analysis is incorporated in most professional analysis and advice. It turns out that many signals exist of a potential manipulation environment and earnings, and other financial information can be reevaluated to better understand economic reality. Part of the analysis requires an understanding of the new institutional framework, including oversight and regulation brought about by Sarbanes-Oxley. Signals of adequate compliance (superb compliance is better) exist and represent a significant part of the earnings magic analysis.

ABOUT THIS BOOK

Given the stock market collapse and one corporate scandal after another, what is a financial professional to do? Stock prices should be based largely on current earnings and earnings potential, but the recent scandals suggest that the earnings numbers presented were not reliable. Executives have incentives to manage earnings to meet analyst forecasts and, thus, increase their own bonuses and stock options. Accounting alternatives allow considerable flexibility, some aggressive and perhaps of questionable ethics. Boards of directors may think they work for the chief executive officer (CEO) rather than the stockholders. Financial analysts working for investment bankers have incentives to puff up the growth potential for investment bank customers. Auditors might push the interests of their corporate clients rather than protect the public interest. Regulators are subject to a political environment not necessarily interested in economic reality.

New regulations should make the financial information environment more reliable and oversight more extensive, but the incentives of key actors have not changed. Presumably executives face a greater threat of being fined, canned, and facing substantial slammer time. How can an investor protect his or her stock portfolio? How can an analyst make accurate projections? The rule is still *caveat emptor,* which means serious analysis when it is difficult to tell which numbers are believable. The premise is that financial reality can be estimated and the relative amount of financial transparency determined—with a little effort. That is the purpose of this book. Based on relatively simple analytical goals and a review of the current regulatory environment, the interested investor or professional can analyze the environment for manipulation and also recast the financial numbers to achieve more accuracy.

The investor/professional should do the analysis, evaluate the major issues, restate the information when appropriate, estimate the financial reality of the corporation, and make decisions accordingly. For example: Invest when the potential for growth exists, when business strategy is reasonable, corporate governance is strong, and when earnings quality is high. When business strategy is questionable, governance is suspect, major financial concerns exist, and earnings quality is considered poor, get out. If the stock is cheap, perhaps take the risk. But know the odds before investing.

This book is designed to provide a relatively straightforward approach specifically to make the analysis doable. Starting with a basic overview strategy, the financial environment is reviewed. Corporate governance, the regulatory environment, the tools available for analysis, and the incentives of major players provide the background for the analysis. The sources of financial data include the annual and quarterly reports, the proxy statement, the financial media, and a whole host of Internet tools.

This is not as daunting as it seems. Specific information provides the foundation for analysis. Several key accounting issues are the primary focus. Individual companies have different areas of concern. For example, pension accounting becomes an issue for analysis only if the corporation has a defined benefit pension plan. This is a big problem for General Motors. If no defined benefit plan exists, check that issue off and go on to the next one. Microsoft, Apple, and most high-tech companies have 401-K plans that are not a problem. (These are defined contribution plans, and the companies have no further retirement obligations to the employees.) With a bit of effort, the analyst can understand the basic business strategy, the strengths and weaknesses of the governance structure, the initial fit to quantitative analysis, and the level of earnings quality after the analysis is complete. An analysis checklist and investment scoring system simplify the process.

We will focus on the Dow Jones Industrial Average (Dow 30)—30 of America's largest and most distinguished corporations. No chance of earnings magic—right? They report economic reality—right? Well, Dow member AIG is the major corporate scandal of 2005. I will demonstrate that auto giant and Dow 30 member General Motors really has negative equity —one definition of financial failure! The Dow has two banks with a trillion dollars in assets (Citigroup and J.P. Morgan) that make markets in derivatives and use special-purpose entities on such a vast scale that it is virtually impossible to estimate the underlying risks involved.

Chapter Summary

A summary of chapter content is shown in Exhibit P.1.

Section 1: Earnings Magic and the Unbalanced Sheet	This section explains the problems, the incentives for abuse, the institutional and regulatory framework, and the information available for analysis.
1. What Is Earnings Magic? Does the Balance Sheet Balance?	Does the CFO need another nickel to meet the analysts' EPS forecast this quarter? Thanks to earnings magic, this is possible. Here is why and how this is possible.
2. Caught in the Act!	Companies do get caught fudging the numbers—here is how and why. A few examples of the big, bad, and ugly are included. These indicate some of the ways to game the system and what to look for in future abuse.
3. The New Accounting	Thanks to the Sarbanes-Oxley Act and a host of new regulations, the institutional framework has improved dramatically to provide quality financial information. Particularly important are the new corporate governance and auditing requirements.
4. Wading Through the Earnings Numbers	This chapter provides a review of basic strategy on finding the relevant financial data, financial analysis techniques that provide considerable information, and the basic tools to dig deeper into the reports.
Section 2: The Big 8 and Dirty 30: Key Accounting Issues That Signal Earnings Magic	This section explains the technical finance stuff made (relatively) easy. These are the 30 issues that can raise concerns and signal potential abuse that financial reality may be missing. The Big 8 are the biggest and baddest of the Dirty 30 and a separate chapter is devoted to each.
5. Key Accounting Issues: An Overview	First things first: An overview analysis indicates major strengths and weaknesses and suggests likely places to look for abuse. A digression on industry issues is included.
6. Stock Options	Stock options were the compensation of choice in the 1990s, especially for high-tech companies. According to GAAP, options do not have to be expensed until 2006. But options dilute equity and are real expenses. The information is available to make these adjustments and evaluate the real economic impact of options (including recalculating earnings to treat options as a compensation expense).
7. Pension Plans and Other Postemployment Benefits	Defined benefit plans mean corporations have long-term obligations to employees. The major issue is whether the pension plan is fully funded (based both on GAAP and financial reality—they are not the same). Also of concern is the amount recorded for pension expense, which can be deceptive. Other postemployment benefits (OPEBs) are additional obligations that are almost always underfunded; there is a difference between GAAP and economic reality for OPEB as well.
8. Revenues	Many corporate scandals involve aggressive revenue recognition (the most infamous ones involve fraud). The information becomes available only after the fact—when they have been caught. The trick is looking

(continues)

EXHIBIT P.1   CHAPTER SUMMARY

8. Revenues (Continued)	for signals of an environment conducive to aggressive revenue recognition.
9. Earnings, Expenses, and Expectations	There are many ways to manipulate (or even to define) the bottom line. Here are some considerations and things to look for.
10. Strange Special Items and Other Things That Should Not Be on the Income Statement	Some companies have special charges every year; other companies have various nonrecurring items more often than not. These are items that are not supposed to be there and can complicate the analysis.
11. Treasury Stock and Dividends	Treasury stock is the buying back of the company's shares in the open market. The most common reason is to "fund" outstanding stock options (to prevent dilution). However, doing this reduces both cash and equity; using treasury stock can signal potential problems and possible manipulation. The other use of cash for investors is to pay dividends. Analyzing stock options, treasury stock, and dividends simultaneously is a good strategy.
12. Off–Balance Sheet Items: Operating Leases and Special-Purpose Entities	Several categories of items do not show up on the balance sheet, with unrecorded liabilities of particular concern. Operating leases are significant for many industries, but note disclosure provides the information needed to reevaluate the outstanding obligations. Special-purpose entities (SPEs) have become common financing techniques over the last 25 years and have extraordinary flexibility to keep liabilities off the balance sheet. Remember that Enron was the SPE manipulation champ.
13. Acquisitions and All That Goodwill	Business combinations have been central to the development of American big business over the last 150 years. Thanks to the accounting magic of business combinations, it is very difficult to see through the real economic impact of acquisitions. A company can "look good" financially going on an acquisition binge when, in fact, the acquisitions have been disasters. If goodwill is the biggest asset category, look out. One interpretation of goodwill is the likely "overpayment" for acquisitions. Another form of off–balance-sheet magic is the use of the equity method to "hide" what are called unconsolidated affiliates. The difficulty is determining when these techniques are used for valid economic purposes and when they are used for manipulation.
14. Dishonorable Mention: The Rest of the Dirty 30	Many financial statement items, complex accounting issues, and audit and corporate governance concerns can signal earnings management and camouflage transparency.
Section 3: Putting It All Together	This is where it pays off—putting it all together in a comprehensive analysis and scoring the relative financial reality.
15. Signals of Financial Excellence and Earnings Magic	Disclosure should be complete, extensive, easy to find and evaluate, and free from obvious distortion. This is true for annual and quarterly reports as well as the proxy

(continues)

Exhibit P.1 Chapter Summary (continued)

15. Signals of Financial Excellence (Continued)	statement and the information available on the company's Web site.
16. A Checklist for Evaluating Financial Excellence	A scoring sheet is developed to evaluate each company; then the accumulated analysis is converted to quality scores, A to F.
17. An Investment Strategy	A simple investment strategy is introduced to incorporate the earnings magic checklist.
18. Searching for Help: Useful Internet Sites	Almost all public information is available on the Internet. This chapter presents the most useful sources and has hints for how to navigate the net effectively.

EXHIBIT P.1 CHAPTER SUMMARY (CONTINUED)

Categories to Investigate Earnings Magic

The keys to evaluating relative financial excellence are summarized in categories in Exhibit P.2.

	Accounting Excellence	Red Flags
Financial and Market Analysis	A quantitative and qualitative overview provides the starting point for further analysis.	Any unusual item, including ratios and big unexplained changes over time.
Big 8	Major areas for earnings magic, including options, pensions, revenue recognition, expenses and bottom line, nonrecurring and special items, treasury stock, off–balance sheet items, and acquisitions.	A whole host of issues including substantial stock options outstanding, underfunded pensions and other postemployment benefits, revenue and expense issues, lots of special items, substantial treasury stock, emphasis on off–balance sheet items, and massive goodwill.
Detailed Financial Analysis	Evaluation of liquidity, credit risk, and other quantitative analysis.	Low liquidity, high leverage, poor or erratic performance, unusual patterns and balances in financial statement items.
Complex Accounting Issues	Additional issues such as derivatives, contingencies, or use of the equity method.	Mainly a qualitative analysis looking for evidence of potential problems.
Corporate Governance	Board composed of competent, independent members, strong auditing and compensation committees, "reasonable" executive compensation based on performance.	Poor board committee structure; outrageous executive compensation at poorly performing companies.
Auditing	The auditor and opinion, including internal control evaluation and audit fees; audit committee.	Late audit report date, internal control weaknesses reported; substantial nonaudit fees.

EXHIBIT P.2 SUMMARY OF CATEGORIES FOR EVALUATING RELATIVE FINANCIAL EXCELLENCE

With financial excellence evaluated in an earnings magic score, most investments would come from the top categories. Buys from lower categories suggest increased risk and would have to be based on other overriding factors, such as a bargain price. This may be considered a part of value investing (or casino investing for the skeptic).

EARNINGS MAGIC AND THE UNBALANCE SHEET

Section 1

EARNINGS MAGIC AND THE UNBALANCED SHEET

Is there any reason to have much faith in the finances of corporations after Enron, WorldCom, and the other financial fiascos? The short answer is a qualified yes. The long answer is the content of Section 1. Real incentives exist for financial executives to cheat, and the institutional environment may be accommodating. The system may be repaired, thanks to Sarbanes-Oxley, energized (and better-funded) regulators, plus the shock of the repercussions (including serious slammer time for key executives) of fraud and failure.

This section defines earnings magic and gives a little history of the corporate crooks, the changes in the regulatory structure, and some financial analysis basics and tools—step one to financial genius. Included are the reasons for continued skepticism. The incentives are still there, companies are still cheating—and getting caught—and the environment has the flexibility to game the system.

Chapter	Discussion
1. What Is Earnings Magic? Does the Balance Sheet Balance?	This chapter provides an overview of the environment, particularly the incentives of participants to cheat.
2. Caught in the Act!	Financial crime doesn't always pay. Enron and the other big corporate scandals are analyzed, with emphasis on the signals of blatant earnings magic.
3. The New Accounting	The rules have changed—Sarbanes-Oxley and other new regulations change the accounting and oversight structures. The key question: Will the New Accounting eliminate the Old Earnings Magic?
4. Wading Through the Earnings Numbers	Sources of financial information and basic number crunching are introduced. These are the tools to start the analysis.

EXHIBIT S1.1 CHAPTER DISCUSSIONS

1

1

WHAT IS EARNINGS MAGIC?
DOES THE BALANCE SHEET BALANCE?

Earnings are an accounting theory and dividends are cash flow.

— Ralph Wanger

After the first of the Wall Street scandals, 10 bad-guy investment
firms paid $1.4 billion in fines. They floated slow apologies.
They were kinda sorry their lying analysts had hyped the prices
of Internet, high tech and telecommunications stocks.
They were really sorry they got caught making all that
money while you were losing yours.

— Jane Bryant Quinn

Investment decisions concentrate on the bottom line (there are several definitions available), with particular attention to earnings per share (EPS). Financial analysis generally assumes this number is accurate. Unfortunately, the numbers on the financial statements may not be correct, resulting in a misstated EPS (i.e., not financial reality). Enron's earnings numbers for 2000 were not close to financial reality, as the 2001 earnings restatements and subsequent bankruptcy demonstrated. This is equally true for the other scandals: WorldCom, Global Crossing, Tyco, Adelphia, and on and on. It turns out that a large percent of corporations incorrectly state earnings. The General Accounting Office (GAO, 2002) found that from 1997 through the first half of 2002, over 900 earnings restatements were issued (involving over 10% of companies listed on major stock exchanges). Consequently, there is considerable evidence that earnings misstatements are common.

What is the problem? The easy answer is *earnings magic*! Companies can be a bit deceptive, aggressively manipulate accounting more or less within existing rules, or commit fraud—all part of earnings magic. But it is not supposed to be like that. Detailed accounting standards exist (called generally accepted accounting principles or GAAP), companies are audited by certified public accountants subject to state licensing and a code of ethics (not to mention securities laws), the role of the board of directors and corporate governance requirements is to oversee compliance, and the Securities and Exchange Commission (SEC) and other regulators are on the job.

The most fundamental accounting issue is the flexibility allowed by GAAP. Firms have considerable accounting choices and incentives to use that flexibility to "game the system," usually to increase earnings. As long as the choices are allowed by GAAP, they most likely will be okayed by the auditors. Executive pay usually is tied to short-term earnings performance (bonuses) and stock price (stock options). Consequently, executives want to make earnings targets, and what better way of doing it than relying on aggressive accounting choices? The process of using accounting alternatives to meet specific goals (usually earnings targets) is called earnings management.

The use of earnings magic (also called aggressive earnings management or earnings manipulation) suggests problems with the income statement. What about the balance sheet? It is supposed to represent the fair values of assets and liabilities, plus ownership interests. Some assets and liabilities actually are stated at fair value (usually the financial items), but many are based on historical costs (most inventory and property, plant and equipment) or not stated at all (including the results of internal research and development, branding, and human resources).

Assets must equal liabilities and equity, but the eclectic mix of valuation techniques results in a confusing jumble of relevant, misstated, and missing information. An additional problem is the relationship between the balance sheet and income statement. As accounting standards move toward fair value—generally swell for relevance on the balance sheet—gains and losses are recognized on the income statement that decimate the concept of the matching principle (i.e., matching expenses to revenues). Thanks to substantial notes and other disclosures, information may be available to better evaluate financial statement results, but with some effort. Considerable effort is required if the company intends deception.

The economic reality problems do not stop with earnings management, however. Auditors are supposed to protect the public and expected to limit the use of earnings management techniques. However, auditors are paid by the clients and often provide substantial (and lucrative) consulting services to their audit clients (which have now been limited by the Sarbanes-Oxley Act of 2002). Because keeping corporate business often means making clients happy, the auditors may be reluctant to restrict the use of earnings management unless it is clear that GAAP is violated. Auditors have appeared to be reluctant to challenge executives even in extreme cases—Enron comes to mind.

Other actors exist in the financial reality-distortion drama. Investment bankers and their analysts and brokers make big bucks from selling banking services and, like the auditors, work to keep the corporate customers happy. Thus, there are incentives to have analysts and brokers promote their corporate customers, irrespective of the underlying financial quality of the corporations. The so-called Chinese Wall that was supposed to create a barrier between analysts and investment bankers collapsed in the 1990s. These practices had been so blatant that major New York bankers paid billion-dollar fines in the last few years and superstar analysts have been banned for life.

The regulators are the watchdogs, but had some embarrassing lapses. Enron was not on the SEC's radar at all before its collapse, for example. During the 1990s, Arthur Levitt, the SEC chairman, was an active reformer and alerted the public to most of the problems. However, the SEC is subject to politics and was underfunded. It turns out that the major accounting firms (now the Big Four), in addition to the corporations, have been major contributors to senators, representatives, and presidential candidates. Major political recipients were strident against the reforms championed by Levitt, threatening legislation and reduced funding. After all, why should the SEC rock the boat when the economy is booming?

After Enron and the other financial scandals, Congress held hearings and passed new legislation. The Sarbanes-Oxley Act of 2002 requires improved corporate governance and established a new audit board and a host of other provisions to beef up regulation. Investors have this new regulatory environment that is supposed to solve the major problems. But it is not yet time to relax. Earnings magic continues. All the groups that had incentives to distort economic reality still have the same incentives.

The Enron bankruptcy of 2001 was the great financial fiasco of the twenty-first century, perhaps the most infamous in U.S. history. Congressional hearings followed. Auditor Arthur Andersen was ruined by criminal prosecution. Executives would be convicted and sentenced to serious slammer time. WorldCom would follow Enron and actually replace Enron as the largest bankruptcy in U.S. history. Other big companies would fall like dominoes, in part for accounting irregularities—Global Crossing, Adelphia, and Tyco, to name a few. Hundreds of companies were forced to restate earnings. A central theme to all these failures was a financial environment that practiced and seemed to encourage earnings magic. Earnings manipulation, driven by corporate greed in a permissive environment, led to stock prices in the stratosphere, then financial collapse for many corporations when the economy turned south and the deception too blatant to continue.

The tech-driven stock bubble burst in 2000, accumulating trillion-dollar losses. Corporate bankruptcies and accounting debacles are old stories, but were unexpected in the New Economy. The shock apparently was that with substantial disclosure requirements, stringent regulation, and high expectations from corporate governance and auditing, these scandals could still happen. In fact, the convergence of the economic downturn and stock market collapse with the scandals was critical. There were plenty of scandals in the 1980s and 1990s: the savings and loan crisis, the related insider trading scandal of Ivan Boesky and Michael Milken, Sunbeam, Waste Management, and Long-Term Capital Management. But the market suffered only minor blips and the economy hardly noticed. These were considered flukes by most investors, not yet perceived as indicators of fundamental institutional problems. Enron might have survived, except for the falling price of its stock. That is the point. High-risk schemes collapse in hard times.

The basic question for financial professionals is how reliable the financial information presented by the corporations being evaluated is for equity investments. If financial reality was 100%, then financial investigation would be easy. Basic financial analysis techniques would work well, without the need for much additional analysis. Of course, 100% is impossible, but close is expected. Techniques exist that give the investor a fighting chance to spot potential problems and perhaps reinterpret financial data into more realistic information. That is a basic goal of this book.

WHAT IS EARNINGS MAGIC?

Given that it may be the scourge of modern American accounting, what exactly is earnings magic? There is less than total agreement on how the term should be defined. Consider the continuum in Exhibit 1.1. (See my book *Detecting Earnings Management* for a more complete analysis of these concepts.)

Earnings management includes the whole spectrum, from conservative accounting through fraud, a huge range for accounting choices. Management takes a relative position on accounting issues, based on some perspective. This can be conservative, with few if any unusual items or unexpected positions, plus thorough disclosure. The result should be close to financial reality and suggest transparency. However, the perspective can be much more aggressive or even fraudulent—earnings magic. If the primary earnings

Conservative Accounting	Aggressive Accounting	Fraud

EXHIBIT 1.1   CONTINUUM

target is the analysts' quarterly EPS forecasts, then earnings management techniques can be quite flexible. Blatant manipulation could be reserved only to reconcile major differences in forecasts and reported EPS. Examples of the range of alternatives and the fit to this perspective are included in Exhibit 1.2. As shown, there are few limits on accounting creativity. Conservative accounting best approximates financial reality, but what is actually reported has to be investigated. Plenty of examples exist for the fraud category: sham sales at Sunbeam, fraudulent depreciation at Waste Management, and capitalization of marketing costs at AOL.

The objective of accounting information is to explain financial reality, including both the performance and the relative financial position of a company. The chief financial officer (CFO), in conjunction with executives and board members, develops a perspective on what this economic reality is (or how to deviate from it in the case of earnings magic) and how it should be

	Conservative	Aggressive	Fraud
Revenue Recognition, Products	After sale, delivery, and acceptance, earnings process complete	Bill and hold; earnings process not close to completion	Fraudulent or nonexistent sale
Revenue Recognition on Services	Services prepaid and have been performed before recognition	Services agreed to but not yet performed	Fraudulent scheme
Inventory	Lower of cost or market faithfully followed	Obsolescent inventory still on the books	Sham rebates on purchased inventory; nonexistent inventory
Asset Reserves (e.g., for Bad Debts)	Conservative use, based on past history	Adjusting reserves to meet earnings targets	Releasing unwarranted reserve amounts to boost income
Accounts Receivable	Conservative credit terms and bad debt allowance	Liberalizing credit policies to expand sales and reduce bad debts by ignoring likely defaults	Fictitious receivables established to support nonexistent sales
Depreciation	Conservative useful life and residual value	Restate useful life and residual value upward	Change estimates or principles beyond reasonable amounts to meet earnings targets
Advertising, Marketing	Expense as incurred	Expenses based on formulas that can be manipulated, marketing costs capitalized	Capitalized and manipulated to meet earnings targets; other costs treated as marketing and capitalized

EXHIBIT 1.2 EXAMPLES OF THE RANGE OF ALTERNATIVES

reported. This is a dynamic process, which can change from quarter to quarter as financial analysts' expectations change. Using this approach, earnings management is the planning and control of the accounting and reporting system to meet the objectives of management. Management incentives might include a combination of meeting analysts' expectations, reporting sustained earnings growth, or achieving a performance goal of an incentive compensation plan.

Most emphasis on earnings management problems focuses on aggressive accounting and fraud, the deliberate misstatement of financial information for the personal benefit of the managers. The term *earnings magic* will be reserved for these two categories, defined as "opportunistic use of earnings management to effectively misstate earnings to benefit managers."

INCENTIVES FOR DECEPTION

Economists focus on opportunism, self-interest with guile; in other words, when people are willing to violate normal ethical boundaries for personal benefit. It is not clear where the boundary is between simple self-interest and opportunism; that distinction probably differs with each individual. Earnings management strategy relates to the full spectrum of self-interested behavior, conservative reporting to blatant opportunism.

Executives in their fiduciary role are expected to be corporate stewards, running the company in the best interests of the shareholders. Presumably the firm should maximize long-term economic earnings. One of the potential problems inherent in corporations is that managers may focus on short-term personal incentives rather than the long-term economic success of the firm. Executives can attempt to maximize salary, bonuses, and other short-term compensation. This can be done through improved business strategy and successful operations. It can also be accomplished, at least in the short-term, through earnings magic.

Most earnings management decisions represent relative timing differences. Revenues and expenses can be increased or decreased in the current period rather than in future periods. Revenues can be increased through aggressive revenue recognition, while expenses can be avoided temporarily by capitalizing certain costs. Gains can be recognized immediately or losses postponed. Troubled companies likely use earnings magic techniques to indicate they are still solvent. However, even successful companies are tempted to manage operating numbers when quarterly earnings are not up to analysts' forecasts.

A number of recent examples of earnings magic have lead to considerable distrust of corporate financial information. WorldCom announced that it had wrongly capitalized some $3.85 billion in operating expenses and then declared bankruptcy in July 2002. The actual amount involved ballooned to over $11 billion. Enron hid a multitude of its operating problems by using insider partnerships and special-purpose entities to keep liabilities, losses, and other bad news off the financial statements. Global Crossing sold fiber cable capacity to other telecommunications companies using long-term contracts, booking the prospective proceeds immediately as operating revenues. Dynegy was subject to a federal probe based on sham trades, again to boost revenues. Just when it appeared that the run of scandals had ended, HealthSouth erupted as another billion-dollar scandal in 2003. More recent scandals hit American International Group (AIG), Fannie Mae, the mutual funds industry, and Krispy Kreme.

A potential component of earnings management is income smoothing, attempting to generate consistent revenue and earnings growth rather than erratic changes. Generally, accrual accounting promotes income smoothing, such as capitalizing costs and allocating these costs over time as expenses using a straight-line method. A typical income smoothing strategy is to increase reserve accounts when earnings are great (called cookie-jar reserves) and reduce reserve accounts during bad periods. This was a blatant earnings magic strategy at Sunbeam and Enron, for example. Companies also can categorize accounting errors or misapplications of GAAP as "immaterial" and effectively hide them as part of "other expenses." This helps give the appearance of high earnings quality or earnings persistence (indicators that core earnings are likely to continue).

The CFO may manage earnings to "just meet" analyst expectations, which may call for an "adjustment" of as little as a penny per share. Bonuses and other incentive compensation are likely based on some performance formula approved by the board. For example, unusual or infrequent items may be excluded from calculating bonuses. In that case, losses would be dumped into these categories. The use of stock options has been more pronounced since the 1990s, with a couple of interrelated problems. First, options normally are not expensed on the income statement, which understates real compensation expense. Second, the options generate big incentives to drive up the stock price, whether justified by economic performance or not.

At some point, the line is crossed to opportunistic behavior. When, for example, obvious operating expenses are capitalized, this is earnings magic. Generally, when earnings magic is detected, the perception of earnings quality of the firm plummets and analysts have to reevaluate and reestimate financial information (a process called normalizing income).

Techniques to decrease current earnings also can be used. This can be part of an income smoothing strategy. Examples include extremely conservative revenue (e.g., delaying recognition of sales) or expense recognition (immediate expensing of items that typically are capitalized). As a high-profit company with antitrust problems, Microsoft has used multiple methods to keep down current earnings. The company usually expenses software development costs that other software providers capitalize. Microsoft also used several categories of reserves, such as operating reserves based on contingencies, "marketing accruals" resulting in advertising expenses less than budgeted, and reserves associated with reducing the useful lives of fixed assets. Microsoft agreed to "cease and desist" certain of these practices based on a 2002 SEC Administrative Proceeding.

An extreme example of loss recognition is the "big bath" write-off. AOL Time Warner wrote off $54 billion in goodwill in the first quarter of 2002, the largest such write-off ever (until topped by WorldCom's $74 billion write-down). Why would managers do this? When the corporation is losing money in the current period and, therefore, no cash bonuses will be paid, it may be a good time to take a large write-off. Doing this is especially effective when the company is in the process of reorganizing. Generally these write-offs are nonrecurring items that are not considered part of continuing operations and may be ignored by some analysts. These losses highlight the reorganization attempt and, because these losses are recorded in the current year, make it more likely that profitability will happen in future years—allowing the managers to get larger future bonuses. Better yet, when new executives are in place, they can blame all the problems and write-offs on the incompetent old team.

Potential areas of earnings magic often are industry specific: the understatement of warranty liabilities for manufacturers; credit losses and loan loss provisions of banks; contingencies for tobacco litigation or environmental damage due to industrial waste; technological change, especially important in high-tech companies (e.g., potential for inventory losses); high receivables and bad debts in retailing; and product liabilities for chemical or drug companies.

THE INSTITUTIONAL FRAMEWORK

Each company should have a review structure in place to monitor the actions of the chief executive officer (CEO), CFO, and other executives, designed to ensure compliance. Executive performance should be reviewed by the compensation committee made up of independent members of the board of directors. Equally important is a separate audit committee made up entirely of independent and financially competent board members and an independent audit, usually by one of the Big Four accounting firms. New securities issues and other financial instruments are handled primarily on Wall Street, with the investment bankers highly regulated by the SEC.

Financial reporting is complex and governed by the extensive standards of the Financial Accounting Standards Board (FASB) and the SEC. There also are industry-driven standards by other regulatory agencies, such as the Federal Energy Regulatory Commission for regulated utilities and the Comptroller of the Currency for financial institutions. Accounting regulatory oversight is extensive. In addition to the regulations associated with specific industries, the SEC is directly and aggressively involved. All actively traded corporations must submit extensive reports to the SEC: the annual 10-K, the quarterly 10-Q, the annual proxy statement, along with other more technical reports, such as the 8-K for significant events outside the normal reporting periods. Given this extensive institutional structure, how is noncompliance, let alone the potential for fraud and other criminal acts, possible?

The institutional environment related to earnings management has the significant factors shown in Exhibit 1.3. These factors are important to understand the environment that led to the recent scandals and the regulatory response to attempt reasonable solutions. They are dynamic, in the sense that they are moving targets, changing with new circumstances. We review the important components of the financial environment next, then turn to the serious work of analyzing the financial reports of the corporate giants.

What Were They Thinking?
The Incentives for Earnings Magic

Okay, it could not have been as blatant as shown in Exhibit 1.4, but the outcomes were consistent with these attitudes. All the fail-safe systems failed.

What Are They Thinking?
Threats to Complete Transparency

Sarbanes-Oxley, increased funding to the SEC and other regulators, real reform for corporate governance, diligent audits, and requirements that CEOs and CFOs know what is really going on in their companies. It should work. What could possibly go wrong? (See Exhibit 1.5.)

Corporate Governance	The governance structure includes the board of directors, the functions of the committees, interaction of the board with management, compensation issues, and auditing.
Auditing	The external auditors evaluate appropriate financial accounting and reporting according to generally accepted accounting principles (GAAP). Auditors must have the ability to discover significant discrepancies with GAAP (competence) and willingness to report the discrepancies to the audit committee or other relevant bodies (independence).
Accounting Regulation and Standard Setting	The Securities and Exchange Commission (SEC) regulates the equity capital market structure, including the stock exchanges and financial reports of some 17,000 public companies. The SEC's Division of Enforcement investigates possible violations of accounting issues and other violations of securities laws. The Financial Accounting Standards Board (FASB) sets accounting standards (GAAP), based on a formal due process.
Earnings Restatements	A financial statement restatement is the revision of public financial information that was previously reported. It represents real evidence of earnings magic.
Investment Banks	Investment banks issue new securities and other financial instruments. Financial analysts provide research on equity investment, including earnings forecasts and buy-hold-sell recommendations. Analysts have incentives to recommend buys on investment banking clients, and brokers are encouraged to sell the new issues.

EXHIBIT 1.3   SIGNIFICANT FACTORS OF THE INSTITUTIONAL ENVIRONMENT RELATED TO EARNINGS MANAGEMENT

Corporate Executives	The pay is incredible, not to mention the perks. But wealth in the millions of dollars is not enough. With my competitors making more than me, greed is insatiable. Let us violate the rules big time. This quarter's earnings per share is all-important. Who cares about the long-term interests of the company?
Corporate Board Member	The CEO is my pal and hired me. Big bucks for little work. The CEO also is the chairman of the board and dominates everything—especially executive compensation. But he is worth it and can handle any problem. I had some worries, but those high-priced lawyers and accountants explained everything.
Auditors	We deal with corporate management. They really hire us, including our lucrative consulting services. Dealing with the board of directors is perfunctory. Audits are essentially priced as commodities, and pricing ignores the high-quality audit risk approach. We have to cut some corners on the audit, especially those internal control evaluations. But we will catch the important stuff. There are some suspicious contracts. Technically they seem to violate the

(continues)

EXHIBIT 1.4   INCENTIVES FOR EARNINGS MAGIC

Auditors (Continued)	rules, but legal positions support the company's positions and the board approved them.
Investment Bankers	We want to dominate new security issues, especially those new dot-com initial public offerings. The stock prices make no financial sense, but that just means greater fees for us. Our financial analysts are on board and have nifty graphs and measures to "prove" these are once-in-a-lifetime investments. The analysts are the key. Because no one is enforcing the "Chinese Wall," we can get a big share of the business.
Financial Analysts (Working for Investment Banks)	The pressure is great to issue only "strong buys" on investment banking clients. Superstar status comes with participating in investment banking deals and ignoring any bad news (and there is plenty of that). Because the "Chinese Wall" no longer exists, I have no choice. But those million-dollar salaries and media attention make it all worthwhile.
Investors	Wow! What a market. All those complex financial ratios are meaningless. Those stock prices are going up and up. The business cycle is dead, and this market will continue for decades. Those business plans predict astronomical revenue growth; no wonder the CEOs get so much money. I am buying on margin, because I can make more money. With all the regulators and oversight, I cannot lose.
Congress	The economy is booming. The stock market is great. This party can go on indefinitely. The campaign contributions just keep rolling in from corporate interests. The SEC and the FASB are trying to dampen the boom. What is this nonsense about expensing stock options? We will squash them if we have to. They know nothing about the New Economy.

EXHIBIT 1.4 INCENTIVES FOR EARNINGS MAGIC (CONTINUED)

Corporate Executives	The incentives have not changed. CEOs and the other big shots get mega-millions in salary bonuses and stock. There is a move away from options to restricted stock and other equity packages (all these alternatives mean compensation expense), but meeting earnings targets is still a major goal.
Corporate Board Members	After being embarrassed and now subject to real reform, directorships are less prestigious and harder work (not to mention the increased liability). The board members are central to effective oversight. If interest in oversight flags, then all bets are off.
Auditors	There was real reform with Sarbanes-Oxley and the creation of the Public Company Accounting Oversight Board (PCAOB). Auditors are supposed to work in the public interest, but incentives still favor pleasing management and the audit committee. This will work well only with diligent effort on the part of the audit committees of corporate boards and PCAOB.

(continues)

EXHIBIT 1.5 WHAT CAN GO WRONG?

Investment Bankers (Continued)	Investment banks were fined a fraction of fees they earned and all claimed to put real "Chinese Walls" in place. Talks with bankers since then do not indicate much repentance. Business as usual will not be unexpected.
Financial Analysts	Financial analysts did not get hammered, and even the most blatant insiders got no jail time. Big-time spin masters Henry Blodgett and Jack Grubman were fined and banned from the business. Not exactly big threats to self-serving behavior.
Investors	Investors saw their wealth plummet. Except for short sellers, most saw big losses. It turns out that standard financial analysis techniques are still important. Bull and bear markets run in cycles, and market psychology is difficult to predict. Much of the stock market still seems overpriced based on the usual market analysis ratios such as price earnings and dividend yields. The past is easy to analyze but the future is unpredictable.
Congress	Congress still depends on campaign contributions and is swayed by lobbyists. They are at it again. The House of Representatives tried to stop the Financial Accounting Standards Board from requiring the expensing of stock options—this is, after all, the evidence of abuse directly associated with options. The business lobby also wants to cut back on parts of Sarbanes-Oxley, especially internal control requirements. There is a direct relationship between relaxing regulations and the probability of future scandals. Stay tuned.

EXHIBIT 1.5   WHAT CAN GO WRONG? (CONTINUED)

WHAT IS FINANCIAL REALITY?

The most common term for ideal financial reporting is *transparency,* but it is not often defined. I would define it as complete disclosure, which includes the information to achieve financial reality, incorporating such FASB-defined characteristics as relevance and faithful representation. The point of financial reality is to use disclosure-adjusted financial statement information to better estimate appropriate income numbers and financial position.

These terms sound great, but they lack clear definitions. The FASB focuses on relevance and reliability as key qualitative characteristics, but these are equally nebulous and often at odds. Fixed assets stated at historical costs, for instance, are reliable but not necessarily relevant. Fair value reporting where an obvious market does not exist may be relevant but not reliable.

The financial statements could represent a summary of financial reality. Net income could be close to "real earnings" for a period. For most purposes, that is assumed to be true. Net income and earnings per share are used for calculating most financial ratios to measure income and market performance, perhaps "good enough" measures.

For a sophisticated analysis of financial reality, financial statements are only the starting point. These represent summary analysis based on GAAP, including all the accounting choices used by management including earnings magic. Complex disclosures exist in notes, Management Discussion and Analysis, and elsewhere. Financial reality can be attempted by making adjustments, both quantitative and qualitative. Key questions include: (1) What earnings number(s) is/are the best approximation(s) of real performance? and (2) What is the financial position including credit risk?

An ongoing debate is between current operations and an all-inclusive or comprehensive approach to measuring earnings. Current operations focus on the basic ongoing performance of a company ("above the line"). All-inclusive includes all gains and losses, which can include all kinds of strange stuff ("below the line"). The earnings numbers for companies minimizing the strange stuff should be about the same under either approach—one indicator of low earnings magic and high transparency. Consequently, a reasonable approach is to include both and show the major adjustments from a financial statement definition of current operations, to arrive at an adjusted comprehensive income number.

A possible starting point is income from continuing operations, which includes operations and is after tax. If companies have no nonrecurring items, the number will be the same as net income. To arrive at an operating performance number, deduct stock options expense (more on this later in the options note) and deduct any strange stuff that is actually reported as part of continuing operations, such as most impairment charges and various restructuring charges (based on notes and Management Discussion and Analysis), plus other possible adjustments, including the impact of these changes on income tax. Compare that amount to net income. If they are not close, it is a signal of possible earnings magic.

Comprehensive income is an all-inclusive measure (usually reported on the statement of stockholders' equity). It includes net income plus other comprehensive income items (e.g., foreign currency translation and marketable security gains and losses). Deduct stock options expense. Recalculate pension and other postemployment benefit expenses by replacing expected return on plan assets with actual return (explained in Chapter 7). Add other adjustments (including tax effects). Comparisons to net income also are useful, although substantial differences are not necessarily indicators of earnings magic.

The balance sheet is the starting point for financial position. The primary adjustments are to include estimates of off–balance sheet items that should be included. Large balances of operating leases (say greater than 10% of total assets) suggest that these are really capital leases in disguise and should be added to assets and liabilities (discounted; see Chapter 12). Pension and other postemployment benefit funded status represents the real net asset or liability position for these items and should replace the amounts actually reported. Other major off–balance sheet items, including contingencies and special-purpose entities, should be noted but are difficult to restate quantitatively. The adjusted amounts should be compared to balance sheet amounts, and, if the differences are large, various financial ratios should be recalculated.

The adjusted totals for both earnings and financial position should be better approximations of financial reality and, at a minimum, suggest the potential impact of earnings magic. However, the primary approach used in Section 3 of this volume is to actually rate earnings magic/financial reality from A to F across the major categories.

2

CAUGHT IN THE ACT!

*Accounting fraud does tend to come in waves, and is
discovered most often after a market collapse, since no
one is interested in investigating much when stock prices
are high and everyone's making big money.*
— Barbara Toffler

*Those who cannot learn from history are
condemned to repeat it.*
—George Santayana

During the boom times, everyone in the market is brilliant: the executives
who oversee sales and earnings growth, the investor who picks only win-
ners, the brokers who have a buy recommendation on all the securities, the
board that gives huge bonuses and stock options to the executives. The auditors and regulators are the spoilsports, whose job is to ruin success. But what
happens in the bad times? Sales drop, earnings disappear, the stocks become
losers, and the cheaters are more likely to be discovered. It is hoped that they
are fired and prosecuted. Perhaps the regulators have a real function after
all. It is how the system functions during the bad times that determines the
long-term success of the companies and institutions involved. Congress holds
hearings, the media pick the heroes and villains, and researchers and historians try to make sense of what actually happened.

There are many theories as to why scandals occur, especially when they
happen in clusters. It could be just a few criminals: the rotten apple theory.
It could be the developing culture that allows or encourages increasingly
egregious acts. It could be based on the particular institutional environment
that encourages or turns a blind eye to unethical or illegal acts. It could be
the specific incentive structures that exist in a company. Finally, the survival
of the fittest theory, related to Joseph Schumpeter's idea of creative destruction. Marginal, high-risk companies can survive when economic conditions

are great (perhaps by manipulation), but not when times are bad—consider many of the high-flying Internet companies from the 1990s, now toast.

The Wisdom of Crowds by James Surowiecki suggests some interesting psychological factors. Surowiecki considered trust central to successful economic systems because of the importance of cooperative behavior. Because trust is expected, corruption is very damaging. He views the stock market bubble of the 1990s as "a perfect breeding ground for corruption":

> In the case of the executives at companies like Enron and Tyco, the short-term gains from self-interest and corrupt behavior were so immense—because they had so many stock options, and because their boards of directors paid them no attention—that any long-term consideration paled by comparison. In the case of Dennis Kozlowski, the CEO of Tyco, for instance, it's hard to see how he could have made $600 million honestly if he had stayed CEO of Tyco. But dishonestly, it was remarkably easy. Investors should have understood that the rules of the game had changed . . . but they didn't.
>
> At the same time, the mechanisms and institutions that were supposed to limit corruption ended up facilitating corruption rather than stopping it. If Goldman Sachs underwrites a stock offering for a company, it's saying that the company has real value, as is Merrill Lynch when one of its analysts issues a buy recommendation. . . . And when Ernst and Young signs off on an audit, it's telling us that we can trust that company's numbers. We are willing to believe Ernst and Young when it says this because its entire business seems to depend on its credibility (pp. 126–127).

Howard M. Schilit's *Financial Shenanigans* (2002, p. 28) identified three reasons for scandals: "(1) It pays to do it, (2) it's easy to do, and (3) it's unlikely that you'll be caught." This fits the rotten apple theory, just a few sleazy leaders who break the law or establish a group conspiracy to expand illegal acts on a broad basis. In almost every case, specific individuals are blamed for the crimes and prosecuted if enough evidence exists. The advantage of the rotten apple theory is its simplicity. Fire the culprits, rely on the Justice Department to prosecute, restructure and restate financial statements, and introduce controls to avoid the same mistakes. More often than not, the original incentives to cheat remain the same.

The twenty-first-century scandals can be blamed on the high-tech, boom-period culture that got out of hand in the 1990s. The 1990s was a greed decade (not necessary much different from other decades, the incentives just were different), with huge executive pay, massive stock options, continuing technology changes, and the pressures of meeting the quarterly earnings targets.

Incentives to meet quarterly earnings get much of the blame for this greedy culture theory, and the theory ties to the other factors. Stock prices continued up as long as the quarterly earnings were always met, but the stocks were pummeled if actual earnings were below forecasts. The fabulous salaries and stock option values depended on what Alex Berenson called *The Number* (2003). His book was subtitled *How the Drive for Quarterly Earnings Corrupted Wall Street and Corporate America*. With a chief financial officer (CFO) a bad apple, earnings manipulation was inevitable.

Different cultures can explain the problems of different periods. The mass-market speculation of the late 1920s allowed stocks bought on margin and open rigging of stock prices. Radio and autos were hot stocks. Stock pyramiding based on debt and inadequate equity dominated utilities and railroads. During the go-go years of the 1950s and 1960s, conglomerates, electronics, and aerospace were the hot stocks, with irrational stock prices. Earnings magic centered on the flexibility of merger accounting, which allowed amazing valuations, gains, and write-offs. Conglomerates were able to post big accounting earnings numbers when economic reality indicated disaster. During the 1980s, hostile takeovers and leveraged buyouts dominated. Earnings magic continued to focus on acquisition accounting, aided by available credit from junk bond king Michael Milken. Increasing the sleaze were the insider trading scandals of Milken, Ivan Boesky, and others and the savings and loan debacle. Different cultures, same result: speculative bubbles followed by crashes. Many of the former geniuses turned out to be incompetent, crooks, or both. New regulations were effective until the next generation of scam artists came up with new tactics for evasion.

The institutional/regulatory structure can be the explanation of economic fiascoes—so claims a prominent perspective in history and economics. It is a reasonable and respected theory. The amazing economic growth of the United States over the last 200 years can be attributed to a combination of natural resources and the legal and economic structure in place. This theory can be used to explain the high-tech growth of the current information age or the Great Depression of the 1930s. Important institutions associated with the corporate scandal story are the regulators, especially the Securities and Exchange Commission (SEC), Internal Revenue Service (IRS), the stock exchanges, and the accounting and auditing standard setters. They do not get high marks for being on top of the problems. However, a significant factor was the political environment: Corporations, auditors, and many others were major contributors to politicians. The politicians came through for the corporations when the SEC and others were determined to clamp down on shady practices: dealing with acquisitions, stock options, special purpose entities, cookie jar reserves, and so on.

Corporate governance practices could be the explanation. The board of directors sets the business strategy and broad policies, hires and evaluates the chief executive officer (CEO) and other key executives, and is the watchdog of corporate performance. The compensation committee approves salaries, bonuses, and long-term compensation. The audit committee picks the auditors and reviews the results of both internal and external audits. A strong board should make scandals difficult, if not impossible. The problem is with weak or complicit boards. In every recent scandal, a lousy board was present when scandals were discovered; some even were complicit. A prominent theory is that requiring a strong, independent board will deter scandals, and recent legislation (especially the Sarbanes-Oxley Act) mandates improved board structure. If this theory is right, scandals should be rare in the future.

Survival of the fittest has a long history in economics. Nineteenth-century economist Herbert Spencer coined the term, based on Darwin's theory of evolution. Business loved the concept and relished squashing competitors. Austrian economist Joseph Schumpeter stressed (1) the importance of innovation as the engine of growth and (2) the downturns of the business cycle to eliminate the marginal firms. Innovation has been the driver of economic growth throughout America's history. The logic of downturns is that the premier firms are forced to increase efficiency and reorganize in the bad times, while the marginal and corrupt firms go bankrupt or are gobbled up by stronger companies. This concept can explain the recent Internet history; a long period of innovation and growth, virtually unlimited capital for stock and bond offerings, followed by overreaching and increased speculation. The best tech firms are doing nicely; most of the rest are gone.

LESSONS FROM THE RECENT SCANDALS

Accounting manipulation, fraud, and various illegal acts are part of the business environment. There are dozens of major failures, frauds, and other measures of massive corruption each decade. The big ones often hit during recessions or periods of other economic problems, as expected. The high-risk firms are the most vulnerable to economic shocks. The recent scandals are no exceptions. The most infamous ones are summarized in Appendix 2.1, including the egregious ones from the 1990s.

Corporate crooks have been creative in perpetrating fraud, but a few common characteristics pop out. The first is the obvious corporate greed. Why do this stuff when you are a corporate mogul making millions? Presumably they expected to get away with it. They also fit the financial-corporate culture described earlier. And earnings magic is part of (and usually central to) most of the scandals. Some of them used brazen and unsophisticated approaches (e.g., WorldCom), while others used new, sophisticated devices to defraud (like Enron). Outrageous manipulation may involve criminal acts, but not necessarily. Federal and state authorities are still prosecuting the most blatant acts, but convictions are not a sure thing.

The Internet craze was a driving force of the stock market bubble. Plenty of manipulation and the initial public offerings (IPOs) were amazing: Huge stock valuations were achieved from dinky companies with little if any profits, despite heroic earnings magic. These companies were only small potatoes in the scandal game. As likely as not, they went bankrupt before their executives had a chance to commit felonies. AOL does get dishonorable mention in the scandal department.

The two industries particularly prominent in the scandals were energy and telecommunications. They usually claimed to be New Economy–Internet companies. Deregulation allowed the stodgy energy companies to become high-tech energy traders using sophisticated derivatives and structured-finance deals. The result was giant profits for the leaders, but big losses when they guessed wrong. Continued big profits meant increasing risks and more complex deals. For Enron and others it also meant hiding the losses in controversial (and perhaps fraudulent) off–balance sheet schemes. The telecommunications industry transformed from monopolist AT&T in the 1970s to a group of dynamic and competitive high-tech giants, all trying to integrate and dominate with new telecommunications methods. Corporate moves to broadband and other new markets led to overcapacity and shady capacity-trading schemes booked as revenues. Despite the deceptive accounting, big losses eventually had to be booked. Global Crossing and WorldCom went bankrupt and became corporate corruption leaders.

It is worth considering Enron in some detail, because that company was the worst—or the best, if you are an earnings magic fan. Enron did it all, starting with a terrible business strategy. No one seemed willing to say no to a deal, no matter how ill conceived. Deal makers earned big bonuses for closing deals, not for making "great deals." Losses were covered over at the end of each quarter through sheer earnings magic.

With Andy Fastow as CFO, no special-purpose entity–based deal was too outrageous to meet earnings targets (especially if he was the so-called outside investor). Amazingly, Fastow was named CFO of the year by *CFO Magazine* and Enron was named best-managed company by *Fortune*. Enron was bad at deal making, but great at public relations.

Fastow set up his own partnership—to do business with Enron. This obvious conflict of interests was approved by the lawyers, auditor, and board of directors. This was idiotic under any circumstances, made worse because Fastow was a crook. Long-term risks were ignored, short-term gain was everything. Investment banks would be punished (denied banking business) if their financial analysts were honest and downrated Enron stock. (The honest analysts likely were fired.) Enron's "first-tier" banks were the most accommodating. The culture was to game every system, with gas trading leading the way. Enron created the gas trading market, was expert at it, and still gamed the system to extract even more profit.

The Enron executives enriched themselves, but all the players were culpable. The audit partners at Arthur Andersen who believed in audit excellence were overridden—after all, the audit and consulting fees were huge. The lawyers at Vinson and Elkins overcame their skepticism and assisted in the shenanigans. The board of directors bought the tales of the executives with less than due diligence. Gosh, the executives seemed to know what they were doing. The investment bankers would write almost any deal (perhaps with shady side agreements) for the banking fees. The SEC allowed the outrageous uses of Enron's mark-to-market schemes and provided less than adequate oversight (partly due to tight budgets). CEO Ken Lay knew the Bushes and many other top politicians and used them to push Enron's interests. Too bad the execs did not use their talents to develop a great business strategy.

The pace of scandal slowed down after 2002 but did not disappear. Health-South, which runs outpatient surgical centers, was caught early in 2003. The company and senior executives were charged with accounting fraud related to deals with MedCenterDirect and Source Medical. The stock was downgraded by Standard & Poor's to CCC, and the New York Stock Exchange suspended trading following an SEC order to halt trading. CEO and founder Richard Scrushy and several other senior executives were fired, as was auditor Ernst & Young. Scandals involving the big investment banks, mutual funds, and mortgage resellers Fannie Mae and Freddie Mac followed. AIG and Krispy Kreme were among the scandals of 2005.

Enron

Enron will be remembered as the biggest recent American scandal, perhaps the premier corporate scandal in American history. It turned itself into a New Economy energy trading company that seemed to succeed at everything it attempted. Enron started as a stodgy gas transmission company when Inter-North Inc. and Houston Natural Gas merged in 1985, with Ken Lay as the first CEO. The resulting merger was loaded with debt, a continuing problem when Enron executives wanted to expand rapidly—new junk bonds do not help the leverage ratios or gas traders looking for counterparties. Enron formed a gas trading company in 1989 run by Jeff Skilling, who would prove to be a major villain in the scandal. Enron would expand into electric utilities, finance, risk management, and, toward the end, a telecommunications company. Why is not easily explained. Based on economic reality, these new enterprises were not particularly successful.

The deregulated gas market increased volatility, because of unreliable prices and supply. Many long-term take-or-pay contracts were replaced by spot market purchases. With this volatility, buying and selling natural gas was no longer creditworthy; thus the need for Enron Gas Services, Skilling's gas trading company, which developed gas futures and other derivatives. Trading profits increased with volatility, and opportunities expanded when California deregulated energy. Enron stuck it to California, and giant electric utilities California Edison and Pacific Gas and Electric declared bankruptcy in 2001.

A big problem with Enron's potential growth was its massive debt load and junk bond rating (later raised to low investment grade and back to junk status before the final collapse). To continue to grow, the company turned more and more to special-purpose entities (SPEs). Skilling hired Andrew Fastow as an SPE specialist, who combined various energy-related assets that were then sold to institutional investors. Fastow created Enron's first SPE, called Cactus, to fund long-term contracts with oil and gas producers.

Rich Kinder's job as chief operating officer (COO) included making sure Enron met its quarterly earnings forecasts, initially through cost savings, then through more gimmicks. Two interrelated schemes were used. The first was to revalue physical assets using "fair value" models, based on Financial Accounting Standards Board Statement No. 125. (This standard was designed to be used only for financial assets.) Profit streams on major projects, such as large power plants, were front-loaded. Thus, earnings were based on deals, not the cash flows that would come over several years. The second scheme involved using the magic of SPEs in virtually any complex context to record earnings. This relied on fair value accounting, called mark-to-market. However, the Enron version was usually mark-to-model because no market existed for complex structured finance transactions and the company's "quant" guys could model the arrangement to give the company whatever profit was needed.

Enron expanded into Enron Development to build power plants around the world and into Enron Broadband, timing the entrance into telecom just before the collapse of that industry. Some projects were profitable, others disasters, but the same SPE magic was used to set up complex deals so Enron could book profits. Not only were Enron's financial statements misstated, but CFO Fastow and other executives enriched themselves by acting as the so-called independent third-party trustees.

Fastow was general partner in LJM and LJM2, both established in 1999 (Enron partnerships that used SPEs, which enriched Fastow while restructuring Enron assets primarily to avoid losses). The board of directors was required to waive its conflict-of-interest requirements. Andersen auditor David Duncan agreed to go along only if the board approved, which it did. At a minimum, these schemes should have been disclosed as related-party transactions and, in many cases, SPEs consolidated in the Enron financial statements. The degree to which the SPEs were mishandled and CFO Fastow was allowed to manipulate them through both the audit committee and auditor Arthur Andersen is quite remarkable. According to Swartz and Watkins (2003, p. 310), Fastow "earned" $58.9 million from LJM and LJM2. Fastow was later convicted of defrauding Enron.

Other companies gained expertise in energy trading, driving down Enron's profitability and pushing it to assume greater risks and to venture into trading areas it had no expertise in. The end result was obvious. Losses, side deals gone bad, and other shady practices caught up with Enron—although complex, fraudulent transactions using SPEs hid the problems for quite a while. In mid-2001 the stock price started dropping, executives bailed out of their options, and SPEs "with no skin" (i.e., no hard assets) could not be kept off the balance sheet, even with accommodating attorneys, auditors, and board members. Enron was forced to restate earnings for the third quarter of 2001 (recorded losses of over $600 million and a $1.2 billion loss of equity), which proved devastating to the company's precarious financial position. Enron's bond rating, which eventually had reached minimum investment grade at BBB, was downgraded to junk status. With no chance of a bailout and no last-minute shenanigans possible, Enron declared bankruptcy in December 2001. Just prior to failure, Enron gave $55 million in bonuses to key executives while firing 4,500 employees.

The Enron story is a pretty good microcosm of all that could go wrong with the high-tech business and the motivations for the stock market bubble of the late 1990s. Executive greed; ruthlessness; a lack of ethical standards; accommodating auditors, law firms, and investment bankers; substantial political contributions used to acquire influence in Washington; and a board of directors asleep at the wheel. The stodgy gas transmission company remade itself as a high-tech conglomerate and, despite obvious high leverage and extreme financial risks, misled investors on its true value.

Worldcom

By the middle of 2002, the financial and political worlds stopped hyper-ventilating about Enron and business as usual returned. Then came the announced bankruptcy of WorldCom on July 22, 2002, after the discovery of almost $4 billion in accounting irregularities in June (later to rise to $11 billion), replacing Enron as the largest failure in history. WorldCom listed assets of $107 billion (and a market cap that peaked at $115 billion in 1999), compared to Enron's $63 billion. Business as usual was no longer possible. Serious reform resurfaced, including a revitalized Sarbanes-Oxley (in a slightly watered-down version of the original Senate version). Former CEO Bernard Ebbers and CFO Scott Sullivan were charged in the multibillion-dollar accounting fraud; former controller David Myers and three others pleaded guilty to securities fraud.

Bernie Ebbers and others started Long Distance Discount Service in 1983. The name was changed to WorldCom in 1995. Growth came mainly through over 70 mergers, with the big one the $42 billion acquisition of tele-com giant MCI in 1998—much larger than WorldCom at the time. Ebbers was a master at using the board of directors to his advantage. As described by Haddad (2002, p. 138):

> Through the 1990s, the then-nine-member board was composed of insiders and execs from acquired companies. [The board] collected plenty of perks—from use of a corporate jet to financial support from Ebbers' in their pet projects. And they piled up loads of WorldCom stock . . . . as many as 10,000 stock options per year. . . . [T]he board O.K.'d megaloans to Ebbers. They backed him through the stupendous expansion of WorldCom—to the brink of its collapse.

At first glance WorldCom looked solid, based on its 2001 10-K. Total assets were $104 billion and stockholders' equity was $58 billion, resulting in a debt to equity ratio of 79.3%. Not bad for a telecom. However, almost $51 billion of the assets were goodwill and other intangibles, while cash totaled less than $1.5 billion. This indicates the significance of acquisitions, but who knows to what extent the goodwill represented overpaying for the acquired companies. In bankruptcy, goodwill is not a real asset, and the $30 billion in long-term debt looks huge. According to the 10-K, earnings were off for 2001, with net income of $1.5 billion compared to $4.1 billion the previous year. Revenues were down and operating expenses up. Net income for the first quarter of 2002 was a less-than-stellar $172 million, down from $610 million for the same quarter in 2001. But even this lousy performance was not correct.

Early in 2002, internal audit found operating expenses charged as capital expenditures, double counting of revenues, and undisclosed debt. New auditor KPMG reviewed the books, old auditor Arthur Andersen was fired. Ebbers resigned in April. On June 25, 2002, WorldCom announced $3.8 billion in accounting errors ($3.1 billion for 2001 and $800 million for first-quarter 2002), mainly by capitalizing "line costs," which are fees to other telecom companies for network access rights. These are operating expenses. With the required restatements, net losses were now reported for both 2001 and first-quarter 2002. CFO Scott Sullivan was fired on the same day. Further review found over $11 billion in operating expenses that were erroneously capitalized.

WorldCom filed for bankruptcy in July 2002. CFO Sullivan copped a plea, and Ebbers was convicted in 2005 of securities fraud and other illegal acts. WorldCom emerged from bankruptcy in 2004 as MCI, after a $74 billion restatement of assets—the biggest restatement ever—and correcting previous accounting errors. It now has a market cap over $8 billion, equity of $4.1 billion, and no goodwill.

Tyco

Tyco started as a research lab in 1960, only to be transformed into a conglomerate through acquisitions. Dennis Kozlowski became president and COO in 1989, then CEO in 1992. He earned his "Deal-a-Day Dennis" nickname with 750 acquisitions, with up to 200 in some years. Earnings magic based on business combination accounting gave the impression of substantial growth and rising earnings. Revenues rose almost 50% a year from 1997 to 2001. With the $6 billion acquisition of ADT Security Services, the deal was structured as a reverse takeover so that Tyco could use ADT's Bermuda registration to shelter foreign earnings. The SEC started an investigation into Tyco's acquisition accounting in 1999 but did not charge Tyco with wrongdoing.

Tyco's acquisition of CIT Group, the biggest independent commercial financial company in the United States, for $9.2 billion in 2001 was a disaster. Deceptive techniques used by Tyco became public with this acquisition, because CIT continued to issue financial statements after the acquisition to continue to maintain a high credit rating. Tyco specialized in "spring loading," notifying the acquired company to modify accounting policies before the acquisition and make various write-offs and adjustments, with the intent of improving the perceived performance of the parent immediately after the acquisition. Before the acquisition date, CIT disposed of $5 billion in poorly performing loans, made downward adjustments of $221.6 million, increased the credit-loss provisions, and took a $54 million charge to acquisition costs (apparently "pushed down" from Tyco). Revenues for CIT were extremely low just before the deal and dramatically increased after the deal. The result was a net loss reported by CIT just before the acquisition date.

After the acquisition, CIT reported net income of $71.2 million. That increased Tyco's earnings for the September 2001 quarter, but luck ran out. Tyco Capital had extreme problems with credit, because it was now tied to Tyco. Ultimately, this new business segment was sold. Tyco recorded this as a discontinued operation (recording an after-tax loss of $6.3 billion). For the year ended September 30, 2002, Tyco had a total net loss of $9.4 billion. The company had goodwill and other intangibles of nearly $33 billion, liabilities of almost $42 billion, and equity of less than $25 billion.

In 2002 Dennis Kozlowski was charged with evading $1 million in New York sales tax on paintings he bought (apparently using noninterest loans from Tyco). He resigned in June. Later he and former Tyco CFO Mark Swartz were charged with 38 felonies from "enterprise corruption and grand larceny" for raiding Tyco of some $600 million (Huffington 2003, p. 35). Kozlowski was convicted in 2005. What is not clear is if Tyco actually engaged in criminal acts. There is no doubt that actions were manipulative and deceptive, but illegality can be hard to prove. Unlike most of the scandal-plagued companies, Tyco did not go bankrupt. It dropped close to 90% of its market value in 2002 but has since recovered half of that back.

Adelphia

John Rigas turned a local cable franchise into a communications empire, including high-speed Internet, cable, and long-distance phone service. In May 2002 Adelphia announced the earnings restatement for 2000 and 2001, including billions of dollars in off–balance sheet liabilities associated with "co-borrowing agreements." The company filed for bankruptcy in June 2002, following an SEC suit charging Adelphia and several executives with extensive financial fraud:

> Adelphia, at the direction of the individual defendants: (1) fraudulently excluded billions of dollars of liabilities from its consolidated financial statements by hiding them in off-balance-sheet affiliates; (2) falsified operation statistics and inflated Adelphia's earnings to meet Wall Street expectations; and (3) concealed rampant self-dealing by the Rigas family. . . . (GAO 2002, p. 122)

Adelphia also created sham transactions and false documents indicating that debts were repaid rather than shifted to affiliates. Self-dealing by

the Rigas family included using Adelphia funds to purchase stock and tim-
ber rights for the Rigas family, construct a golf club, pay off margin loans
of various family members, and purchase several condominiums.

The financial statements of Adelphia indicate a company with problems.
The last 10-K filed before bankruptcy (for fiscal year ended December 31,
2000) showed a net loss of $548 million, with losses also in 1998 and 1999.
The last 10-Q (for the September 2001 quarter) also showed continuing losses.
Of $21.5 billion in total assets, $14.1 billion were intangibles (primarily
goodwill). Liabilities totaled $16.3, while equity was only $4.2 billion. That
is, after they cooked the books!

Adelphia indicates the importance of corporate governance. Included
on Adelphia's nine-member board of directors were five Rigas family members, John as chairman and CEO, three sons, and a son-in-law. Son Timo-
thy also was CFO and son Michael was an executive vice president. Rigas,
two sons, and two former Adelphia executives were indicted on criminal
charges for conspiracy, bank fraud, and securities fraud. Rigas was convicted
in 2004.

What Happened at Arthur Andersen?

Guilty. The foreman of the Houston jury pronounced the verdict on Arthur
Andersen. The firm obstructed justice by shredding tons of paper related to
the firm's audit work at Enron Corp. The firm was effectively out of business by the middle of 2002, after a mostly illustrious 90-year history. The
conviction was reversed by the Supreme Court in 2005, but too late to save
Andersen.

Arthur Andersen founded his firm in Chicago in 1913, stressing integrity
and consistency (including the "One Firm" concept) as the keys to success.
Along with the other large auditing firms, Andersen received most of its revenues from auditing until the 1980s. As pointed out by Byrne (2002, p. 2):
"in the '80s came the rise of the management-consulting business, a broader,
less quantitative, and more lucrative line of work that involved a much higher
degree of salesmanship. Slowly, auditing went from being the soul of the
firm to a loss leader used to attract and retain the consulting contracts. Just
as the vast riches represented by stock options helped corrupt ethics at some
corporations, consulting helped push Andersen and its rivals off course."

It did not start with Enron. Andersen had a history of "aggressive auditing," accommodating clients in most circumstances. As stated by Toffler
with Reingold (2003, p. 62): "in the new world, clients had become too valu-
able to defy. The distortion of the Tradition now meant you could best serve
the client—and therefore, keep the client—by keeping it happy." In May 2001

Andersen paid $110 million to settle shareholders' claims at Sunbeam Corp. Then it paid almost $100 million more to settle claims at Waste Management Inc. and $7 million to settle the SEC case for Waste Management's audits. The final judgment from Waste Management included a permanent injunction forbidding Andersen from deceiving anyone in the future. WorldCom also was an Andersen client. Ironically, both Enron and WorldCom were listed among the four most important clients of Andersen (Toffler with Reingold 2003).

The crisis at Andersen was summarized by Byrne (2002, p. 2):

> The collapse of Andersen represents an unimaginable failure of leadership and governance. It raises questions about the anachronistic governance structure imposed by a private partnership, a structure better suited to a local enterprise than a global organization. In many ways, Andersen was more like a loose confederation of fiefdoms covering different geographic markets than an integrated company. Checks and balances were few and frequently ineffective. Insular and inbred, Andersen was unable to respond swiftly to crises or even to govern itself decisively. It took the firm five months to elect [Joseph] Berardino as CEO. Once in office, he was unable to fire a partner without a two-thirds vote of Andersen's 1,700 partners around the world. Even as the firm was engulfed in turmoil, some partners squabbled over who should be its public spokesman. If it was the head of Andersen's U.S. business, rather than Berardino who was CEO of the worldwide firm, perhaps the crisis could have been confined to America, some thought. Berardino's emphasis on growth over audit quality, his reluctance to walk away from big clients with questionable accounting, and a stunning ignorance of potentially crippling issues all contributed to the firm's undoing.

A key question is to what extent the remaining Big Four are similar to Andersen. The signals are at best mixed on evidence of contrition. One former regulator thought another firm would follow Andersen into oblivion, due to similar behavior. The one clear outcome of increased regulation, especially Sarbanes-Oxley, is that audit fees are up dramatically. It is hoped that the new regulatory requirements will increase the competence and confidence in auditing, along with the fees.

They Just Keep Coming

Despite vastly improved corporate governance, increased regulation and enforcement, real slammer time for the big offenders, and big bucks paid to auditors, earnings magic did not go away. Other financial players including investment banks and mutual fund companies have their own recent dirty laundry. The incentives to cheat did not go away, and neither did the arrogance to expect to get away with it. The good news is the level of blatant acts has diminished; the bad news is nowhere near the catastrophic level of Enron or WorldCom. In other words, ordinary corruption. Nothing to stimulate more outraged senators and representatives demanding new hearings — except for Fannie Mae and Freddie Mac, since they are "government-sponsored enterprises." News coverage is on the business page rather than the front page. No big impact on the economy or stock market. Just the specific companies' stock prices getting pummeled.

Question: How long will the somewhat contrite behavior last? Most players are on the straight and narrow, because of better corporate governance, plus more diligent audits and regulators (who are also better funded). But that can change. Another bull market, more deals, and budget cuts at the SEC would signal greater earnings magic potential. Stay tuned.

APPENDIX 2.1

A SUMMARY OF THE MAJOR SCANDALS

TWENTY-FIRST CENTURY SCANDALS

Company	Year	Auditor	Description
Enron	2001	Arthur Andersen	Declared bankruptcy on December 2, 2001, after restating earnings in 3rd quarter 10-Q, indicating major problems with special-purpose entities. Ongoing investigations by the SEC, Justice Department, and others; executives indicted and convicted; class action lawsuits filed.
Global Crossing	2002	Arthur Andersen	Overstated revenue and earnings over network capacity swaps and then declared bankruptcy; investigated by SEC and Federal Bureau of Investigation.
WorldCom	2002	Arthur Andersen	Recorded improper expenses of $3.8 billion, then declared bankruptcy; under investigation for accounting fraud and other violations; almost $11 billion in improper expenses uncovered. Former CEO Bernie Ebbers convicted of securities fraud and conspiracy.
Tyco	2002	Pricewaterhouse-Coopers	Conglomerate with questionable practices on accounting for acquisitions and other issues. Restated 1999–2001 financials based on merger-related restructurings plus other problems with reserves. CEO and CFO convicted.
Adelphia	2002	Deloitte & Touche	Cable TV operation charged with overstating earnings; former CEO John Rigas convicted of looting the company, which went bankrupt.
Imclone	2002	KPMG	Insider trading conviction against former CEO for selling stock after Food and Drug Administration rejected a new drug; alleged to have tipped off Martha Stewart and other friends and relatives.
Merrill Lynch; Salomon; Smith Barney; Credit Suisse; Goldman Sachs; J.P. Morgan; and others	2002	Various	Major investment banks settled with the New York Attorney General, SEC, and other regulators on deceptive stock analysis and other brokerage-related practices, similar to Merrill Lynch earlier. Essentially, analysts were praising banking clients no matter *(continues)*

Company	Year	Auditor	Description
Merrill Lynch; and Others (Continued)			what, in violation of the "Chinese Wall" between analysis and investment banking. The total fine was a combined $2 billion or so, plus other sanctions and agreement to correct deceptive practices.
HealthSouth	2003	Ernst & Young	Accused of accounting fraud involving $1.4 billion in earnings and $800 million in overstated assets. Former CFO and others pleaded guilty to fraud charges. Former CEO Richard Scrushy made about $250 million from the scam. Amazingly, Scrushy was acquitted of all criminal charges.
Mutual Funds Scandals	2003	Various	Mutual funds have only limited SEC regulation requirements and poor corporate governance yet have been considered highly ethical. That changed when New York Attorney General Eliot Spitzer sued them on several counts. Some pundits considered the mutual funds scandals as egregious as Enron's.
Fannie Mae	2004	KPMG	$9 billion restatement from derivative accounting valuations and extensive payouts to ousted executives. CEO Franklin Raines and CFO Timothy Howard were fired at the end of 2004.
American International Group (AIG)	2005	Pricewaterhouse-Coopers	Improperly accounted for reinsurance transactions, overstating net worth some $1.7 billion. Chairman Hank Greenberg resigned. Previously AIG paid substantial fines to the SEC and Justice Department for structuring deals that violated insurance accounting regulations. Additional investigations are ongoing.
Krispy Kreme	2005	Pricewaterhouse-Coopers	Internal report showed "egregious accounting" to inflate earnings, including shipping high-margin doughnut-making equipment to franchisees far in advance, booking revenue but franchisees did not pay until it was actually installed.

SCANDALS FROM THE 1990s

Company	Year	Auditor	Description
Waste Management	1997	Arthur Andersen	In 1997 Waste Management had the largest earnings restatement up to that time, $1.4 billion, for the 1992–1997 period, associated with understated expenses including inflated useful lives and salvage value of fixed assets.

(continues)

Company	Year	Auditor	Description
Sunbeam	1998	Arthur Andersen	Al Dunlap was hired in 1996 to turn the company around. Sunbeam was profitable by 1997, due to premature revenue recognition, channel stuffing, bill and hold, ignoring returned merchandise, and other problems. After an internal investigation, Dunlap was fired and Sunbeam wrote off $1.2 billion in earnings.
Cendant	1998	Ernst & Young	Conglomerate that gobbled up many well-known firms, including Ramada, Coldwell Banker, and Avis. HFS acquired CUC International to form Cendant, but after the acquisition, fraud was discovered in sales and receivables. Cendant lost billions in market value and eventually settled a shareholder suit for $2.8 billion.
Rite Aid	1999–2000	KPMG	This retail drugstore chain had a multitude of accounting issues, many related to acquisitions; auditor KPMG resigned in 1999. Misstatements were related to maintenance costs capitalized; leases recorded as sales; compensation costs capitalized; charges for store closures not expensed; improper inventory and cost of goods sold. SEC investigation and class action lawsuits filed. Company's $1.6 billion restatement was the largest up to that time.

Adapted from Giroux 2004 (pp. 25–26, 28).

3

THE NEW ACCOUNTING

A regulatory climate that does not appreciate that the financial
developments over an extended period of good times will tend
to breed the financial environment that leads to the likelihood of
crisis and hard times will not serve this economy well.
— Hyman Minsky

Krispy Kreme's woes stemmed in part from a common 1990s-era
practice: Setting earnings-per-share targets for Wall Street
analysts and then pushing to beat them by a penny.
— Mark Maremont and Rick Brooks

The regulatory and oversight framework imposed on corporate America was substantial in the 1990s but fatally flawed. Virtually all oversight authorities, from the corporate boards of directors, to the auditors and the Securities and Exchange Commission (SEC), were lax or complicit. Thanks primarily to the Sarbanes-Oxley Act of 2002 (SOX), the entire structure has been overhauled and a host of new systems put into place — the New Accounting. The effectiveness of this system has a big effect on the potential for earnings magic and will be reviewed critically. SOX is the starting point, followed by the impact of the law on corporate governance, responsibilities of senior executives, auditing, accounting standard setting, and SEC enforcement.

SARBANES-OXLEY TO THE RESCUE

SOX has 11 titles, each divided into sections. The most important topics are referenced by section number. Title I created the Public Company Accounting Oversight Board (PCAOB), a quasi-governmental board to regulate auditing of public companies. Title II banned several nonaudit services to improve perceived auditor independence. Title III promotes corporate responsibility by requiring the chief executive officer (CEO) and chief financial officer (CFO) to certify that the financial reports are correct. Title IV on enhanced financial disclosure includes Section 404, which requires a management report on internal controls, the biggest sticking point in costly new audit requirements. Title VI requires the stock exchanges to address conflicts of interests by securities analysts, which has been done. Additional titles increased SEC funding, required research reports by the Government Accountability Office (GAO), SEC and others, and increased corporate, white-collar, and criminal fraud penalties.

Corporate Governance

Corporate governance is the structure in place to oversee the management of an organization and the first line of defense for avoiding, detecting, and eliminating financial abuse. A weak governance structure is more likely associated with misleading accounting information. The board of directors has two vital functions: to provide (1) a broad overview on operating policy and strategic planning and (2) corporate oversight. It is up to the board of directors to ensure that the business strategy in place is viable and that operations follow this strategy. The boards of Enron, WorldCom, and the other financial fiascos all had irresponsible governance characteristics. New regulations emphasize governance requirements because of this obvious relationship.

SOX includes relatively little direct guidance on corporate governance. Instead, SOX shifted the responsibility to the oversight of the SEC and specific rules adopted by the stock exchanges. The new rules are summarized later in this chapter.

The corporate governance in place is detailed in the annual proxy statement of each corporation. A review of recent proxy statements indicates how effective SOX has been in enhancing corporate governance. This is particularly true of companies that have had a history of poor governance and are fighting off any attempts to improve governance. Walt Disney is an interesting example. Chairman and CEO Michael Eisner dominated the company and eliminated virtually all executive and board opposition, in spite of obvious blunders. With SOX requirements, 9 of 12 Disney board members are independent; Eisner was stripped of the chairmanship and announced his retirement. He still managed to make over $8 million in salary and bonuses in 2004. Even corporations with a history of excellent governance, such as General Electric, have shown improvements and enhanced proxy statement disclosures.

Audit Requirements

SOX mandates extensive changes in the audit process. These include the creation of the new audit regulator (PCAOB), new requirements for corporate audit committees, the banning of many nonaudit services by the auditor to improve perceived auditor independence, required rotation of audit partners, and additional audit-related requirements including the certification of internal controls by both the auditor and corporate executives.

Several of the new requirements are considered controversial, especially banning nonaudit services and the new internal control reports. Former chairman of the SEC Arthur Levitt was particularly vocal on auditor independence and had a big influence on Congress. However, academic research (at least so far) does not support this allegation. Basically, research suggests no evidence that nonaudit services influence auditor independence. It is more difficult to criticize internal control requirements—the concept of adequate internal controls has been central to auditing for decades and also has been required by federal law, long before SOX. Most of the complaints so far have been related to the high costs, compared to expected minimal benefits, and the overregulation of the auditors in the field.

The future importance of the PCAOB is not known with any certainty. This is a new category of regulation. In the past, auditors have been regulated by state laws, state licensing requirements, and oversight by the American Institute of Certified Public Accountants (AIPCA, essentially the trade association of auditors and other accountants). The SEC under former chairman Harvey Pitt had difficulty picking the five-member board. Despite the slow start, the PCAOB is now running effectively under Chairman William McDonough. The board has issued three audit standards and a set of rules, plus proposed rules and briefing papers. Audit Standard No. 2 on internal control audit and related rules is particularly important. The reports of the initial inspections of the Big Four were completed in 2004, and inspection reports are available on the PCAOB Web site. So far, the PCAOB is active and professional; its long-term effectiveness has yet to be determined.

Executive Responsibility for Financial Reporting and Internal Controls

Section 302 of SOX requires that both the CEO and CFO certify that each periodic report (10-K and 10-Q) filed with the SEC "fairly presents, in all material respects, the financial condition and results of operations of the issuer." Because Section 906 of SOX indicates that failure to meet the criteria could result in a fine up to $1 million and 10 years in jail (up to $5 million and 20 years if the executives willfully provide false information), the presumption is that these executives will pay particularly close attention to the financial statement details. The CEOs at Enron, WorldCom, and other financial fiascos claimed ignorance of the accounting fraud. This excuse will not fly under SOX. Corporate executives have been signing off for the last few years, presumably confident in the basic transparency of their financial statements. However, former HealthSouth CEO Richard Scrushy was subject to this provision and acquitted on all counts.

Increased Financial Disclosure

Financial disclosure was extensive before SOX. However, not everything was disclosed adequately or even disclosed at all. Enron's special-purpose entities are a glaring example of critical misreported and unreported arrangements. There was (and still is) plenty of latitude for (almost) complete transparency, but only if companies are willing. The scandals make it clear that many companies were not willing. The open question is: Are most corporations attempting transparency? One goal of financial regulation is mandating complete disclosure whether companies are willing or not.

SOX requires more disclosures in specific areas where disclosures have been lacking in the past. Under SOX Section 401, the SEC is required to issue new rules on off–balance sheet transactions and pro forma presentation. The SEC also is required to report on special-purpose entities, which was accomplished in 2005. The SEC now requires that off–balance sheet arrangements must be disclosed in Management Discussion and Analysis (MD&A), including a table summarizing certain contractual obligations, critical accounting policies, and estimates. These off-balance transactions include contracts or transactions with unconsolidated entities and various contingencies and various obligations associated with derivatives. To comply with SOX Sections 401 and 409, the SEC also includes new Regulation G, which requires disclosure of pro forma results ("non-GAAP financial measures"), including the most directly comparable financial measure from generally accepted accounting principles.

SOX Section 409 encourages the SEC to require corporations to make public disclosures in a "rapid and current basis." The SEC adopted rules to accelerate 10-K and 10-Q filings, from 90 days after the end of the fiscal year to 60 days (beginning in 2006); the deadline for 10-Qs was decreased from 45 days to 30 days, again beginning in 2006. The SEC also is required by SOX Section 408 to review each company's reports at least once every three years.

The most significant disclosure issues are based on new Financial Accounting Standards Board (FASB) pronouncements. The FASB has been encouraged to move toward principles-based rather than rules-based pronouncements, integrating pronouncements with international accounting standards (a process called international convergence), and solve all the big issues of the day, from special-purpose entities and derivatives to stock options and revenue recognition.

Funding the SEC and Other Organizations

A key regulatory problem for federal agencies has been a lack of funding. Thus, over 70 years the SEC has been curtailed mainly by budget cuts rather than changing legislation. During the 1990s the role of the SEC was expanded and economic growth increased the size and number of public companies regulated (not to mention new industries based on the new high-tech technologies and more complex financial contracting), while SEC budgets remained tight. This meant that the SEC had to prioritize its responsibilities and focus on what were considered key areas. Much of the SEC effort in the later 1990s was on initial public offerings (IPOs), especially for Internet and other New Economy companies. Many of these IPOs recorded only losses, had poor operating and governance structures, used blatant accounting manipulation, and in more typical circumstances would never have gone public. The SEC did its best to stop the most extreme abuse. In the meantime, relatively little effort was put into the annual evaluation of established companies—Enron, for example.

The FASB faced somewhat different circumstances. Although the FASB is supposed to be independent, much of the funding came mainly from corporate and accounting-related groups (indirectly through the Financial Accounting Foundation). These groups expected substantial influence for these bucks. The FASB is subject to the jurisdiction of the SEC. The SEC comes under political pressure from Congress (and indirectly from lobbyists and others), which reacts to campaign contributors. These campaign contributors can be the same groups that fund the FASB. The FASB was not underfunded, but FASB's standard-setting process has always been political. It is difficult to establish the most appropriate accounting standards if Congress claims it will eliminate your organization and corporate sources threaten to eliminate all future funding.

SOX and other federal legislation dealt with funding for the SEC, FASB, and the brand-new PCAOB. SEC funding comes directly from Congress as an annual appropriation. Since SOX, funding levels have been substantially improved and staff levels increased. The fiscal year 2005 budget was $913 million, up 13% from the previous year. By comparison, the fiscal year 2000 budget was only $377 million. Thus, the funding level of the SEC increased almost two and a half times over five years.

PCAOB funding is based on SOX Section 109, which states that the PCAOB's budget will be funded by the "issuers." Annually, the board completes its budget (which must be approved by the SEC), and "accounting support fees" are set based on the market value of publicly traded companies with over $25 million in capitalization. The 2005 total budget outlays for the PCAOB was $137.1 million (up from $103.3 million in 2004), and accounting support fees were $136.1 million. This procedure should provide adequate funding and more independence to the PCAOB. SOX Section 109 also funds the FASB using the same approach; that is, charging corporations for FASB operations.

Why Is SOX Important?

Despite the additional regulatory burden and implementation costs, SOX has been a demonstrable success and the key to understanding the new accounting. The major points are (1) the specific SOX mandates, such as the creation of the PCAOB and specific audit committee requirements, and (2) the requirements for action by the SEC and other groups, such as new corporate governance rules of the major stock exchanges and the new SEC rules on financial disclosures.

SOX really got the ball rolling: corporate governance, enhanced responsibilities for the senior corporate executives, an invigorated and better-funded SEC, and substantial changes in auditing requirements. The role of the FASB and other groups, such as investment bankers and analysts and attorneys, were directly and indirectly influenced by SOX. The process has been dynamic as well and complex and uncertain, but obvious progress has been made.

CORPORATE GOVERNANCE: THE FIRST LINE OF DEFENSE

Corporate governance provides the stewardship to oversee the management of an organization. It is up to the board of directors to ensure that the business strategy in place is viable and that operations follow this strategy. The corporate governance environment is the first line of defense for avoiding, detecting, and eliminating financial abuse. From an investor perspective, the governance structure signals the amount of reliability expected in the financial reporting system. A weak governance structure is more likely dominated by the CEO, which could result in poor earnings quality.

It took the market collapse of 2000 and the scandals that followed to reveal the extent of the problems associated with poor governance. From an earnings magic perspective of major corporations, the environment for abuse starts at the top, the board of directors. The members of the board and the existing corporate governance structure are significant signals of the potential for earnings manipulation and opportunistic behavior. Thanks in part to beefed-up regulations, the current governance structure is more likely to limit further abuses. The problem is that management incentives for abuse have not changed much.

SOX requirements for corporate governance shifted the burden to the SEC and stock exchanges to formulate new rules. The New York Stock Exchange (NYSE) and Nasdaq rewrote governance standards for the listed companies. Important new rules include the requirement that a majority of board members must be independent; executive sessions would take place without the presence of management; and new rules for the audit, compensation, nominating, and governance committees. All of these committees would be composed of independent directors.

The enhanced role of the audit committee to dominate the hiring, compensation, and replacing independent auditors, plus oversight of the audit functions (both internal and external), is particularly important. These requirements are based on SOX Section 301 and new SEC requirements.

Evaluating the corporate governance environment is a qualitative analysis, based on a review of the proxy statement (with additional information found in the annual report, corporate Web site, and other sources). Despite the complexity of the topic, an analysis of governance will pay dividends—so to speak. Three corporate governance areas are particularly important: (1) the CEO and board of directors, (2) executive compensation, and (3) auditing.

The Board of Directors and the CEO

The chief executive officer and other senior executives are normally responsible for day-to-day operations and developing plans and strategies for board approval. The professional responsibilities of these leaders are extensive, and they are rewarded with substantial compensation. How they function is central to the overall success and future potential of the corporation, as well as to the establishment of the earnings management environment of the firm.

Topic	Concerns
Role of the CEO	Strong CEO, usually also the chairman of the board, with little or no control by the board; alternatively, weak CEO or poor fit to the job.
Composition of the Board	Lack of independence: too many company executives, major customers or suppliers, friends, or relatives of the CEO.
Committees of the Board	Few committees exist beyond minimum requirement; obvious lack of competence or independence of committee members.
Compensation and Commitment of Board Members	Overly generous compensation, which may make them less objective on possible earnings management issues; compensation not tied to performance; board members not putting in an adequate amount of time and effort.

Exhibit 3.1   Concerns Associated with the Board and CEO

Particular concerns associated directly with the board and CEO are shown in Exhibit 3.1.

The information needed to evaluate these concerns is found in the annual proxy statement, issued after the annual report and before the annual stockholders' meeting. The proxy statements will give a brief biography of each board member, state whether they are independent, and provide a summary of board compensation.

The composition of the board, the number of board members, and the board's committee structure are major signals of the earnings magic potential. Key factors could be the relative indifference of the board (true at Enron), ability or willingness to stand up to a strong CEO, and possible collusion of board members in questionable acts. A desirable board is made up primarily of outsiders and picked for competence rather than because they are friends of the CEO. Deviations signal potential problems. The number of board members, the relative split between internal (company executives and directors with direct connections to the firm) and external members, background and training, performance requirements, and compensation are issues to review.

The existence of board committees is important to the specific performance of the board. Many of the crucial board functions are directed to specific committees. All major corporations now are required to have an audit committee and a compensation committee, and firms may have additional committees as well. Committee structure and composition should be reviewed to ensure independence and relative competence. The number of meetings held by the specific committees during the year gives some indication of the relative seriousness of the committee members.

Compensation packages for board members, CEOs, and other executives will differ substantially from one company to another. Compensation can include cash payments, bonuses, stock options and other equity interests, and various perquisites. The compensation package should be commensurate with the responsibilities and time commitments required. The specific composition of the package also may be an indicator of the expected behavior of the board.

Executive Compensation

The board of directors must have a compensation committee. The board determines executive compensation and generally approves employee compensation and benefits. The annual compensation decisions for senior executives are summarized in the proxy statement. Employee compensation and benefits are summarized in the notes to the annual report, including detailed notes for pension plans, stock options, and other compensation agreements.

Executive compensation has four basic components: (1) base salary; (2) bonuses, which are usually based on current earnings performance; (3) long-term compensation, usually stock options (with restricted stock and stock appreciation rights common alternatives); and (4) various perquisites. Base salary is normally limited because of IRS regulations on deductibility; however, performance-based salary, including bonuses, is effectively unlimited. Base salary usually is not an earnings management concern.

Bonuses can be important, because executives subject to large bonuses have increased incentives to meet bonus targets. Bonus targets typically are based on a specific definition of earnings, which means that executives would tend to focus on that specific target. Consequently, if the target is based on some definition of income from current operations (called above the line), earnings magic strategies are expected to dump losses as nonrecurring items (called below the line). Stock options became more popular in the 1990s and, with the booming stock market, became a huge source of wealth to executives. Consequently, the executive mind-set seemed to focus on whatever it took to ensure that stock prices continued to ratchet up. Perquisites vary substantially, and the evaluation must be done on a case-by-case basis.

Executive compensation-related concerns are listed in Exhibit 3.2.

Consider the compensation of IBM chairman and CEO S. J. Palmisano. According to the 2005 proxy statement, his 2004 base salary was $1.66 million, he received a bonus of $5.575 million, and he was awarded 250,000 options and other compensation of almost $2 million. Not bad: Cash compensation of over $9 million plus a bunch of options. This seems reasonable

Topic	Concerns
Composition of the Compensation Committee	Members must be outsiders but specific composition may hint as biases.
Functions and Authority of the Committee	Lack of authority to adjust compensation to focus on executive performance.
Specific Compensation Packages	Actual compensation paid does not match actual firm performance.
Poor-Performing Companies	Overcompensation of executives based on actual performance.
Companies with Previous Abuse	Particular concern that compensation packages changed to increase compensation rather than match compensation with economic performance.

EXHIBIT 3.2 CONCERNS RELATED TO EXECUTIVE COMPENSATION

given that IBM's revenues were up 8% to $96 billion, while net income improved 11% to $8.4 billion.

Auditing

Corporations have both external audits and internal audit departments, which are the responsibility of the audit committee. Given the recent corporate scandals and the perceived deficiencies of external auditors, this oversight function is vital. Audit committees are now required by the major stock exchanges.

Potential concerns associated with the audit function are outlined in Exhibit 3.3.

Most of these are now nonissues thanks to SOX. SOX and related regulations by the stock exchanges require that all audit committee members are independent and that the committee chair is a "financial expert." Most of the nonaudit services have been banned, particularly high-cost specialties, such as information technology, that give the perception of lack of independence. However, the audit opinion still might be qualified or the audit report late. Both events signal potential conflict between auditor and client.

The role of the audit committee should be described in detail in the proxy statement, including the members, the role of the committee, analysis of the selection process of the external auditor, how the auditor is to be evaluated, and fees paid to the auditor. The auditor's report or opinion is presented in the financial statement section of the annual report. The content indicates whether there is an unqualified ("clean") opinion or if specific problems exist. Almost all opinions are unqualified ("the statements present

Topic	Concerns
Composition of Audit Committee	Potential lack of competence or independence, based on committee composition.
Audit Procurement	Poor audit procurement practices (i.e., the process for selecting the auditor); lack of disclosure on procurement practices.
Nonaudit Services	Fees for nonaudit services excessive; potential for lack of auditor independence.
Audit Opinion	Qualified opinion, indicating dispute with auditor; late audit report date.
Auditor Oversight	Committee oversight inadequate; does not spend enough time for due diligence or fails to pursue problems brought up by the auditors.
Internal Control Weaknesses	Thanks to Sarbanes-Oxley Sections 302 and 404, increasing focus on controls means more announcements of control weaknesses. Reported control weaknesses are a likely red flag signal of earnings magic.

EXHIBIT 3.3 POTENTIAL CONCERNS ASSOCIATED WITH THE AUDIT FUNCTION

fairly the financial position and results of operations . . . in accordance with GAAP"). A qualified or other opinion is a red flag. The date of the opinion indicates when the audit was completed; a relatively early date suggests a relatively problem-free audit. Corporations initially had 90 days to issue the 10-K from the end of the fiscal year; auditor's reports coming close to or exceeding the 90 days may be a red flag. The SEC has accelerated filing dates to 60 days for 10-Ks for fiscal years beginning in 2006.

It is still a good idea to check the audit fees (and nonaudit fees) charged, the auditor's report date, and the number of days from fiscal year end to the 10-K filing date. According to its 2004 10-K, giant pharmaceutical company Pfizer was audited by Big Four firm KPMG, which issued a clean (unqualified) opinion 55 days after the end of the fiscal year; the 10-K was submitted on February 28, 2005, 59 days after fiscal year-end. According to the proxy statement, the audit fee was $25.5 million, or 64.9%, of total fees paid to KPMG. The relatively long period before the audit opinion date (55 days) and the sizable amount of nonaudit fees (including $11 million for tax work) are minor concerns.

Internal control weaknesses are supposed to be reported on the 10-Q, 10-K, and 8-K filings. Two Dow 30 firms reported internal control weaknesses in 2004, AIG and General Electric. Accounting research shows that disclosures are increasing because of SOX. However, not all of these disclosures are major, and it will take some effort to determine which ones are particularly important (e.g., oversight controls over nonroutine transactions or poor review systems by senior financial management). The good news is that research evidence indicates that auditors are spending more effort on firms with material weaknesses.

NEW PERSPECTIVE AT THE FASB

The Financial Accounting Standards Board is responsible for financial accounting standard setting in the United States for corporations and nonprofit organizations. It is the basic source of generally accepted accounting principles. The FASB has an agenda based on current issues, a formal process that includes substantial research and public input, a theoretical perspective based on the *Conceptual Framework,* and an approach for solving today's accounting problems. The most important changes to the FASB have been the funding sources (now the market-traded corporations, based on SOX rules), a shift from rules-based to principles-based standards (or at least the perception of a change), more interaction with the International Accounting Standards Board (IASB) to attempt international convergence of accounting standards, and the focus on accounting issues highlighted by the scandals, such as special-purpose entities, stock options, and derivatives. These were FASB issues earlier, but now the FASB is likely to be more decisive when confronting conflict, as it has been given something of a federal mandate.

A major criticism of U.S. GAAP, and more specifically the standards issued by the FASB, has been that they tend to be rules-based rather than principles-based. A major point of comparison was U.S. GAAP (and the resulting accounting scandals) compared to European and other foreign commercial accounting standards, which are perceived to be principles-based (with fewer scandals). A principles-based system relies on conceptual principles, with general agreement of the accounting and reporting goals and consistency across the various aspects of the financial statement components, operating performance recognition, and disclosure requirements.

Sarbanes-Oxley required the SEC to study principles-based accounting, which was done in 2003. The study critiqued the current U.S. system and provided evidence of both rules-based standards with the expected deficiencies and a review of recent FASB attempts to adopt a more principles-based approach. The FASB response: "The Board agrees that the objective and underlying principles of a standard should be clearly articulated and prominently placed in FASB standards. . . . [T]he understandability of its standards could be improved by writing its standards in ways that (a) clearly state the accounting objective(s), (b) clearly articulate the underlying principles, and (c) improve the explanation of the rationale behind those principles and how they relate to the conceptual framework" (FASB 2004, pp. 2–3).

Recent FASB pronouncements required market value or other fair value measures for financial instruments. For example, derivatives, which are contracts "derived" from other financial instruments, are recorded at fair value (Statements of Accounting Standards [SFAS] No. 123), pension assets use fair value and liabilities are discounted using complex formulas (SFAS No. 87 and others), business combinations are now limited to the purchase method which records all acquisition assets and liabilities at fair value (SFAS No. 141), and stock options use fair value calculations (SFAS No. 123). This focus on fair value is expected to accelerate.

The SEC report on principles-based accounting recommended the need for convergence; that is, the movement toward global GAAP. Both IASB and FASB have agreed to work together on this process. There is general consensus on some issues but differences on others. An additional difficulty is the different legal systems. The United States, Britain, and most former British colonies are common-law countries, which share many legal and regulatory similarities. The remaining European countries and most other countries use civil law, based on extensive civil codes. FASB and IASB are working together on a short-term convergence project on issues that can be solved quickly. There are also a number of joint projects, which the two boards are conducting simultaneously, including revenue recognition and business combinations. A major research project identified substantive differences between U.S. and international GAAP. The FASB and IASB agreed that a Conceptual Framework improvement project should be undertaken jointly.

The FASB Web site (www.fasb.org) is a useful starting point for recent pronouncements and current issues that may change GAAP in the near future. Available by the middle of 2005 were summaries of all FASB pronouncements issued, 153 statements (plus a revised Statement No. 123), and 46 interpretations. Also important are exposure documents that likely will become pronouncements in the near future. Accounting standards are changing, and the FASB Web site is the place to stay on top of the action.

THE SEC IN ACTION

The SEC was established with the Securities Exchange Commission Act of 1934 to regulate financial markets, delegating accounting standard setting to the private sector—now the FASB. A major problem of the SEC was an inadequate budget and too small a staff. This was demonstrated when the SEC announced that the last review of Enron before its 2001 collapse was done in 1997. SEC funding has been greatly increased and responsibilities have been added, thanks in part to SOX. Despite the staffing and other problems, the SEC established the EDGAR system, which makes the 10-K, 10-Q, proxy statement and many other documents available online. In addition, Regulation FD (for full disclosure) requires that when companies talk to financial analysts, the information be made available to everyone at the same time.

According to its Web site: "The primary mission of the SEC is to protect investors and maintain the integrity of the securities markets. . . . [A]ll investors, whether large institutions or private individuals, should have access to certain basic facts about an investment prior to buying it. To achieve this, the SEC requires public companies to disclose meaningful financial and other information to the public, which provides a common pool of knowledge for all investors to use to judge for themselves if a company's securities are a good investment." The SEC oversees key securities players, including stock exchanges, broker-dealers, investment advisors, and mutual funds. The SEC brings 400 to 500 civil enforcement actions annually against individuals and companies that violate securities laws, such as insider trading, accounting fraud, and providing false or misleading information.

The SEC oversees the FASB and issues additional accounting rules on top of FASB standards. This is an ongoing process, with increased effort since SOX, including accelerated filing of 10-K and 10-Q reports being phased in from 90 and 45 days to 60 and 30 days, respectively. As a SOX mandate, the SEC sets the rules for corporate internal control reports, including management responsibilities and assessment. The SEC beefed up its requirements for MD&A disclosures, including discussion of all major off–balance sheet transactions, especially those infamous special-purpose entities (SPEs). Pro forma earnings are still allowed, but limited by SEC rules. There are new detailed accounting rules on revenue recognition (including buy/sell arrangement and service contracts), leases, statement of cash flow presentations, business combinations, marketable securities, contingencies, pensions, SPEs, segment disclosures, derivatives, fair value reporting, and loan losses.

ANALYSTS AND INVESTMENT BANKERS

As pointed out by Berenson (2003), the quarterly earnings per share (EPS) analyst forecast is "the Number." Most companies meet or beat the forecast most of the time, and a few consistently meet this forecast quarter after quarter, year after year. The system rewards the companies with high earnings growth and the ability to always meet expectations with a price premium, usually defined as an above-market price earnings ratio (PE). Companies, especially high-tech and other high-PE firms, that fail to meet the forecasts can expect to have their share price pummeled—bad news for executive compensation contracts. This focus was in place throughout the 1990s and proved to be a significant element in the earnings scandals. The system is still in place, and companies are enticed to manage earnings to meet or beat forecasts. How can financial information be used to ensure financial reality?

Analysts can have a major impact on stock price, although forecasting is hardly an exact science. Independent analysts make forecasts on a combination of their own detailed analysis plus "insider information" furnished directly from the company. However, analysts who work for investment banks (called sell-side analysts) have substantial conflicts of interests. Investment banks make huge fees from underwriting new issues, and analysts are considered part of the "banking team," assisting in due diligence, presenting favorable information in investor road shows, making positive recommendations on the client, and even bringing in banking business. It is difficult to maintain the "Chinese Wall" between banking and analysis in this environment. The incentives of the analyst are entirely one-sided: to support the client and the new issue. Why would a client use an investment bank whose superstar analyst badmouths the company? Jack Grubman (Salomon Smith Barney, later a part of Citigroup, in telecom), Mary Meeker (Morgan Stanley, Internet), and Henry Blodgett (at Merrill Lynch, also Internet) were the superstar analysts who seemingly never met an investment client they did not like in the 1990s. They all continued to make buy recommendations as their investment bank clients crashed and burned. Both Grubman and Blodgett paid big-time fines and were barred for life from financial analysis.

Thanks to SOX, there have been rule changes. New regulations have been issued by the SEC and stock exchanges. Generally, sell-side conflicts of interest must be disclosed, including public appearances by analysts. "Quiet periods" exist that limit analysts of banking clients from issuing any recommendations about new security around the issue dates or trading in the new issues. Other rules are designed to make analysts more independent, barring promises of favorable research, changing analyst compensation procedures, and so on. These minor changes certainly do not fundamentally change the obvious conflicts of interest, especially the incentives for positive ratings by analysts. The SEC basically warns the investing public to be aware of these conflicts: Do not depend on sell-side analysts.

In summary, the new accounting is in place, and changes continue at a rapid pace. Most of these changes are good news, suggesting more transparency and more competent oversight. But earnings magic will not go away, nor will the incentives of key actors to game the system. Investors and analysts need to be aware of the New Accounting, including the more problematic areas, such as corporate governance, auditing, and sell-side financial analysts' recommendations.

4

WADING THROUGH THE EARNINGS NUMBERS

Financial reporting should serve as an anchor during bubbles, to check speculative beliefs.

—Stephen Penman

The function of rating agencies in a crisis is to go out on the battlefield and shoot the wounded.

—Martin Mayer

By 2006, companies are required to submit an annual report, Form 10-K, to the Securities and Exchange Commission (SEC) within 60 days of the end of the fiscal year. A company can also issue a separate annual report that has most of the information in the 10-K plus lots of pretty pictures. The quarterly report, 10-Q, is submitted within 30 days of the end of the fiscal quarter. These reports are almost immediately made available to the public over the Internet from the SEC's EDGAR system and from the companies' Web sites. Usually within a few days or weeks of the end of the quarter, companies issue earnings announcements, which could include an income statement and balance sheet. Consequently, this level of information generally is available quickly. Thanks in part to Regulation FD, companies are expected to "simulcast" their earnings announcements and other financial press releases that are presented to analysts and other financial specialists.

The financial statements and the explanatory notes represent the most significant disclosures of these reports and will be the central focus for analyzing earnings magic. These financial statements are based on generally accepted accounting principles (GAAP), primarily established by the Financial Accounting Standards Board (FASB). In addition to the financial statements and notes are the Management Discussion and Analysis (MD&A) and additional explanatory materials, such as a chief executive's letter. These are used primarily to explain the company's current operations, business strategy, market and business risks, and future expectations.

Corporations also issue proxy statements annually, before the annual stockholders' meeting. These statements concern issues to be voted on by the stockholders and are useful to evaluate corporate governance. Stockholders vote on directors, and considerable information is given on each prospective director. Proxy statements include information on board, audit, and compensation committees. Important information is presented on the audit, including auditor, audit cost, and nonaudit fees. Executive compensation is presented in some detail; it is particularly important to understand management performance incentives. As more disclosures on corporate governance are required, the proxy statement becomes increasingly important to evaluate the earnings magic environment.

The purpose of financial accounting is to provide financial information to internal and external parties to make reasonable decisions on investment, credit, supply, and so on. The FASB not only establishes GAAP, but also continues to develop a conceptual framework to determine the objectives and fundamental "theory" on what financial information should be incorporated and how it should be measured. The basic financial reports and other relevant information are described in this chapter. Also included is a discussion of earnings quality, including useful quantitative and qualitative techniques.

CONTENTS OF THE 10-K

The basic format of the 10-K is governed by SEC requirements. Most components are required; others are common but voluntary. Exhibit 4.1 shows

Section	Description
Management Letter	Optional section that could be from the president, CEO, CFO, chairman, or others. It is usually optimistic and presents the most cheerful information possible.
Financial Highlights	Optional summary, usually focusing on operations (income statement) information for two or more years.
Mission Statement or Objectives Statement	Occasionally stated separately from the MD&A, presumably to emphasize the distinct business strategy of the corporation.
Various Types of Management Reports	The executives' responsibility for financial statements is presented, often next to the auditor's report; other reports are common for some companies and industries.

(continues)

EXHIBIT 4.1   MAJOR COMPONENTS PRESENTED IN THE 10-K

Management Discussion and Analysis (MD&A)	Required section containing extensive analysis of business strategy, current operations, business risks, and future projections (which can be presented in a separate "forward-looking statement").
Financial Section	Includes all financial statements, the auditor's report, and notes to the financial statements. This is the heart of the annual report.
Auditor's Report	A standard opinion related to the financial audit. It is signed in the name of the audit firm (usually one of the Big Four), dated at completion perhaps within a month after the end of the fiscal year, and states an opinion in one or more paragraphs. Almost all opinions are "clean," meaning there are no exceptions (audit problems usually lead to a qualified opinion—essentially the auditor disagrees with the client). The auditor's internal control report often is presented as part of the auditor's report.
Income Statement	Comparative analysis for the last three years, explaining the operations over each year associated with sales and other revenues, operating expenses, and various nonoperating gains and losses (most of which are considered nonrecurring items), resulting in net income. Earnings per share on a basic and diluted basis also are presented.
Balance Sheet	The position statement at the end of the fiscal year, listing the book values of the major categories of assets, liabilities, and owners' equity, compared to the previous year.
Statement of Cash Flows	Comparative statement over the last 3 years explains the changes in cash of the period in three major categories (mostly using the indirect method): (1) cash flows from operations starts from net income and adds back depreciation and other accruals, plus changes in other current items; (2) cash from investing, including capital expenditures; and (3) cash from financing, including sale or purchase of stock, debt instruments, and dividend payments.
Statement of Stockholders' Equity	Statement (also called statement of changes in stockholders' equity or something similar) that comes in a variety of formats and generally presents three years of changes in equity by categories, including other comprehensive income.
Notes	Explain the accounting policies used by the corporation and present detailed information of various accounts and categories of financial information. These can be extensive and important for analyzing earnings management potential.
Operating Summary	A required 5-year summary (many companies extend this to 10 or more years) of significant financial and nonfinancial information. Financial data include operations (sales, net income, earnings per share, etc.), balance sheet items (working capital, assets, equity, various ratios), and cash flow items. Nonfinancial information tends to be industry-specific.

Adapted from Giroux (2004), pp. 48–49.

EXHIBIT 4.1   MAJOR COMPONENTS PRESENTED IN THE 10-K (CONTINUED)

the major components, presented in a typical order in the 10-K. Terminology and specific content vary by company, although standardization by industry is common.

Financial Section

The balance sheet shows the financial position of a company at the end of the fiscal year. The assets are the resources of the firm. The liabilities and equity are the "sources" of assets, explaining how they were financed by creditors or owners (also called the stakeholders). This is demonstrated in the accounting equation: Assets = Liabilities + Stockholders' Equity. Current assets usually are disclosed separately from long-term assets, as are current and long-term liabilities.

An income statement summarizes the relative operating success of business performance for the fiscal year. The statement is comparative, including the current and the two previous years. Basically, the form is sales and other revenue less all expenses (plus and minus gains and losses) to arrive at net income. Major categories of expenses include cost of sales, other operating expenses, and nonoperating (nonrecurring items and others). Net income is then stated on a per share basis as earnings per share. The format is more or less standardized based on GAAP to include several basic components. Substantial differences in reporting format exist, usually by industry.

The statement of cash flows evaluates cash receipts (inflows) and cash payments (outflows) for the year into three categories: operations, investing, and financing activities. The focus of cash flows from operations (CFO) is cash effects of transactions that involve net income. The indirect method starts with net income and then adds back noncash items such as depreciation and amortization as well as changes in noncash current items (receivables, inventory, payables and so on). Most often, CFO is positive because net income is normally positive and noncash expenses such as depreciation increase CFO. Cash flows from investing (CFI) include capital expenditures and investments. Generally CFI is negative because investments are uses of cash. Cash flow from financing (CFF) includes the acquisition or disposal of equity and debt as well as the payment of dividends. Then cash is reconciled from the beginning balance to the ending balance.

The final required statement is the statement of stockholders' equity, which reconciles the various components of equity for three years. Alternative formats are allowable. In most cases, the beginning equity balances are stated for the beginning of the year; additions and deletions are presented for each of the three years to arrive at current year-end balances for all major components. Particularly important is the reconciliation of other comprehensive income items, because these gains and losses are not part of net income.

Notes

The Notes section may be the longest part of the 10-K. The first note is "The Summary of Significant Accounting Policies," which reviews specific accounting policies (essentially how GAAP is being applied) for major income statement and balance sheet categories. The important information is the specific accounting choices made; for example, first-in, first-out (FIFO) for inventory rather than last-in, first-out (LIFO) or another method.

The remaining notes review specific reporting areas in detail. Unique items the company used during the current year, such as restructuring or specific nonrecurring items, usually come next, followed by detailed item-by-item disclosures. Formats differ. Most often companies start with either the balance sheet or income statement and disclose major categories down that statement. The last item presented tends to be quarterly information.

Usefulness of the Proxy Statement

The proxy statement is an SEC-required annual report, in advance of the corporation's annual stockholders' meeting. The stockholders will be expected to vote on directors and various other issues. Based on current SEC and stock exchange requirements, stockholders vote on executive compensation issues and the selection and fee structure of the auditor. The purpose of the proxy statement is to present the stockholders with the information they need for informed voting. The statement provides considerable information on the existing and proposed board of directors, on board and executive compensation, and on the auditor, including fees charged and nonaudit services provided. Consequently, the proxy statement can be extremely useful in evaluating corporate governance and the overall earnings management environment.

EARNINGS QUALITY

What characteristics are most useful in evaluating reporting quality and, implicitly, the potential earnings quality of a corporation? Four items seem particularly important: (1) a well-defined business strategy, (2) the corporate governance structure, (3) relative report completeness and timeliness, and (4) transparency. Any evidence of earnings magic suggests poor quality, that is, unreliable information.

Well-Defined Business Strategy

Evaluating the business strategy of a corporation is a qualitative analysis to determine the relative effectiveness of this strategy compared to the industry and economic condition the firm faces. If the company cannot articulate a viable business strategy in its MD&A and other sources, it is unlikely that the financial reporting will demonstrate current and continued operating success. Tyco's conglomerate strategy of acquiring unrelated companies did not make much sense, but acquisition earnings magic jacked up the earnings numbers.

This evaluation is called qualitative analysis for a reason. It requires judgment. For several years AT&T attempted to enter virtually all telecommunications markets. The concept was a fully integrated telecom, where consumers could come to AT&T to solve their communication needs. This AT&T strategy meant buying a number of high-priced firms in various telecom segments or developing these segments internally. Unfortunately, technology problems and competition almost brought AT&T to financial ruin. This business strategy proved to be a failed one, but it looked like a winner at the start. AT&T acquirer SBC may succeed at a similar strategy, aided by continued technical innovations, beneficial regulatory rulings, and a more disciplined approach.

Dell has a relatively simple business strategy of cost leadership. Through a variety of efficiency measures (including selling directly to the customer and an effective just-in-time inventory system), Dell is the low-cost producer of personal computers. It uses a low price strategy to increase market share and enter new business hardware areas. It is number one in market share and profit, based on a winning strategy rather than earnings magic.

CORPORATE GOVERNANCE STRUCTURE

The corporate governance structure is the first line of defense for quality reporting and avoiding financial abuse. The board of directors and its committees should provide an objective review of corporate strategy, compensation and compensation incentives, financial audit decisions and review, and overall evaluation of the success for the executives and corporate operations. A high-quality, independent board that takes its roles seriously and is not beholden to the CEO and other executives provides considerable

assurance that earnings manipulation and other mischief will not be toler-
ated. By the same token, a board largely of insiders, friends of the CEO, and
interlocking boards with other companies, particularly those of suppliers
and customers, signals significant concern.

Corporations are improving corporate structures, partly in response to
new rules by stock exchanges and other bodies. But the specific characteristics need to be reviewed, with considerable information on the board in the
proxy statement. The review should include compensation agreements and
audit characteristics, also found in the proxy statement.

Reporting Completeness and Timeliness

Financial reports can be 100-page monsters, but still be incomplete and not
timely. How can reporting be incomplete? The companies have strict SEC
guidelines for when reports must be issued. How can they be untimely? Granted,
completeness and timeliness are relative terms. Some companies always wait
until the last acceptable date to file. Many companies present no more than
the minimum acceptable information and then present it in a confusing fash-
ion. A few companies miss the time deadlines and present reports that violate
GAAP disclosure standards—indicators of real chaos.

The earliest financial information is the earnings announcement at the
end of each quarter. The faster companies announce earnings within a couple of weeks of the end of the period. In addition, the information might be
relatively complete, including financial statements and substantial discussions of operations and any issues of concern, such as restructuring or nonrecurring items of any kind. Such companies file the 10-K and 10-Q early,
and they tend to provide detailed information on key operating and financial items.

Other companies follow with a considerable lag. Typically, relatively
little is disclosed during earnings announcements, and it may be deceptive,
such as focusing on pro forma earnings rather than GAAP-based earnings.
Quarterly and annual reports tend to follow this same pattern, with the companies often filing on the last possible day. Confusing and incomplete reports
tend to be in the late-reporting camp.

Reporting completeness means including all necessary information to
make informed judgments on financial reality. Consider special-purpose
entities (SPEs). Thanks to Enron, SPEs went from an obscure category of
structured financing contracts used for ordinary operating purposes to the
well-known means to pull virtually anything off the balance sheet. In the
Enron era, SPEs did not have to be reported and most companies did not
report any, although major companies used SPEs routinely. The situation has

changed with recent SEC and FASB standards. There should be disclosure in the notes and MD&A on SPEs, whether they are used or not. In practice, completeness and understandability varies by company.

Transparency

Transparency means that all financial information is observable and fully reported, at least within reason. Opaque reporting in good times can lead to optimistic illusions that can bid up stock prices (think Enron). When the bad news hits, nothing can be believed and prices collapse: "You go from believing everything to believing nothing" (Friedman 2000, p. 173).

Several areas can be frustrating, starting with the previously mentioned SPEs. A related area of concern is derivative accounting. Derivatives are usually reported in the notes based on fair value. However, it is difficult to determine if a company is, in fact, hedging (the usual claim) or speculating. Several companies explain the rationale and underlying finances of derivatives in detail (e.g., J.P. Morgan), but this is not standard practice.

Another example is segment reporting. Limited segment reporting is required by GAAP, and reporting is often very limited. Major corporations are complex and global. Consequently, industry and geographic segments are widespread and usually complicated. The first problem is the extreme flexibility in defining a segment. There is no obvious standardization, and complexity does not help. At a minimum, revenues and operating income should be stated for each segment, but often they are not. Disney, for example, has extensive information on the four operating segments it reports; however, if you want to evaluate Miramax or ABC (which Disney owns), you are out of luck—they are part of Studio Entertainment and Media Networks and not reported separately. Consequently, an area extremely important to analysts can lack usefulness.

Evidence of Earnings Magic

Companies do not admit to manipulation. They have to be caught in the act, but that is the job of regulators. Outsiders look for signals of possible earnings magic. The primary method of gathering evidence is the relatively detailed analysis of the financial statements and related information. Evidence also comes from external sources. The SEC initiates investigations of unacceptable practices with some frequency, but it is limited in the number of companies it can investigate fully because of funding constraints. The business press reviews company problems and can highlight potential magic in the making.

A recent Government Accountability Office (GAO, the General Accounting Office until the 2004 name change) report (2002) demonstrated that earnings restatements have become a plague. About 15% of Standard & Poor's 500 firms restated at least once from 1997 to 2002, with revenue recognition the most common category. The existence of restatements signals evidence of past earnings magic. The restatement trend has continued since the GAO report.

A summary of the major reporting quality components is shown in Exhibit 4.2.

CAN EARNINGS MAGIC BE DETECTED?

Most large American corporations are run by competent, relatively honest and trustworthy executives who use earnings management sparingly. U.S. GAAP tends to be conservative, and most firms follow conservative alternatives (e.g., delaying revenue recognition until the earnings process is complete). Most CFOs probably attempt to smooth earnings over time and, perhaps, tweak quarterly earnings to meet analysts' forecasts. From an outsider's perspective, there is no reason to assume anything. Earnings magic

Component	Discussion
Well-Defined Business Strategy	The corporation's operations are derived from a reasonable business strategy within a given industry. It should be well explained in MD&A.
Corporate Governance Structure	Corporate governance provides the strategic planning and monitoring of the corporate executives and business strategy effectiveness. If the structure is loose, earnings magic is a greater concern and reporting quality is more suspect. The proxy statement is the primary source of information.
Reporting Completeness and Timeliness	The 10-K and 10-Q must be published within 60 days and 30 days, respectively (beginning in 2006). Early reporting for these plus earnings announcements and other reports are indicators of timeliness. GAAP establishes certain reporting requirements and minimum reporting. Actual reporting should at least meet the minimum requirements.
Transparency	Financial information and results of operations should be clear to the reader and in a form that is both simple to analyze and complete.
Evidence of Earnings Manipulation	Evidence of past earnings magic substantially reduces reporting quality, partly because of the specific manipulation practices but also because of the lack of reporting credibility.

EXHIBIT 4.2 MAJOR REPORTING QUALITY COMPONENTS

can be rampant even if difficult to detect, and corruption and greed could be on a vast scale. Consequently, a detecting strategy should be part of the analysis process.

The first step is a subjective or qualitative analysis, which follows from the reporting quality components just described. Current financial operations should follow from the stated business strategy. For example, acquisition and various partnership arrangements fit some business strategies but not others. Corporate governance is particularly important. The board should be independent, competent, have necessary committees, and be compensated appropriately. The qualitative review suggests the initial expectations and level of skepticism.

Now comes a more detailed quantitative review, which can cover specific categories or be quite comprehensive. The most significant are the Big Eight, items that are likely to signal possible manipulation. Beyond that are other areas that suggest problems, the rest of the Dirty 30. For example, consider Maytag as a possible equity investment. The company had a great dividend yield over 3.3% and could be undervalued based on a forward price earnings ratio of 13.6. However, Maytag lost money in fiscal 2005 and had negative stockholders' equity thanks largely to $1.4 billion in treasury stock (repurchase of its own stock). Evaluating this equity position becomes the focus, because the analysis would go forward only if the investor still considered Maytag a viable investment candidate after this preliminary finding. (Note that archrival Whirlpool is in the process of acquiring Maytag.)

General Electric is one of the largest, oldest, and most respected American companies. It is a huge, global conglomerate, but has suffered some bad press over former CEO Jack Welch's retirement package, successor Jeff Immelt, and a number of accounting practices. GE restated 2004 earnings, and the audit report indicated internal control weaknesses. The global operations are complex, as are the business strategy and financial operations. Just to make things particularly difficult, a large part of GE's operations is GE Capital Services, with quite different financial and accounting practices from the various industrial segments. The good news for GE is that the company's annual report is detailed and the writing style and analysis are relatively easy to follow, which is not true of all companies.

A quantitative analysis can be calculated around the financial statements and then address a number of additional issues of concern. The analysis starts with cash and other current assets and liabilities related to liquidity. Then property, plant and equipment, and other long-term assets are studied. Leverage concentrates on liabilities (primarily long-term liabilities), then "hidden" liabilities: potential liabilities, such as contingencies as well as off–balance sheet liabilities. Stockholders' equity includes several "cross-over" areas, such as treasury stock, comprehensive income, and relationships to stock options and dividends.

Analyzing operations starts with revenues and works down the income statement to net income and earnings per share. Ultimately, this is where earnings magic is summarized. Cash flows from operations are related to performance. Various calculations may signal possible earnings magic. There are expected relationships, for example, among revenue, cost of sales, receivables, and bad debts reserve. Unusual comparisons and trends are likely magic signals.

The cash flow statement includes investing and financing activities, which provide information useful for the evaluation of the overall business strategy relative to operations. Ultimately, all transactions convert to cash, and it is difficult to manipulate both accruals and cash simultaneously.

When earnings magic signals pop up, they often show up in clusters, because the financial statements are interrelated. Thus, Maytag has negative stockholders' equity and negative earnings. It shows up in standard performance and leverage ratios. The cash flow statement shows an acquisition of treasury stock as a negative cash flow item under financing activities. A more detailed analysis indicates the importance of treasury stock for reducing equity, and the stock options note indicates the relationship of options to treasury stock.

Companies with poor operating performance, especially net losses after a period of profitability, usually have concerns pop up like weeds. Gateway Computer started running net losses in the December 2000 quarter after years of high-tech success, with serious losses since then. Performance ratios continued to be large and negative (a $568 million loss in 2004), as were cash flows from operations. Stockholders' equity continued down as losses increased. Corporate announcements, MD&A, and various footnotes detailed the multiple approaches to restructuring. The company attempted to control costs, shut down foreign operations, and beef up cash and liquidity. The potential areas of earnings management shifted accordingly, with particular emphasis on how the restructuring activities were accounted for and if the company was boosting performance through manipulation.

Gateway did not meet the 90-day deadline for filing its 10-K for fiscal year 2002. Instead, it petitioned the SEC for an extension. The 10-K filing was issued on April 15, 2003, two weeks late. The net loss for 2002 was $298 million. (Note that Gateway filed on time in 2003 and 2004.) The detection strategy for Gateway shifted from evaluating the real growth potential of the company to evaluating survival probabilities.

Given the immense amount of quantitative financial data available, the analysis strategy is to develop a structured approach that standardizes important information for comparative purposes. Financial information is relevant when it is compared over time for the firm, then compared to competing firms and economy-wide measures of performance and financial position.

Comparing High-Tech Companies— Common-Size Analysis

Four high-tech companies are part of the Dow 30: Microsoft, Intel, IBM, and Hewlett-Packard. A quantitative analysis of these firms would start with a common-size analysis. The balance sheet and income statement in a simplified form can be presented in dollar amounts and then standardized as percentages. All balance sheet items are stated as a percent of total assets, and all income statement items are stated as a percent of sales or total revenues. Abbreviated financial statements for several years and across firms in the industry can provide a useful overview of the operating performance and financial health of the firm. Common-size analysis can be used as a useful starting point for a firm's operations and financial position. Assuming a primary interest in Microsoft, common-size statements would be (in millions and percentages) as shown in Exhibit 4.3.

These standardized statements provide considerable information and can be interpreted quickly. Microsoft was exceptionally profitable, with a return on sales of 22.2%. This is the best of the group (only slightly higher than Intel), but substantially lower than the previous year. Gross profit was about the same, but selling, general and administrative, and other expenses were higher. Microsoft has a balance sheet to love, with an immense cash balance of $60 billion (but down in fiscal year 2005); low receivables, inventory, and property, plant and equipment; plus a big equity position at over 80% of assets. Microsoft's competitors have reasonable balance sheets with considerable cash, working capital, and equity, with IBM the lowest of the group. This suggests no obvious operating problems, but an analysis of Microsoft should focus more on expenses than other aspects.

Financial Ratios

A ratio converts the financial data to percentages. This provides one approach to standardize financial information for useful comparisons. The major ratio categories and the questions they attempt to answer are shown in Exhibit 4.4.

Each ratio provides a somewhat different analysis. A company may have substantial current assets but little cash. A company with high leverage may

Common-Size Income Statements

Fiscal Year Ended	Microsoft 6/30/04	Microsoft 6/30/04	Microsoft 6/30/03	IBM 12/31/04	H-P 9/31/04	Intel 12/25/04
Revenue	$36,835	100%	100%	100%	100%	100%
Cost of Revenue	6,716	18.2	17.7	62.6	75.3	42.3
Gross Profit	30,119	81.8	82.3	37.0	24.7	57.7
SG&A Expense	13,306	36.1	26.8	20.0	13.8	13.6
Net Income	8,168	22.2	31.1	8.5	4.4	22.0

Common-Size Balance Sheets

Fiscal Year Ended	Microsoft 6/30/04	Microsoft 6/30/04	Microsoft 6/30/03	IBM 12/31/04	H-P 9/31/04	Intel 12/25/04
Cash and Marketable Securities	$60,592	65.6%	61.6%	9.7%	17.0%	53.8%
Receivables, Net	7,987	8.6	9.7	27.8	28.6	8.3
Inventories	421	0.7	0.8	3.0	9.3	5.4
Total Current Assets	70,566	76.4	74.1	43.0	56.3	50.0
Fixed Assets, Net	2,326	2.5	2.8	13.9	8.7	32.8
Total Assets	92,389	100	100	100	100	100
Total Current Liabilities	14,969	16.2	17.6	36.5	37.5	16.6
Total Liabilities	17,564	19.0	23.3	72.8	50.7	19.9
Total Equity	74,825	81.0	76.7	27.2	49.3	80.1

EXHIBIT 4.3   MICROSOFT COMMON-SIZE STATEMENTS

suggest a red flag. High leverage increases credit risk but improves return on equity. High leverage could result from too many long-term bonds, high accounts payable, or the acquisition of treasury stock. These causes of high leverage would be interpreted differently.

Does the company have the cash to pay its bills? Most current assets are converted to cash, and most current liabilities are paid in cash when due. Accounts receivable are credit terms given to customers on sales. Some percentage of receivables will become delinquent and end up as bad debts. The

Liquidity	Does the company have enough cash and current assets to pay obligations as they come due?
Activity	How efficient are the operations of the company?
Leverage	What is the mix of equity to debt?
Performance	How profitable is the company?

EXHIBIT 4.4   MAJOR RATIO CATEGORIES AND QUESTIONS THEY ATTEMPT TO ANSWER

Ratio	Calculation	Discussion
Current	Current Assets / Current Liabilities	Standard ratio to evaluate working capital.
Cash	(Cash + Marketable Securities) / Current Liabilities	Only cash and cash equivalents considered for payment of current liabilities.
Operating Cash Flow	Cash Flows from Operations / Current Liabilities	Evaluates cash-related performance (as measured from the Statement of Cash Flows) relative to current liabilities.

Exhibit 4.5 Common Liquidity Ratios

credit terms that companies give is an important component related to revenue analysis. A company can increase sales by expanding credit sales to higher-risk customers. Doing this will increase revenue in the short term, but receivables will increase and bad debts can be expected to rise. Inventory represents goods available for sale, either purchased or manufactured. Large inventory may signal relatively inefficient operations. Also, excess inventory or rising inventory levels may be a red flag related to potentially obsolete inventory or operating problems.

Current liabilities are obligations to be paid or liquidated with current resources, usually within one year. The largest category usually is accounts payable, the amount owed to suppliers. Companies may have a policy of delaying payments as long as possible to conserve cash.

Working capital is net current assets (total current assets – total current liabilities), one measure of liquidity. Because cash and other current assets are needed to pay current obligations, negative working capital is problematic.

Common liquidity ratios are shown in Exhibit 4.5.

Liquidity ratios are calculated for Microsoft and competitors in Exhibit 4.6.

Basically, the higher the liquidity ratios, the better. Microsoft has very high liquidity ratios, followed closely by Intel. IBM and H-P are low average. What is the downside of high liquidity? Critics claim better uses can

	Microsoft	Microsoft	IBM	H-P	Intel
Year	2004	2003	2004	2004	2004
Current	4.7x	4.2x	1.2x	1.5x	3.0x
Cash	4.0x	3.5x	26.6%	45.4%	2.1x
Operating Cash Flow	97.7%	1.1x	38.5%	17.8%	1.6x

Exhibit 4.6 Liquidity Ratios for Microsoft and Competitors

Ratio	Calculation	Discussion
Inventory Turnover	COS / Average Inventory	Measures inventory management. Manufacturing inventory should be turned over rapidly rather than accumulating in warehouses.
Receivables Turnover	Sales / Average Accounts Receivable	Measures the effectiveness of credit policies and level of receivables compared to sales.
Total Asset Turnover	Sales / Average Total Assets	Represents the overall (comprehensive) efficiency of assets to sales.

EXHIBIT 4.7 COMMON ACTIVITY RATIOS

be made of the cash. The company should invest in new projects, expand research and development, or increase dividends.

Activity or turnover ratios are measures of efficiency, and the higher the better. Typically, the numerator is an operating measure, such as sales (revenues) or cost of sales (COS), and the denominator is a balance sheet measure, such as inventory or receivables. Thus, operating flows are measured against asset and other levels. Common activity ratios are shown in Exhibit 4.7.

The operating measures occur over the fiscal period. Therefore, the most appropriate comparison is the average balance sheet measure for the denominator. This is measured as $\frac{1}{2}$ (beginning balance + ending balance), equivalent to half of this year's balance plus half of last year's balance. Note that inventory turnover uses COS as the numerator; all other activity ratios use sales (or total revenue) as the numerator.

Turnover ratios are shown in Exhibit 4.8.

Microsoft's activity ratios are not that good, and the total asset turnover less than 1 means that sales are less than total assets (in this case only about 40% of assets).

Activity ratios can be converted to days "held," measures that are easily compared across firm, as shown in Exhibit 4.9.

Day's ratios for Microsoft and competitors are shown in Exhibit 4.10.

	Microsoft	Microsoft	IBM	H-P	Intel
Year	2004	2003	2004	2004	2004
Inventory Turnover	12.7x	8.7x	19.3x	9.2x	5.6x
Receivables Turnover	4.7x	4.3x	3.1x	3.9x	8.7x
Total Asset Turnover	42.8%	43.7%	90.1%	1.1x	71.8%

EXHIBIT 4.8 TURNOVER RATIOS

Ratio	Calculation
Average Days Inventory in Stock	365 / Inventory Turnover
Average Days Receivables Outstanding	365 / Receivables Turnover
Length of Operating Cycle	365 [(1 / Inventory Turnover) + (1 / Receivables Turnover)]; equivalent to average days inventory + average days receivables outstanding

EXHIBIT 4.9 ACTIVITY RATIO CALCULATIONS

	Microsoft	Microsoft	IBM	H-P	Intel
Year	2004	2003	2004	2004	2004
Average Days Inventory in Stock	28.7 days	42.0 days	18.9 days	39.7 days	65.2 days
Average Days Receivables Outstanding	77.7 days	84.9 days	117.7 days	93.9 days	42.0 days
Length of Operating Cycle	106.4 days	126.9 days	136.6 days	133.3 days	107.2 days

EXHIBIT 4.10 DAY'S RATIOS FOR MICROSOFT AND COMPETITORS

Ratio	Calculation	Discussion
Debt to Equity	Total Liabilities / Total Stockholders' Equity	Direct comparison of debt to equity stakeholders and the most common measure of capital structure.
Long-Term Debt to Equity	Long-Term Liabilities / Total Stockholders' Equity	A long-term perspective of debt and equity positions of stakeholders.
Debt to Market Equity	Total Liabilities at Book Value / Total Equity at Market Value	Market valuation may represent a better measure of equity than book value. Most firms have a market premium relative to book value.

EXHIBIT 4.11 COMMON LEVERAGE RATIOS

	Microsoft	Microsoft	IBM	H-P	Intel
Year	2004	2003	2004	2004	2004
Debt to Equity	23.5%	30.4%	2.7x	1.0x	24.8%
Long-Term Debt to Equity	3.5%	7.5%	1.3x	26.6%	4.0%
Debt to Market Equity	6.4%	6.7%	66.3%	63.4%	6.1%

EXHIBIT 4.12 LEVERAGE RATIOS FOR MICROSOFT AND COMPETITORS

Converting to days represents the same results, although it is easier to evaluate. These results indicate relatively poor efficiency for the group. Microsoft has almost a month's inventory in stock and an operating cycle of about three and a half months. However, this is similar to the other high-tech firms. Because high tech is usually associated with efficiency, these results are unexpected. By comparison, Dell had average days inventory of 3.6 days and an operating cycle of 33.2 days, the expected numbers for high-tech manufacturing.

Leverage considers the capital structure of the firm and the evaluation of the relative risk and return associated with liabilities (especially long-term debt) and equity. Common leverage ratios are shown in Exhibit 4.11.

Debt is defined as total liabilities, an oversimplification but easy to determine and compare across firms. Total equity at market value is defined as closing stock price at some specific date multiplied by number of shares outstanding at the end of the fiscal period under study.

Leverage ratios for Microsoft and competitors are shown in Exhibit 4.12.

Microsoft and Intel have extremely low leverage, making them essentially impervious to default. H-P also is not bad, while IBM has mediocre ratios. Note that in all cases debt to market equity is much less than debt to equity, indicating that market values are substantially higher than book values.

Leverage ratios are relatively easy to interpret for credit decisions: the lower the better. As debt increases, the potential for credit default decreases. The interpretation for equity investment decisions is more difficult, because increasing debt increases return on equity. Leverage sends a big earnings magic signal. High leverage suggests a corporation that has too much debt and therefore incentives to camouflage as much debt as possible—think Enron. The incentives are there to use operating leases, special-purpose entities, and other debt-hiding techniques.

Profit means business. The only commercial reason for a corporation to exist is to make a buck. Big profit, including evidence of future earnings growth, means lofty market valuation. Several profitability ratios consider different aspects of earnings performance.

Common profitability ratios are shown in Exhibit 4.13.

Ratios for Microsoft and competitors are shown in Exhibit 4.14.

Microsoft's 2004 profitability ratios are consistently lower than 2003, which will need explaining in a more detailed analysis. Microsoft's operating margin and return on sales are the highest of the group and extremely high for any company. Because of poor total asset efficiency, return on assets is much smaller than return on sales, generally true for the competitors. Return on equity is a mediocre 12%, because Microsoft has little leverage—the one

Ratio	Calculation	Discussion
Operating Margin	(Sales − COS) / Sales	Captures the relationship between sales and manufacturing (or merchandising) costs.
Return on Sales	Net Income / Sales	Measures the relationship of the bottom line to sales and thus captures sales to total costs of sales.
Return on Assets	Net Income / Average Total Assets	Measures the firm's efficiency in using assets to generate earnings. Alternatively stated, it captures earnings to all providers of capital.
Pretax Return on Assets	Earnings Before Interest and Taxes / Average Total Assets	Measures earnings from operations on a pretax and preinterest expense basis.
Return on Equity	Net Income / Average Stockholders' Equity	Measures earnings to owners as measured by net assets.

EXHIBIT 4.13   COMMON PROFITABILITY RATIOS

downside of a massive equity position. Note that IBM's high leverage results in a return on equity (ROE) of almost 30%. Consequently, Microsoft's performance does not look quite so stellar.

Ratio analysis provides information on a percentage basis, useful for comparisons over time and across firms and industries. However, the limitations of ratio analysis are important. Relative size is deemphasized. Being a large or small firm may be particularly important. The largest firm in a mature industry is less likely to achieve rapid growth, but it may continue to dominate an industry at adequate performance levels well into the future. A small firm may have potentially unlimited growth potential, but market share may be hard to achieve when facing much larger competitors.

A basic assumption of financial ratios is that the numbers used are correct. Basic income statement and balance sheet numbers can be misstated or manipulated in a variety of ways. Managers have earnings magic incentives,

	Microsoft	Microsoft	IBM	H-P	Intel
Year	2004	2003	2004	2004	2004
Operating Margin	81.8%	82.3%	37.4%	24.7%	57.7%
Return on Sales	22.2	31.0	8.8	4.4	22.0
Return on Assets	9.5	13.6	7.9	4.6	15.8
Pretax Return on Assets	13.6	20.0	11.4	5.8	22.0
Return on Equity	12.0	17.7	29.3	9.3	19.7

EXHIBIT 4.14   RATIOS FOR MICROSOFT AND COMPETITORS

the result being fallible financial statement numbers. A primary purpose for additional accounting analysis is to determine to what degree the financial statement numbers can be relied on. If the ratio analysis is not reliable, the results are less useful for decision purposes.

Why Crunch These Numbers?

Crunching and evaluating numbers is a lot of work. Is it worth it? The basic reason to do so: This is the starting point for understanding a complex corporation. For example, Microsoft has many unique features that are more obvious from a quantitative analysis, and it turns out that there are possible deficiencies. Microsoft has lots of cash and low leverage. That is something to cheer about, except for its mediocre ROE. At 12% this is comparable to "dogs of the Dow," lowly performers that usually pay high dividends. Perhaps a better big company high-tech bet would be IBM—lots of leverage, a lower return on sales of 8.8%, but a loftier ROE at 29.3%.

There is little indication from this quick analysis that Microsoft has incentives to game the system. Why would the company hide liabilities? What would be the point of manipulating cash flows? The incentives would seem to be higher for IBM (high leverage, low cash, and lower return on sales compared to Microsoft).

Section 2

THE BIG 8 AND DIRTY 30: KEY ACCOUNTING ISSUES THAT SIGNAL EARNINGS MAGIC

This is the somewhat technical stuff to understanding corporate financial reality. There is no earnings magic section in the annual report, and companies never claim they manipulate anything. But there can be flashing neon signals of "red flag, red flag" if you know where to look. Here are eight of them, plus a couple of dozen dishonorable mentions along the way. Stock options are the place to start: "worry-free" compensation that provides whopping incentives to fudge the numbers every quarter. Revenue recognition is the most likely category of earnings magic; however, revenue signals of manipulation are hard to find. Here are the Earnings Magic Big 8 and the rest of the Dirty 30.

Chapter	Discussion
5. Key Accounting Issues: An Overview	The Earnings Magic Big 8 each gets a separate chapter; the remaining Dirty 30 get dishonorable mention in the last chapter of this section.
6. Stock Options	The big incentive for earnings magic: load up the CEO with options and see if earnings are reported honestly.
7. Pensions and Other Postemployment Benefits	Defined benefit plans and employee commitments can be expensive, deceptive, and represent billions in obligations. Given the many calculation alternatives (e.g., expected rate of return), this is magic heaven.
8. Revenues	The most likely category of earnings magic: Let's beef up sales. Timing is everything—almost everything; there are still fraudulent sales.
9. Earnings, Expenses, and Expectations	What is the bottom line? To arrive at the magic earnings number, if revenue manipulation is not enough, then mess with expenses.

(continues)

EXHIBIT S2.1 THE BIG 8 AND THE REST OF THE DIRTY 30

Chapter (Continued)	Discussion
10. Strange Special Items and Other Things that Should Not Be on the Income Statement	Nonrecurring and other special items show up on the income statement, sometimes frequently—they are unexpected and usually bad news.
11. Treasury Stock and Dividends	Why buy back your own shares? This use of cash to decrease equity seems to be a loser—unless you want to increase share price and jack up EPS.
12. Off–Balance Sheet Items: Operating Leases and Special-Purpose Entities	Why record liabilities at all? Avoid reporting obligation whoppers with operating leases and special-purpose entities.
13. Acquisitions and All That Goodwill	Buy competitors and really demonstrate acquisition magic; remember, those big goodwill numbers do not represent real assets. Accounting tricks can camouflage merger disasters.
14. Dishonorable Mention: The Rest of the Dirty 30	There are a whole host of other items, including specific financial statement categories such as those related to leverage, complex accounting issues like derivatives, as well as auditing and corporate governance issues.

EXHIBIT S2.1   THE BIG 8 AND THE REST OF THE DIRTY 30 (CONTINUED)

5

KEY ACCOUNTING ISSUES: AN OVERVIEW

Used properly, accrual accounting is about timing, not about creating profits where none exist.

— Alex Berenson

Most of the scandals that provided a catalyst to the passage of the [Sarbanes-Oxley] Act did indeed involve transactions that were structured so as to present information in a manner inconsistent with the underlying economics.

— SEC report on off–balance sheet arrangements

With most accounting items, only the insiders would have a clue whether earnings magic is present. It is obvious after fraud is discovered, when the details are presented. Prior to manipulation disclosure, it is the *signals* of potential earnings magic that are important. The big daddy of possible abuse is stock options, the prime motivator of scandals in the 1990s, and that earnings magic wonder—"costless" compensation. Billions of dollars of off–balance sheet obligations can be committed with pensions and other postemployment benefits (OPEB). Revenue recognition abuse has been widespread and documented in detail—after the fact, of course. Other issues scream "look out" when they are present. Many of these, such as operating leases, are well known; others are quite obscure, such as the equity method used for affiliates. The increasing use of mark-to-market derivatives is problematic. Then there are the special-purpose entities (SPEs) of Enron fame. All of these are valid financial techniques. The problem is they can be misused—but when? That is the focus of this section.

When do standard performance measures truly represent economic reality? In a simple world, an earnings number, such as net income, could be that perfect measure. If earnings per share (EPS) come close to reality and future EPS numbers are easily predicted, then financial analysis would be easy. Unfortunately, the financial world is complex and filled with players not much interested in economic reality. Accruals shift cash flow timing to better measure earnings performance—at least in theory. The income statements and balance sheets usually are kept fairly simple, but the greater details are presented in notes and Management Discussion and Analysis (MD&A). Most of these disclosures follow the relatively rigid requirements of generally accepted accounting principles (GAAP), but, for a variety of reasons, considerable flexibility exists.

In an environment where earnings management incentives exist, how is earnings magic detected? The preliminary analysis is an income statement overview to determine the reasonableness of the numbers presented, compared to previous periods and close competitors. Common-size and percentage changes from previous periods indicate basic relationships and reasonableness of changes over time. Earnings magic is possible virtually anywhere, and certain signals increase the probability of manipulation.

EARNINGS MAGIC

When are earnings magic incentives strong? When expected earnings performance is threatened. Managers may have incentives to "signal" strong performance numbers rather than high-quality earnings. Doing this would seem to be a losing strategy long term, but the mind-set may be entirely short term. Making quarterly earnings targets seems really important when big bonuses hang in the balance. See Exhibit 5.1 for earnings situations that increase manipulation potential.

Perhaps the most common earnings management strategy is to maintain a near-constant growth rate in earnings. This can be achieved by maintaining the high levels of operating performance and efficiency expected with a viable business strategy. That strategy is consistent with high-quality earnings. However, the chief financial officer can use income smoothing, with "cookie jar reserves" and various adjustments to operating accounts, to make sure those quarterly earnings rise period after period. Doing this gives the appearance of quality earnings and can be difficult to detect.

Short-term performance can be managed by: (1) adjusting operations to reduce (or increase) maintenance, research and development (R&D), or employee training; or (2) accounting choices that change numbers rather than actual performance. "Tweaking" accounting numbers to meet quarterly expectations, such as sales of assets for gains or adjusting allowance accounts, seems to be common. However, the level of manipulation can increase to the point of fraud or other criminal acts. WorldCom's capitalization of some

Dilemma	Description
Earnings are below consensus analysts' forecasts.	Many CEOs consider meeting quarterly forecasts sacrosanct. Large stock price drops often follow missed forecasts (also called a "negative earnings surprise"). This is the big motivator for manipulation.
Earnings will be slightly below zero.	Reporting a small net loss sends a strong signal of poor performance. Better to at least make a small profit.
Earnings are slightly below the previous period.	A small decrease is often viewed as a negative (e.g., the percentage change is negative). This is a strong incentive for "tweaking" earnings.
Earnings are close to violating debt covenants.	Violating debt covenants puts the company in technical default on debt, which could lead to bond downgrading and other negative consequences.
Maximizing bonuses and other compensation agreements.	Managers could be sensitive to the specific bonus and other incentive agreements. How bonuses are constructed (e.g., above the line versus below the line) can be useful for understanding management incentives for earnings management.
"Big-bath" write-offs.	Managers may have incentives to take large losses if current bonuses will be zero; additional losses will not affect current compensation but may boost future compensation. Write-offs are likely to take the form of nonrecurring or special items.

Adapted from Giroux 2004, p. 111.

EXHIBIT 5.1   EARNINGS SITUATIONS THAT INCREASE MANIPULATION POTENTIAL

$11 billion of operating costs was one of the most extreme examples. It is now clear that Enron used the most blatant quarter-by-quarter manipulations conceivable.

Earnings magic incentives increase under specific circumstances. Net income just above zero, slightly above the previous period, or at or slightly above analysts' consensus quarter after quarter suggests earnings magic at work. Researchers have found exactly these trends. For example, companies often report a small net income, but seldom a small net loss. The potential for debt covenant violations should be evaluated from a credit risk perspective, based on standard ratio analysis, consideration of information available on outstanding debt, and external sources, such as bond ratings. Big-bath write-offs should be obvious from evaluating nonrecurring items on the income statement and additional information related to restructuring charges and other unusual circumstances.

Based on quantitative and qualitative techniques, a number of signs can indicate earnings magic potential, as shown in Exhibit 5.2. The list in the exhibit is not complete, but it indicates useful approaches to signal possible earnings magic.

Topic	Concern	Detection Strategy
Stock Options Outstanding	Big options packages for senior executives increase the incentives to cheat.	Options note disclosures indicate number of options outstanding and *pro forma* impact on net income.
Pension and OPEB Funding Levels	Large net underfunding, especially if off–balance sheet.	Pension and OPEB notes that disclose funding levels and funded status.
Revenue Recognition Policies	Aggressive recognition policies that can overstate revenues.	Note 1 on accounting policies states revenue recognition policies.
Relative Amounts of Sales and Other Revenue Items	Unusual amounts may indicate problems.	Common-size and percentage changes; comparisons over time and to competitors.
Comparison of Cost of Sales to Revenues	Unusual amounts or relationships may suggest problems.	Common-size and percent changes, operating margin; changes over time and comparison to competitors.
Declining or Erratic Net Income	Negative patterns are "bad news," but circumstances are important. Mergers, restructuring, and industry-related cycles are possible reasons.	Standard quantitative analysis; comparisons over time and to competitors; evaluate reasons for this behavior (notes, MD&A) plus analysts' forecasts of future earnings.
Net Loss	A net loss should be considered a potential red flag for financial analysis, requiring further analysis.	Same as above.
Nonrecurring Items, Other Special Items	Infrequent and unusual items should be rare, and their presence is a concern.	Income statement line items and note disclosure; qualitative evaluation of item(s). How often used—check back perhaps five years.
Treasury Stock	Large amounts of treasury stock reduce equity and shares outstanding, and may jack up stock prices.	Treasury stock normally listed on the balance sheet and recent acquisitions in the statement of cash flows.
Operating Leases	Big amounts of operating leases.	Leasing note: Calculate total operating leases outstanding; calculate as a percentage of total assets.
Special-Purpose Entities	Massive use of SPEs, designed to eliminate debt on the balance sheet.	MD&A and note disclosure; discussion should indicate usage and amounts; key question is the fit to business strategy and operations.
Acquisitions	Big goodwill balance, possible indicator of overpaying on acquisitions.	Goodwill reported on balance sheet or in notes: calculate as a percentage of total assets.

(continues)

EXHIBIT 5.2   SIGNS THAT INDICATE EARNINGS MAGIC POTENTIAL

Topic	Concern	Detection Strategy
Working Capital	Negative working capital and low cash balances suggest liquidity problems.	Current ratio less than 1; low cash percentage.
Cash from Operations and Free Cash Flow	The purpose of performance is to generate cash; cash from operations and free cash provide alternative indicators of performance problems.	Compare cash from operations to net income; calculate free cash flows as (1) cash from operations less cash from investing and (2) cash from operations less capital expenditures.
Credit Risk	High leverage (and, to a lesser extent, liquidity) increases credit risk.	Calculate leverage and liquidity ratios; consider bond ratings; calculate Altman's Z-score.
Derivatives	Derivatives are supposedly used as hedges to reduce risks, but can be used to speculate and increase risk.	Review notes and MD&A disclosure for completeness and reasonableness.

Adapted from Giroux 2004, p. 112.

EXHIBIT 5.2   SIGNS THAT INDICATE EARNINGS MAGIC POTENTIAL (CONTINUED)

INDUSTRY ISSUES

Company operations and financial disclosures tend to look like those of competing firms. Pharmaceuticals have relatively low cost of sales but high R&D and marketing expenses. Retailers have high cost of sales and low or zero R&D. Auto manufacturers typically have financial arms that have lots of debt and very little in common with manufacturing. They also have huge pension and other postemployment benefit liabilities. High-tech companies usually have low pension obligations but substantial stock options.

From an analyst's perspective, industry is critical. Areas of concern are often industry related. For example, operating leases are common among airlines and retailers. Because they are a common industry practice, the relative level of operating leases is particularly important as an indicator of off–balance sheet financing. Stock options are big items at newer high-tech companies and are a concern as the percent of options to shares outstanding increases. Pharmaceuticals and tobacco companies have substantial contingencies. Financial institutions have large amounts of liabilities, loan losses, and are likely to use SPEs for structured financing. When evaluating a particular company, it should be compared to close competitors.

The analysis of earnings magic issues will focus on the Dow 30, which are introduced in Appendix 5.1.

APPENDIX 5.1

A DIGRESSION ON THE DOW

The Dow Jones Industrial Average (Dow 30) is the most famous U.S. market index. The Dow 30 represents a convenient group of dominant firms that represent one definition of the market and will be used throughout the book. Charles Dow, who founded the *Wall Street Journal* with partner Edward Jones in 1889, invented the Dow. Dow's first index of 11 railroads was started in 1884, with the first all-industrial average in 1896. That list included American Cotton Oil, American Sugar, American Tobacco, Chicago Gas, General Electric, Distilling & Cattle Feeding, Laclede Gas, National Lead, North American, Tennessee Coal & Gas, U.S. Leather preferred, and U.S. Rubber. Only General Electric is still part of the index. On the first day, the index was 40.94; it dropped to 28.48 on August 8 of that year, its lowest point on record. The list changed over time and increased to 30 firms in 1928. Only General Electric and General Motors remain from that list, plus Standard Oil of New Jersey is now Exxon-Mobil.

The current list is tabulated in Exhibit 5.3, with basic market information for comparison. This includes market capitalization (stock price times shares outstanding, market cap in billions), price-to-book (market cap divided by stockholders' equity), and dividend yield—all based on stock closing prices at July 13, 2005.

Mean (average) values for the Dow 30 can be used as estimates of market averages. The average Dow corporation had a market cap of $123 billion. Amazingly, General Motors had the lowest market cap, at $20 billion, despite revenues of almost $200 billion. Thus, the market considers GM a company in trouble (declining market share, high pension and retirement costs). Exxon-Mobil had the largest market cap, at $380 billion, followed closely by GE and four other companies over $200 billion. These are big companies.

The market ratios are in a "normal range" of market-traded corporations. Market-to-book is the relative market "premium" over book value.

Company	Market Cap	Price-to-Book	Yield
3M (MMM)	$ 57.4	5.6	2.10%
Alcoa (AA)	23.9	1.8	2.20%
Altria (MO)*	135.6	4.2	4.50%
American Express (AXP)	67.0	4.2	0.90%
American International Group (AIG)	156.6	1.9	0.70%
Boeing (BA)	53.5	4.6	1.40%
Caterpillar (CAT)	33.8	4.4	1.70%
Citigroup (C)	237.8	2.2	3.70%
Coca-Cola (KO)	103.2	6.3	2.50%
Du Pont (DD)	43.8	3.8	3.20%
Exxon-Mobil (XOM)	379.5	3.7	1.80%
General Electric (GE)	373.1	3.3	2.50%
General Motors (GM)	20.2	0.8	5.60%
Hewlett-Packard (HPQ)	70.3	1.8	1.30%
Home Depot (HD)	88.4	3.7	0.90%
Honeywell (HON)	30.8	2.7	2.20%
IBM (IBM)	131.6	4.3	0.90%
Intel (INTC)	171.2	4.6	0.90%
J.P. Morgan (JPM)	124.6	1.2	3.90%
Johnson & Johnson (JNJ)	191.7	5.7	1.80%
McDonald's (MCD)	37.1	2.5	1.90%
Merck (MRK)	67.4	4.0	4.80%
Microsoft (MSFT)	277.4	5.8	13.00%**
Pfizer (PFE)	200.5	3.0	2.70%
Procter & Gamble (PG)	136.1	7.8	1.90%
SBC Comm. (SBC)	79.0	2.0	5.40%
United Technology (UTX)	52.6	3.5	0.80%
Verizon (VZ)	95.3	2.5	4.60%
Wal-Mart (WMT)	209.8	4.4	1.10%
Walt Disney (DIS)	52.4	2.0	0.90%
Average	$123.4	3.6	2.73%

* Name change from Philip Morris.
** Includes special dividend.

EXHIBIT 5.3 CURRENT LIST OF DOW JONES 30

Assuming that the net asset position (book value) represented real economic value, then market-to-book should be about 1. Market-to-book is one measure to locate possible bargains. As a rule of thumb a market-to-book less than 1 suggests that the liquidation value is greater than market value, a possible buying opportunity for value investors. The average market-to-book was 3.6, with GM the only company with a market-to-book less than 1. Coke and Procter & Gamble had ratios greater than 6. High values suggest firms with great earnings potential; in any case, the stock price is more likely representative of earnings power rather than book value.

Dividend yield is particularly important to income investors, which includes retirees and others who depend on cash return. The average yield was 2.7% (higher than the average yield of the Standard & Poor [S&P] 500, which is about 2%). All companies paid a dividend, with the range from 0.7% for AIG to 6.4% for GM. (The 13.0% yield for Microsoft is a fluke, associated with a one-time special dividend of $3 a share.)

Limited financial statement information for the Dow 30 also is presented in Exhibit 5.4 (based on the last four quarters, generally through the second quarter of 2005).

Company	Revenue*	Current Ratio	Debt/Equity	ROE
3M (MMM)	$ 20.2	1.4	0.28	33.5%
Alcoa (AA)	24.2	1.1	0.53	10.3
Altria (MO)**	65.0	1.4	0.78	33.2
American Express (AXP)	28.9	1.9	2.80	22.6
American International Group (AIG)***	90.4			
Boeing (BA)	52.5	0.7	1.00	16.9
Caterpillar (CAT)	32.1	1.4	3.20	31.2
Citigroup (C)***	81.6			16.2
Coca Cola (KO)	22.2	1.2	0.42	30.3
Du Pont (DD)	27.6	1.9	0.75	18.8
Exxon-Mobil (XOM)	279.1	1.4	0.08	28.4
General Electric (GE)	157.8	1.7	3.30	17.5
General Motors (GM)	191.5	3.7	11.40	1.9
Hewlett-Packard (HPQ)	83.3	1.5	0.19	9.3
Home Depot (HD)	74.5	1.2	0.09	22.3
Honeywell (HON)	25.9	1.3	0.53	12.1
IBM (IBM)	97.0	1.2	0.78	29.2
Intel (INTC)	35.6	2.7	0.02	21.0
J.P. Morgan (JPM)***	44.7			6.3
Johnson & Johnson (JNJ)	48.6	2.2	0.08	28.8
McDonald's (MCD)	19.5	1.0	0.59	18.5
Merck (MRK)	22.7	1.4	0.41	32.8
Microsoft (MSFT)	38.9	2.9	0	19.1
Pfizer (PFE)	53.1	1.5	0.29	13.6
Procter & Gamble (PG)	55.5	0.9	1.30	38.5
SBC Comm. (SBC)	41.0	0.5	0.67	9.9

(continues)

EXHIBIT 5.4   DOW 30 LIMITED FINANCIAL STATEMENT INFORMATION

Company	Revenue*	Current Ratio	Debt/Equity	ROE
United Technology (UTX)	38.2	1.2	0.33	21.6
Verizon (VZ)	72.4	0.7	1.00	21.9
Wal-Mart (WMT)	291.4	0.8	0.70	23.6
Walt Disney (DIS)	31.5	1.2	0.49	9.8
Average	$ 71.6	1.3	.53	20.0%

* Revenue in millions.
** Name change from Philip Morris.
*** Financial companies typically do not separate current from noncurrent items.

EXHIBIT 5.4   DOW 30 LIMITED FINANCIAL STATEMENT INFORMATION (CONTINUED)

Revenues are an alternative measure of size and ranged from $19.5 billion for McDonald's to $291.4 billion for Wal-Mart. Generally, larger revenues are associated with a larger market cap. The revenue/market cap relationship varies by industry, and GM is a notable exception because of market share and employee issues that pummeled the bottom line. The current ratio is the most common liquidity measure, and five companies had ratios below 1; that is, negative working capital. Long-term debt to equity is a standard leverage measure, with high ratios increasing credit risk (the probability of default or declaring bankruptcy). The ratio ranged from zero for Microsoft to 11.4 for GM, another indicator of GM's problems. Financial institutions such as J.P. Morgan, Citigroup, or AIG tend to have larger ratios. Companies with large financial components, including GE, GM, and CAT, also have substantial leverage. Return on equity (ROE) is the most influential performance ratio, which ranged from 1.9% for GM (again at the "bad news" end) to 38.5% for Procter & Gamble. Note that P&G had negative working capital and a high price-to-book. Integrating all the anomalous financial information is one reason successful analysts deserve the big bucks.

Appendix 5.2

DOW—Industry, Description

Company	Industry	Description (from Yahoo!)
3M (MMM)	Conglomerates	3M Company operates as a diversified technology company. The company has seven segments: Health Care; Industrial; Display and Graphics; Consumer and Office; Safety, Security, and Protection Services; Electro and Communications; and Transportation. 3M Company markets and sells its products directly to users as well as through wholesalers, retailers, jobbers, distributors, and dealers worldwide. The company was founded in 1902. It was formerly known as Minnesota Mining and Manufacturing Company and changed its name to 3M Company in 2002. 3M is headquartered in St. Paul, Minnesota.
Alcoa (AA)	Aluminum (Metals)	Alcoa, Inc. produces primary aluminum, fabricated aluminum, and alumina. It also markets consumer brands to its customers. The company was formed in 1888 and is based in Pittsburgh, Pennsylvania.
Altria (MO)	Cigarettes (Consumer)	Altria Group, Inc. operates as a holding company that engages in the manufacture and sale of various consumer products. The company, through its wholly owned subsidiaries, Philip Morris USA, Inc. and Philip Morris International, Inc., engages in the manufacture and sale of cigarettes and tobacco products. The company sells tobacco products to wholesalers and retail organizations, including chain stores and the armed services worldwide. Altria, through its subsidiaries, offers snacks, beverages, cheese, grocery, and convenient meals. The company was formerly known as Philip Morris Companies, Inc. and changed its name to Altria Group, Inc. in 2003. Altria Group is based in New York City.
American Express (AXP)	Financial	American Express Company and its subsidiaries provide travel-related services, payment services, financial advisory services,

(continues)

Company	Industry	Description (from Yahoo!)
American Express (Continued)		and international banking services worldwide. The company was founded in 1850 and is headquartered in New York City.
American International Group (AIG)	Insurance (Financial)	American International Group, Inc., a holding company, offers insurance and investment products and services to commercial, institutional, and individual customers in the United States and internationally. It operates through four segments: General Insurance, Life Insurance, Financial Services, and Retirement Services and Asset Management.
Boeing (BA)	Aerospace/ Defense	The Boeing Company operates in the aerospace industry worldwide. It has four segments: Commercial Airplanes, Integrated Defense Systems (IDS), Boeing Capital Corporation (BCC), and Other. The Boeing Company was founded in 1916 and is headquartered in Chicago, Illinois.
Caterpillar (CAT)	Farm and Construction Machinery	Caterpillar, Inc. manufactures construction and mining equipment, diesel and natural gas engines, and industrial gas turbines. It operates in three segments: Machinery, Engines, and Financial Products. The company was formed as Caterpillar Tractor Co. in 1925, pursuant to the merger of The Holt Manufacturing Company and the C. L. Best Tractor Co. Caterpillar Tractor Co. changed its name to Caterpillar, Inc. in 1986. The company is headquartered in Peoria, Illinois.
Citigroup (C)	Bank (Financial)	Citigroup, Inc. operates as a financial services holding company, which provides a range of financial services to consumer and corporate customers worldwide. It operates in five segments: Global Consumer, Global Corporate and Investment Bank, Global Wealth Management, Global Investment Management, and Proprietary Investment Activities.
Coca-Cola (KO)	Beverages (Consumer Goods)	The Coca-Cola Company engages in manufacturing, distributing, and marketing nonalcoholic beverage concentrates and syrups worldwide. The company also produces, markets, and distributes juices and juice drinks as well as water products. The company was organized in 1886 and is headquartered in Atlanta, Georgia.
Du Pont (DD)	Chemicals	E. I. du Pont de Nemours and Company (Du Pont) operates as a science and technology company. It engages in a range of fields, including biotechnology, electronics, materials science, safety and security, and synthetic fibers. The company operates in seven segments: Agriculture and Nutrition; Coatings

(continues)

Company	Industry	Description (from Yahoo!)
DuPont (DD) (Continued)		and Color Technologies (CCT); Electronic and Communication Technologies (ECT); Performance Materials; Safety and Protection; Pharmaceuticals; and Textiles and Interiors. Du Pont was founded in 1802 and is headquartered in Wilmington, Delaware.
Exxon-Mobil (XOM)	Integrated Oil	Exxon-Mobil Corporation operates as a petroleum and petrochemicals company. It primarily engages in the exploration, production, and sale of crude oil and natural gas; and the manufacture, transportation, and sale of petroleum products. The company also manufactures and markets basic petrochemicals.
General Electric (GE)	Conglomerates	General Electric Company engages in the development, manufacture, and marketing of various products for the generation, transmission, distribution, control, and utilization of electricity. The company operates through 11 segments: Advanced Materials, Commercial Finance, Consumer Finance, Consumer and Industrial, Energy, Equipment and Other Services, Healthcare, Infrastructure, Insurance, NBC Universal, and Transportation. General Electric Company was created pursuant to the merger of Edison General Electric Company and Thomson-Houston Electric Company in 1892. The company is based in Fairfield, Connecticut.
General Motors (GM)	Automobile	General Motors Corporation engages in the design, manufacture, and marketing of cars and light trucks worldwide. It operates through Automotive and Financing and Insurance Operations (FIO) segments. General Motors was founded in 1908 and is headquartered in Detroit, Michigan.
Hewlett-Packard (HPQ)	Computer Systems	Hewlett-Packard Company provides products, technologies, solutions, and services to consumers, businesses, and governments worldwide. It operates in seven segments: Personal Systems Group (PSG), Imaging and Printing Group (IPG), Enterprise Storage and Servers (ESS), HP Services (HPS), HP Financial Services (HPFS), Software, and Corporate Investments. Hewlett-Packard was founded in 1939 by Bill Hewlett and Dave Packard and is headquartered in Palo Alto, California.
Home Depot (HD)	Home Improvement Stores	The Home Depot, Inc. operates as a home improvement retailer in the United States, Canada, and Mexico. The company provides its products and services through Home Depot and EXPO design center stores. Its Home Depot stores sell a range of building materials, home improvement products, and lawn and garden

(continues)

Company	Industry	Description (from Yahoo!)
Home Depot (HD) (Continued)		products, as well as provide various installation services. The Home Depot, Inc. was founded in 1978 and is based in Atlanta, Georgia.
Honeywell (HON)	Conglomerates	Honeywell International, Inc. provides aerospace products and services; control technologies for buildings, homes, and industry; turbochargers; automotive products; specialty chemicals; fibers; and electronic and advanced materials. It operates in four segments: Aerospace, Automation and Control Solutions, Specialty Materials, and Transportation Systems. Honeywell International was incorporated in 1985 and is headquartered in Morris Township, New Jersey.
International Business Machines (IBM)	Computer Systems	IBM operates as an information technology company worldwide. It operates in six segments: Global Services, Systems and Technology Group, Personal Systems Group, Software, Global Financing, and Enterprise Investments. The company was incorporated in 1911 as the Computing-Tabulating-Recording Co. and changed its name to International Business Machines Corporation in 1924. IBM is based in Armonk, New York.
Intel (INTC)	Semiconductor (Technology)	Intel Corporation operates as a semiconductor chip maker that supplies technology solutions for the computing and communications industries. The company's products include microprocessors; chipsets; motherboards; flash memory; communications infrastructure components, including network and embedded processors; wired and wireless connectivity products; products for networked storage; application processors; and cellular baseband chipsets. Intel Corporation was founded in 1968 and is based in Santa Clara, California.
J.P. Morgan (JPM)	Banks (Financial)	JPMorgan Chase & Co. operates as a global financial services company in the United States. It operates in six segments: Investment Bank, Retail Financial Services (RFS), Card Services, Commercial Banking, Treasury and Securities Services (TSS), and Asset and Wealth Management (AWM). The Investment Bank segment delivers products and services.
Johnson & Johnson (JNJ)	Pharmaceuticals	Johnson & Johnson engages in the manufacture and sale of various products in the healthcare field primarily in the United States. It operates through three segments: Consumer, Pharmaceutical, and Medical Devices and Diagnostics (MDD). Johnson & Johnson was founded by Robert Wood Johnson in 1887. The company is headquartered in New Brunswick, New Jersey.

(continues)

Company	Industry	Description (from Yahoo!)
McDonald's (MCD)	Restaurants	McDonald's Corporation engages in the operation and franchising of McDonald's restaurants worldwide. McDonald's Corporation was founded by Ray Kroc in 1955. The company is based in Oak Brook, Illinois.
Merck (MRK)	Pharmaceuticals	Merck & Co., Inc. engages in the discovery, development, manufacture, and marketing of a range of products to improve human and animal health. The company's products consist of therapeutic and preventive agents, sold by prescription, for the treatment and prevention of human disorders. Merck & Co. was established in 1891 and is headquartered in Whitehouse Station, New Jersey.
Microsoft (MSFT)	Software (Technology)	Microsoft Corporation engages in the development, manufacture, licensing, and support of a range of software products for various computing devices. Microsoft was founded in 1975 by William H. Gates III. The company is headquartered in Redmond, Washington.
Pfizer (PFE)	Pharmaceuticals	Pfizer, Inc. engages in the discovery, development, manufacture, and marketing of prescription medicines for humans and animals as well as consumer healthcare products worldwide. It operates in three segments: Human Health, Consumer Healthcare, and Animal Health. Pfizer was incorporated in 1942 and is headquartered in New York City.
Procter & Gamble (PG)	Consumer Goods	The Procter & Gamble Company engages in the manufacture and marketing of a range of consumer products, worldwide. It operates in five segments: Fabric and Home Care, Baby and Family Care, Beauty Care, Health Care, and Snacks and Beverages. The company was founded in 1837 by William Procter and James Gamble. Procter & Gamble is headquartered in Cincinnati, Ohio.
SBC Communications (SBC)	Telecom Services	SBC Communications, Inc. provides telecommunications services primarily in the United States. It offers various services and products, such as local exchange services, wireless communications, long-distance services, Internet services, telecommunications equipment, and directory advertising and publishing services. SBC Communications was incorporated in 1983 and is headquartered in San Antonio, Texas.
United Technology (UTX)	Conglomerates	United Technologies Corporation provides high-technology products and services to the building systems and aerospace industries worldwide. It operates in six segments: Otis,

(continues)

Company	Industry	Description (from Yahoo!)
United Technology (UTX) (Continued)		Carrier, Chubb, Pratt and Whitney, Hamilton Sundstrand, and Sikorsky. United Technologies was incorporated in 1934 and is headquartered in Hartford, Connecticut.
Verizon (VZ)	Telecom Services	Verizon Communications, Inc. provides communications services primarily in the United States. The company operates through three segments: Domestic Telecom, Domestic Wireless, and Information Services. The Domestic Telecom segment provides local telephone services in 29 states and the District of Columbia. Verizon was incorporated in 1983 under the name Bell Atlantic Corporation. The company changed its name to Verizon Communications, Inc. in 2000 following a merger with GTE Corporation. Verizon is based in New York City.
Wal-Mart (WMT)	Discount Stores	Wal-Mart Stores, Inc. operates retail stores in various formats. The company primarily operates in two segments, The Wal-Mart Stores and The SAM'S CLUB. The Wal-Mart Stores segment includes its Discount Stores, Supercenters, and Neighborhood Markets in the United States as well as Walmart.com. The company was incorporated in 1969 and is based in Bentonville, Arkansas.
Walt Disney (DIS)	Entertainment	The Walt Disney Company, through its subsidiaries, operates as a diversified entertainment company worldwide. It operates in four segments: Media Networks, Parks and Resorts, Studio Entertainment, and Consumer Products.

Adapted from Yahoo! Finance (finance.yahoo.com).

6

STOCK OPTIONS

A firm that substitutes stock compensation for cash compensation increases reported earnings, an egregious way to inflate earnings.

—Stephen Penman

While on the subject of self-interest, let's turn again to the most important accounting mechanism still available to CEOs who wish to overstate earnings: the non-expensing of stock options.

—Warren Buffett

Stock options as a form of employee pay have been used for decades but were not common until the 1990s. The Revenue Act of 1950 made options for employees both legal and practical. As stock prices started rising, options became more lucrative—and the compensation of choice for greedy executives. Because option costs were not expensed, they were considered a zero-cost compensation. Options were also an expense for tax purposes when exercised. What a deal! Why pay big salaries when options could be heaped on executives and workers instead? Start-ups became big option issuers, and corporations large and small added options to executive pay packages. Before the stock bubble some 65 companies had over a billion shares of options outstanding, including 10 Dow 30 stalwarts.

Economics theory indicated that options give employees a greater incentive to promote the interests of shareholders. Harvard Professor Michael Jensen was an early proponent and coauthored an influential *Harvard Business Review* article in 1990. The school of hard knocks proved that options made meeting quarterly earnings targets an executive obsession—and the prime motive for extreme earnings magic. Jensen later recanted on options somewhat, but insisted that executives still should hold considerable equity interests including various forms of "incentivised options," such as cost-of-capital-indexed options.

The scandals at Enron, WorldCom, and the rest are linked directly to the fixation on stock price caused by massive options payments. The evidence suggests that corporate executives insisted on always meeting analyst forecasts, because stock prices could get pummeled when targets were missed by as little as a penny a share. As management's focus should be long term, this short-term fetish could be disastrous, as it was at Enron.

Current generally accepted accounting principles (GAAP) recommend expensing options but require note disclosure of options outstanding and the pro forma impact of options on net income as if they were expensed. Under recently revised GAAP (SFAS No. 123R), companies will have to expense options beginning in 2006. Until then, options are a serious earnings magic issue, but the impact can be estimated using note disclosure. After options are required expenses, the issue shifts to the details of estimating options values and procedures during the transition period—available estimation and reporting alternatives provide continuing earnings management leeway. It should be noted that whether options are expensed or not has no effect on cash flows; instead, expensing options decreases the incentives for issuing options because of the direct impact on earnings. Other ownership-related compensation alternatives should be more effective than options. Of course, all require expensing.

THE (SLIGHTLY) COMPLICATED ACCOUNTING STUFF

Options permit the holder to purchase stock at a set price (the exercise price) over some fixed time period. The most common price is the closing market price of the stock at the issue date. At that price (or higher), the company is not required to record compensation expense. Expensing options would decrease net income and increase the volatility of earnings (because the expense is based on changes in fair value associated with the changing stock price).

The Financial Accounting Standards Board (FASB) decided to require the expensing of options in the early 1990s, and the political fight was on. As former Securities and Exchange Commission (SEC) chairman Arthur Levitt put it: "Whenever the FASB tried to crack down by tightening accounting standards, it ran into a phalanx of corporate, Congressional, and auditor opposition" (Levitt and Dwyer 2002, p. 107). High-tech and other corporate lobbyists bombarded the SEC and Congress. FASB was "antibusiness"; earnings per share (EPS) would drop; American firms could not compete; innovation would be stifled. Connecticut Senator Joe Lieberman led the charge, with plenty of help from Republican and Democratic pols—a strange form of nonpartisanship. Lieberman's legislation would have crippled the FASB, requiring the SEC to ratify every FASB pronouncement and specifically barring the SEC from enforcing FASB's option expensing requirement. Levitt advised the FASB to back off, which the board did.

The result was SFAS No. 123 in 1995, which allows companies to either: (1) expense the estimated cost of stock options using complex options pricing models (primarily the Black-Scholes model) to estimate the value of options, or (2) provide pro forma disclosures in the notes—that is, calculate net income as if options were expensed. Most companies use note disclosure rather than expensing options, although many companies, including Dow 30 giants General Electric and Microsoft, switched to expensing options. SFAS No. 123 requires considerable disclosure when options are not expensed. This information can be used to reevaluate the impact of options and normalize earnings by restating net income on a pro forma basis and recalculating performance and market ratios on that basis.

When executives or employees exercise stock options, which are classified as nonqualified stock options for tax purposes, the employee pays cash to the company equal to the exercise (or strike) price determined at the date of grant. The company records this transaction as an increase in paid-in capital. In addition, the difference between the market price and exercise price (essentially the "profit" from holding the options) represents a tax benefit to the company (i.e., it is a tax-deductible item) and a tax liability to the employees. When companies use the disclosure method and do not expense the options, the tax gain should be reported directly to stockholders' equity rather than on the income statement. The tax benefit potentially could have a large impact on cash from operations. For example, Oracle's tax benefit for 2000 of $1.2 billion was more than half of cash from operations. In summary, not expensing stock options creates considerable earnings management concerns. Fortunately, disclosures are extensive enough to conduct considerable analysis and reestimate earnings.

Options became a popular form of management and employee compensation in the 1990s. With the stock market crash beginning in early 2000, the price of stocks and therefore the value of options dropped precipitously and often became worthless (the term *underwater* was widely used).

Why would executives, directors, and employees prefer stock options rather than higher salaries or cash bonuses? The advantage of the options is the one-direction participation in the success of the company. As the stock price increases, the value of the options rises. If the stock price plummets, the employee does not exercise the options. Stock prices of high-tech companies have a history of substantial price increases (also many failures), so options have the potential to generate substantial wealth. Real tax advantages also exist for both the company and recipients.

Lowenstein (2004) cited Disney chief executive officer (CEO) Michael Eisner as the option king for poor performance. During the 1990s and early 2000s, Eisner collected some $800 million in options and other compensation while Disney's stock price fell. As Lowenstein put it: "Never has a CEO reaped such a fortune from such prolonged mediocrity" (p. 51). Eisner had plenty of competition. Oracle CEO Larry Ellison made $706 million in 2001, while Oracle's stock return was a negative 57%. Enron executives cashed out before the company's bankruptcy in 2001, with similar stories at the other financial fiascoes of 2001–2002.

Why would a corporation want to use options? First, as long as the exercise price is the market price or higher at issue date, no compensation expense needs to be recorded. In terms of the income statement, it can be a zero-cost form of management compensation. Second, presumably it makes the incentives of the managers identical to the owners of the company. Because the benefit of options is future ownership and managers increase the value of the options by increasing the value (i.e., stock price) of the company, management incentives parallel owner incentives. Firms can recruit successful and high-priced executives and retain existing managers and employees by issuing stock options liberally. Doing this has been widely used as a so-called low-compensation strategy for high-tech start-ups. Finally, the tax deductibility of exercised nonqualified options is beneficial.

The FASB was at it again after the corporate scandals, trying to require expensing of options. This was achieved in 2004, with SFAS No. 123R, no thanks to continued lobbying and congressional roadblocks—the usual suspects. Options have to be expensed by 2006 ("as of the beginning of the first interim or annual reporting period that begins after June 15, 2005"), although additional alternatives are allowed to determine options valuation.

THE COST OF STOCK OPTIONS

What is the financial downside to stock options? There are real costs, whether reported on the income statement or not, that can be recognized. The first impact of stock options is the increase in number of shares outstanding (actual and prospective), resulting in stock dilution. The earnings of the company have to be spread over more shares, decreasing EPS. The impact of future dilution is estimated by using diluted EPS. If this has a potentially large impact on future EPS, it is an earnings magic signal.

Consider the four tech companies from the Dow 30, all expected to be large issuers of options. They did not disappoint; however, Microsoft has been expensing options since 2003. In other words, Microsoft has been recognizing the real cost (at least a reasonable estimate) of options as part of compensation. Thanks to FASB's revised Statement 123, the others will be forced to start expense options shortly. The number of options outstanding is presented in an options note; shares outstanding are presented on the balance sheet. These are summarized for fiscal year 2004 in Exhibit 6.1.

Potential dilution is estimated using the ratio of options to shares outstanding. Dilution over 10% could be considered significant. Microsoft has the lowest percentage, at 8.8%, because outstanding options are down substantially (down from 1,796 million options in 2001). Beginning in 2004, Microsoft shifted to restricted stock in place of options and allowed employees to transfer options to J.P. Morgan. The other three tech firms have hundreds of millions of options outstanding, all greater than 10% of shares outstanding. Across the Dow 30 (see Appendix 6.1) outstanding options averaged 228 million, 9.0% of shares outstanding. Twelve firms had options greater than 10% of outstanding shares, with Hewlett-Packard topping the list at 18.9%. Of course, GMs options are underwater.

Because of the potential dilution, pro forma calculations of the expense impact of stock options are important. The necessary information is available in note disclosure, which presents Net Income—Reported compared to Net Income—Pro Forma. Pro forma net income represents the estimated stock options expense as if included in income. Microsoft has no such calculation because options are already expensed and included in income (some $5.7 billion in 2004). The other firms are (2004 fiscal year, in millions) as shown in Exhibit 6.2.

The pro forma difference was substantial for all three (reducing net income more than the arbitrary 10%), with H-P leading the way at over 20%. In other words, these three companies have lots of options and they have a

Company	Stock Options Outstanding (Millions)	Shares Outstanding (Millions)	Options to Shares Outstanding
Microsoft	949	10,771	8.8%
Hewlett-Packard	550	2,911	18.9
Intel	884	6,253	14.1
IBM	252	1,646	15.3

EXHIBIT 6.1   FISCAL YEAR 2004 SUMMARY OF OUTSTANDING STOCK OPTIONS AND SHARES

	Hewlett-Packard (Millions)	Intel (Millions)	IBM (Millions)
Net Income—Reported	$3,497	$7,516	$8,430
Net Income—Pro Forma	2,779	6,245	7,479
Difference	718	1,271	951
% Difference	20.5%	16.9%	11.3%

EXHIBIT 6.2   PRO FORMA DIFFERENCES

big impact on net income. It makes sense to recalculate performance ratios (e.g., return on assets) using the pro forma income numbers as a better measure of economic earnings. Across the Dow 30 (see Appendix 6.2), options decreased net income an average 5.2%. Only four of the Dow 30 had options that reduced net income more than 10%, with Hewlett-Packard topping the list.

STOCK OPTION CONCERNS

Earnings magic concerns and detection strategies are outlined in Exhibit 6.3.

Calculating dilution potential and option expense represents the most obvious impact of stock option use. After the tech bubble collapse in early 2000, large numbers of outstanding options were quickly underwater (stock price below exercise price). That is the risk of options. Note that equity investors face the market risk of declining share price all the time. The execs with underwater options have lost nothing except the potential for the vast rewards of stock price gains, while investor losses are real. Revaluing options

Topic	Concern	Detection Strategy
Dilution	Substantial dilution potential (perhaps equal to 10% or more of outstanding shares).	Outstanding options at year-end (note disclosure) divided by shares outstanding at year-end.
Option Expense	Substantial percent of net income (perhaps 10% or more).	Note disclosure on pro forma net income; calculate % impact.
Revaluing (or Reissuing) Options	"Underwater options" revalued regularly.	Revaluations announced in option note; check for rationale and frequency.
Use of Treasury Stock	Treasury stock as a poor use of cash plus reducing equity; used as a rationale for options-issuing companies and not paying dividends.	Evaluate treasury stock magnitudes on balance sheet and changes on statement of stockholders' equity, plus note or MD&A disclosure.

EXHIBIT 6.3   EARNINGS MAGIC CONCERNS AND DETECTION STRATEGIES

(actually, reissuing new options to replace "underwater options") essentially rewards executives for the past lousy performance; that is, they can now make money as stock prices rise from the new lows. Apple replaced CEO Steve Jobs's 27.5 million options with 5 million shares of restricted stock in 2003, valued at $75 million. The restricted stock is a reasonable alternative, because Jobs will feel both the pain and gain as Apple's stock price rises and falls.

Firms may use the practice of issuing options year after year, whether stock price is going up or down. The executives of mediocre companies receiving options in down years are essentially guaranteed substantial compensation if the stock returns to its previous price. This is true of companies with poor returns relative to the market. If stocks average 10% growth a year and Stuck Co. averages only 2%, Stuck Co. executives still get a big return if they receive substantial options. Stockholders should be none too happy about this.

The relationship of stock options with treasury stock and dividend policy can be an important one and possibly suggests the emphasis on so-called long-term executive compensation to the possible detriment of investors. The options/treasury stock/dividend relationship is partly based on relative philosophy. Historically, corporate success has been measured in terms of dividend payments. Using cash for treasury stock can be a smokescreen for maintaining stock prices (advantage to options holders) rather than paying dividends. Because options holders benefit only from share price and not dividends, where is the incentive for execs to pay dividends?

ALTERNATIVES TO STOCK OPTIONS

There are several stock ownership alternatives to options. These include restricted stock, phantom stock, and stock appreciation rights (SARs). These alternatives tend to be more flexible than stock options, but the benefits (usually increases in fair value) usually are treated as compensation expenses by the corporations.

Restricted stock is a grant of stock to an employee in which the employee's rights to the shares are limited until the shares vest and no longer subject to the restrictions. Typically, the employee may not sell or transfer the shares of stock until they vest, at which point the employee has full ownership of the stock. The restrictions usually involve working for a certain number of years or until specific performance goals have been met. Awards provide service or performance targets for employees to achieve before actually receiving shares or having the right to acquire shares. Unlike stock options or stock appreciation rights, restricted stock retains some value for employees even if the price goes down. Microsoft shifted to restricted stock in 2004, as did many other firms.

Phantom stock is a promise to pay a bonus in the form of the equivalent of either the value of company shares or the increase in that value over a period of time. It is taxed as ordinary income at the time it is received. Stock appreciation rights are similar to phantom stock, except they provide the right to the monetary equivalent of the increase in the value of a specified number of shares over a specified period of time. As with phantom stock, this amount is usually paid in cash, but could be paid in shares. SARs can be granted in tandem with stock options to help finance the purchase of the options and pay taxes due when the options are exercised. SARs and phantom stock are designed to provide employees with the economic benefits of stock ownership without any actual transfer of stock occurring.

Given the increased flexibility associated with restricted stock, phantom stock, and SARs, they are expected to become increasingly common. Stock options are less popular with stockholders, who have seen bloated compensation paid to inept executives and the corresponding dilution of outstanding shares. Because these alternatives require the recognition of compensation expense, the awards should be more modest than stock options. With the FASB's expensing of options in 2006, restricted stock and the other alternatives should become even more popular, because they can be tailored to individual corporate incentive structures.

Earnings management concerns will continue with restricted stock, phantom stock, and SARs. Of most concern are the relative level of compensation to senior executives and the specific terms of compensation agreements. The actual and potential rewards should be commensurate with actual performance and should provide appropriate incentives to managers. Analyzing stock-based compensation requires the qualitative evaluation of disclosures in the proxy statements and 10-K.

APPENDIX 6.1

STOCK OPTIONS OUTSTANDING FOR THE DOW 30

Company	Stock Options*	Shares Outstanding*	Options to Shares Outstanding
3M Co.	78	774	10%
Alcoa Inc.	90	1,663	5%
Altria Group Inc.	75	2,060	4%
American Express	132	1,249	11%
American International Group	54	2596	2%
Boeing Co.	25	832	3%
Caterpillar Inc.	41	343	12%
Citigroup Inc.	331	5,195	6%
Coca-Cola Co.	183	2,409	8%
Disney (Walt) Co.	221	2,000	11%
Du Pont (E.I.) De Nemours	98	994	10%
Exxon-Mobil Corp.	181	6,401	3%
General Electric Co.	286	10,586	3%
General Motors Corp.	107	565	19%
Hewlett-Packard Inc.	550	2,911	19%
Home Depot Inc.	86	2,185	4%
Honeywell International Inc.	58	850	7%
Intel Corp.	884	6,253	14%
International Business Machines Corp.	252	1,646	15%
J.P. Morgan Chase & Co.	376	3,556	11%
Johnson & Johnson	229	2,971	8%
McDonald's Corp.	167	1,270	13%
Merck & Co.	236	2,028	12%
Microsoft Corp.	949	10,771	9%
Pfizer Inc.	635	8,754	7%
Procter & Gamble Co.	276	2,544	11%
SBC Communications Inc.	214	3,301	6%
United Technologies Corp.	44	511	9%
Verizon Communications	271	2,775	10%
Wal-Mart Stores	80	4,234	2%
Average	240.3	3,140.9	9%

*In millions.

97

APPENDIX 6.2

STOCK OPTION INCOME EFFECT FOR THE DOW 30

Company	Net Income Reported*	Net Income Pro Forma*	Difference*	% Difference
3M Co.	$ 2,990	$ 2,841	$ 149	5%
Alcoa Inc.	1,310	1,275	35	3%
Altria Group Inc.	9,416	9,404	12	0%
American Express	3,445	3,261	184	5%
American International Group	9,731	9,693	38	0%
Boeing Co.	NM	NM	NM	NM
Caterpillar Inc.	2,035	1,874	161	8%
Citigroup Inc.	17,046	16,894	152	1%
Coca-Cola Co.	NM	NM	NM	NM
Disney (Walt) Co.	2,345	2,090	255	11%
Du Pont (E.I.) De Nemours	1,780	1,752	28	2%
Exxon-Mobil Corp.	25,330	25,228	102	0%
General Electric Co.	16,819	16,667	152	1%
General Motors Corp.	2,805	2,791	14	0%
Hewlett-Packard Inc.	3,497	2,779	718	21%
Home Depot Inc.	5,001	4,843	158	3%
Honeywell International Inc.	1,281	1,239	42	3%
Intel Corp.	7,516	6,245	1,271	17%
International Business Machines Corp.	8,430	7,479	951	11%
J.P. Morgan Chase & Co.	4,466	4,284	182	4%
Johnson & Johnson	8,509	8,180	329	4%
McDonald's Corp.	2,279	2,129	150	7%
Merck & Co.	5,813	5,338	475	8%
Microsoft Corp.	NM	NM	NM	NM
Pfizer Inc.	11,357	10,783	574	5%
Procter & Gamble Co.	6,481	6,156	325	5%
SBC Communications Inc.	NM	NM	NM	
United Technologies Corp.	2,788	2,673	115	4%
Verizon Communications	7,831	7,760	71	1%
Wal-Mart Stores	NM	NM	NM	NM
Average	6,812.04	6,546.32	265.72	5%

* In millions.

7

PENSIONS AND OTHER POSTEMPLOYMENT BENEFITS

*The CFA Institute . . . recently commented that, because the
pension and other postemployment benefit accounting standard
"fails to provide full recognition in the financial statements of the
effects on the firm of the pension and postemployment benefit
contract, a huge and very costly burden has been shifted to those
for whom the statements are prepared, analysts and other users."*
— SEC report on off–balance sheet issues

Once again, pensions and other postemployment benefits (OPEB) have become financial and political issues. During the 1990s, thanks largely to the stock market boom, most defined benefit pension plans were overfunded—in other words, flush with investments valued much higher than projected pension obligations. That changed with the market crash. More companies moved into the red (became underfunded), with much of the underfunding not recognized on the balance sheet. The pension/OPEB underfunding combination makes a grave matter worse. The potential of big bankruptcies with major under-funding make it a political issue, since the Pension Benefit Guaranty Corpo-ration, the federal agency responsible for making good on pension liabilities, also is underfunded.

Larger employers generally provide pension benefits, either defined contribution plans or defined benefit plans. Firms with defined benefit plans and a large labor force have substantial obligations, which may or may not be fully funded. Generally accepted accounting principles (GAAP) for defined benefit plans are complex and currently based primarily on Statements of Financial Accounting Standards (SFAS) Nos. 87 and 132 (revised in 2003). Many corporations also have committed themselves to obligations for ben-efits to employees who have retired early or have left the firm for other rea-sons (OPEB). SFAS No. 106 requires these commitments to be recognized as liabilities, and the accounting is similar to that of defined benefit pension plans.

During the 1990s, most companies' pension plans benefited from the bull market with overfunded pension plans. That is, pension-invested plan assets zoomed up in value and were greater than calculated pension obligations. Pensions are recorded as "net pension assets" (if overfunded) or "net pension liabilities" (if underfunded) on the balance sheet. When the stock market bubble burst, companies struggled to make a buck, and many moved from overfunded to underfunded status. Because of tax incentives (actually lack of them, because OPEB contributions to investment plan assets were generally not tax deductible), the pension/OPEB combination could be really underfunded.

Thanks to how pensions are recorded and the "smoothing requirements" of pension accounting, the underfunding potential is not obvious on the balance sheet for two reasons. First, few companies actually report net pension assets (or liabilities) and net OPEB obligations (almost always a liability) as separate line items on the balance sheet. They are usually part of "other net assets" (or liabilities). Second, pension GAAP does not recognize the full amount of changes in the market value of the pension (and other adjustments) on the financial statements. Much of these "adjustments" are spread out (smoothed) over a decade or so. The information is presented in a detailed and complex note or two, which is where to go to determine financial reality.

PENSION PLANS

A pension is a long-term contract to provide retirement benefits to employees. Under a defined contribution plan, the employer and/or employees makes periodic cash payments, usually based on a percentage of salary. The employer's contributions are compensation expense. The accumulated total investment including portfolio earnings represents the "retirement "fund," under the direction of the employees and subject to federal requirements.

Defined benefit plans specify the retirement benefits the employee will receive. The most common plans are "pay-related" and determined primarily on some definition of "final salary" and length of service. Assume Grumpy Gary's Gimpy Gismos' defined benefit plan provides a 3% of final salary retirement benefit for each year of service. Foreman Mitty Smitty retires after 30 years, making a final salary of $100,000; therefore, his annual retirement benefit is 3% × 30 × $100,000, or $90,000. The employer manages the retirement fund, makes cash payments to provide pension assets that are invested in securities portfolios, gives cash payments to retirees, and handles all pension-related calculations and journal entries. Thus, the employer specifies the commitments and bears all the risk associated with meeting the pension obligations. Management of the pension plan must comply with extensive GAAP requirements and federal law, based primarily on the Employee Retirement Income Security Act of 1974 (ERISA).

The incentives to offer pension plans are substantial. Pension contributions (both employer and employee) are income tax–exempt to the employees, and taxes on pension assets and earnings are deferred until the employee retires—usually at a lower tax rate than when the employee was working. It is more difficult for the employer, because an annual pension expense is calculated (with net increases in fair value of plan assets reducing the expense). Cash contributions to plan assets also might be required.

The pension is part of the employee compensation package and may make employees more loyal to the company. In a defined benefit plan, dual incentives can exist. The company may feel paternalistic for employees' retirement and thus guarantee retirement benefits. Also, pension accounting for a defined benefit plan allows considerable judgment, and there is substantial room for earnings magic. GAAP require considerable income smoothing for defined benefit plans.

Defined contribution plans are based on employee and employers' cash contributions, usually a percentage of employee salary (with employer contributions usually tied to employee contributions). The employee typically has investment portfolio options and generally has "ownership" of the portfolio after some vesting period. The company essentially has no additional obligations after the cash contributions are made.

Defined Benefit Plans: The Balance Sheet and Net Pension Assets

The plan assets of a defined benefit plan represent the fair value of the investment portfolio used to fund current and future retirement benefits, made up primarily of stocks, bonds, and other earning assets. The end-of-period plan assets essentially include the fair value of the plan assets at the start of the period, plus the return on plan assets, cash contributions from the employer and employees, less retirement payments during the period.

General Electric has a set of defined benefit pensions to be proud of. It has lots of plan assets, is fully funded (overfunded actually, with more plan assets than total pension obligations and a low pension expense relative to net income). We will use GE as a reasonable example of pension reporting.

GE's presentation of fair value of plan assets (presented in note 6) for 2004 was:

(in $ Millions)	Principal Pension Plans		Other Pension Plans	
	2004	2003	2004	2003
Balance at January 1	$43,879	$37,811	$3,035	$2,064
Actual Gain on Plan Assets	4,888	8,203	292	264
Employer Contributions	102	105	370	183
Participant Contributions	163	169	31	25
Benefits Paid	(2,367)	(2,409)	(230)	(148)
Acquired Plans	—	—	868	373
Exchange Rate Adjustments and Other	—	—	286	274
Balance at December 31	$46,665	$43,879	$4,652	$3,035

GE had over $51.3 billion in plan assets at fair value ($46,665 + $4,652 —the principal and other pension plans must be added together), up from almost $47 billion at the end of 2003. The major reasons for the increase in plan assets were that the benefits paid of $2.6 billion were more than off-set by the actual gain in value of the investment portfolio, which went up by $5.8 billion.

The projected benefit obligation (PBO) is the present value of amounts the employer expects to pay retired employees based on employee service to date and expected future salary at retirement (as adjusted by various actu-arial assumptions including average retirement age, mortality rates after retirement, number of employers staying to retirement, etc.). A separate table shows GE's PBO calculations, which totals $47,213 million, up $4.5 billion from 2003.

The funded status of the pension plan is the fair value of plan assets less the PBO. This is the "real" net asset position (if overfunded, or net liability position if underfunded)—that is, financial reality. The funded status of GE (from the note disclosures presented above, in millions) is $51,317 − $47,213 = $4,104. GE's plan is overfunded by $4.1 billion. As important as funded status really is, it is not the amount actually recorded on the balance sheet. Recording funded status would result in volatility in the balance sheet amount, primarily because the fair value of plan assets can fluctuate widely from year to year—especially from stock market gyrations.

GAAP requires various smoothing devices to limit the fluctuations (extremely annoying for earnings magic analysis). GE's calculations, which include all the smoothing components, are:

(in $ Millions)	Principal Pension Plans		Other Pension Plans	
December 31	2004	2003	2004	2003
Funded Status	$ 6,696	$ 6,052	$(2,592)	$(1,828)
Unrecognized Prior Service Cost	1,260	1,571	45	36
Unrecognized Net Actuarial Loss	7,481	7,588	1,662	1,184
Net Amount Recognized	$15,437	$15,211	$ (885)	$ (608)

GE starts with funded status as described above. Total funded status is $6,696 − $2,592, or $4,104 million. To that are added adjustments, defined in Exhibit 7.1.

The "net amount recognized" is the net asset value recorded on the balance sheet, $15,437 − $885 = $14,552. The impact of the adjustments is an increase in net pension assets of $10,448 million ($14,552 − $4,104). What? That is almost $10.5 billion added to assets that is play money—it does not exist. Stated another way, that $10.5 billion is off balance sheet. It is a combination of previous losses in plan assets and increases in obligations due to changes in future benefits that are not recorded.

The reason to record "play money" is to minimize volatility in the financial statements. The logic is that pensions are long term and should not have an "unnecessary" immediate impact on earnings and obligations. Instead, these gyrations are spread out over a decade or so. In other words, it is a form of mandatory income smoothing. It deemphasizes pension volatility but also violates financial reality. The information is in the notes, and further analysis is necessary.

Defined Benefit Plans: The Income Statement and Pension Expense

Now the income statement—where the smoothing affects earnings. Each year the employer recognizes the net expense (pension cost), which includes

Item	Definition	Discussion
Unrecognized Prior Service Cost	The impact of plan amendments, usually increasing pension cost	Amortized over the average remaining employee service life.
Unrecognized Net Actuarial Gain or Loss	Reestimates of PBO based on restated estimates	Usually amortized over the average remaining employee service life.

EXHIBIT 7.1   ADDED ADJUSTMENTS TO GE'S CALCULATIONS

annual service cost and interest cost (roughly the increase in the projected benefit obligation) plus or minus other adjustments. Essentially, the entry is a debit to pension expense and a credit to pension liability. However, one of the adjustments is to record the expected return on plan assets, not the actual return. The amount is an estimated average return percentage times the beginning balance of plan assets. It is always a positive, because it is a percentage based on average return.

The result for GE shows a 2004 pension expense (shown as "total cost") of $255 million, or 1.5% of net income (before tax). The GE calculation for 2004, compared to the two previous years (in millions), is:

(in $ Millions)	2004	2003	2002
Expected Return on Plan Assets	$(4,258)	$(4,245)	$(4,245)
Service Cost for Benefits Earned	1,438	1,375	1,245
Interest Cost on Benefit Obligation	2,516	2,390	2,288
Prior Service Cost	317	252	221
Net Actuarial Loss (Gain) Recognized	242	(544)	(905)
Total Cost	$ 255	$ (772)	$(1,396)

Definitions of key pension cost items are presented in Exhibit 7.2.

The major expenses are service and interest costs of about $4 billion, offset by expected return on plan asset of $4.3 billion. Consequently, the net expense is a relatively low $255 million for 2004. Note that GE had "net pension income" for both 2002 and 2003; in other words, a "negative pension

Item	Definition
Expected Return on Plan Assets	Expected long-term rate of return multiplied by the operating fair value of plan assets at the beginning of the year.
Service Cost for Benefits Earned	Actuarial present value of benefits earned during the period.
Interest Cost on Benefit Obligation	Increase in future pension payments (benefit obligation) beginning PBO multiplied by the discount rate.
Prior Service Cost	Prior service cost (based on plan amendments) amortization for the current period.
Net Actuarial Gain Recognized	Changes in actuarial assumptions (can be net gain or loss); gain reduces pension cost.
Income from Pensions (Usually Pension Expense)	The pension cost (the net pension expense) recorded on the income statement.

EXHIBIT 7.2   DEFINITIONS OF KEY PENSION COST ITEMS

expense." The pension plans actually increased GE's net income (before tax) by almost $1.4 billion in 2002.

But wait a minute. That is using expected return, an estimate, and not financial reality. Financial reality can be calculated by substituting the actual gains on plan assets of $5,180 ($4,888 + 292, found on the table of fair value of plan assets) for expected return. That calculation is $255 + $4,258 − $5,180 = −$667. In other words, if economic reality is important, GE had net pension income of $667 million because the actual return on plan assets was greater than expected return by $922 million. It is not clear how useful this calculation is because of the year-to-year volatility of stock returns, which the Financial Accounting Standards Board thinks should be smoothed.

In summary, the key points for GE are: (1) the company is substantially overfunded, $14.6 billion in terms of the amount actually recorded on the balance sheet; (2) but overfunded by $4.1 billion based on funded status, some $10.5 billion less and a better measure of economic reality; (3) the net pension expense was $255 million, or about 1.5% of net income, but the actual return on plan assets was $5.2 billion, or almost $1 billion more than expected; and (4) none of this is obvious from looking at the balance sheet or income statements, because all the pension amounts are presented as part of "other items" rather than separate line items. Thus, analyzing the pension note is necessary to better understand economic reality.

Earnings Magic and the Dow 30

Pension accounting for defined benefit plans has an "off–balance sheet" focus with the important information not directly disclosed on the financial statements. Accounting procedures are based on a substantial set of assumptions, primarily actuarial rate assumptions and GAAP requirements for smoothing procedures that incorporate a number of undisclosed assumptions. Given this structure, there are a number of specific concerns as well as procedures to better understand the real impact of defined benefit pension plans.

Key issues are shown in Exhibit 7.3.

Some of these concerns are obvious from the previous discussion of GE; others need further explanation. How significant are they for the Dow 30?

Twenty-six of the Dow 30 have defined benefit plans (see Appendix 7.1). The balance sheets for 2004 looked great, with total overfunding (a net asset position) of over $119 billion, an average of $4.6 billion per company. Only 4 of the 26 had a net liability position, with Exxon-Mobil leading the way at $2.7 billion underfunding—unexpected since Exxon-Mobil was the earnings champ for 2004 at over $25 billion.

Topic	Issue
Economic Position	Pension plan "real" funding level based on funded status. This can be substantially different from what is reported.
Reported Funding Level	"Reported" pension plan amount and comparison to funded status.
Pension Expense	What is the pension expense? What does it mean if "negative"?
Expected Return on Plan Assets Compared to Actual Return	The actual annual return can be substantially different from expected return, which is always positive.
Actuarial Assumptions	Aggressive assumptions for discount rate, expected return on plan assets, and rate of compensation increases. Changing rates can change the amounts recognized.
Actuarial Assumption Trends	Looking at changes in rates over time may suggest earnings management.

EXHIBIT 7.3   KEY ISSUES

Here's the scary part. Twenty-two of the 26 were underfunded based on funded status—that is financial reality. Seventy-three percent of America's most successful firms really had underfunded pension plans. The underfunding averaged $1.8 billion a firm, $46.9 billion total. In other words, these companies reported pension net assets of $119 billion, while in fact they were underfunded by $46.9 billion—that is a swing of $166 billion that represent off–balance sheet obligations.

GE, overfunded both on a reporting and funded status basis, was not typical. More typical was 3M, with an overfunded net asset position of $2 billion and an underfunded status of $1.1 billion. That shift of almost $3.2 billion was nearly 22% of total assets. General Motors shifted from a net asset position of about $35 billion to a negative $7.5 billion funded status, a swing of over $42 billion.

There is nothing unusual about the Dow 30. A recent Securities and Exchange Commission (SEC) report entitled "Arrangements with Off–Balance-Sheet Implications" (SEC 2005) found that 81% of the large firms in the sample had defined benefit plans, with a combined underfunding based on funded status of over $85 billion but overfunded on the balance sheet by almost $90 billion. Extrapolating to the entire population of traded corporations, the SEC estimated that over $400 billion in real pension obligations was off balance sheet; that is the estimated balance sheet net asset position of $212 billion less the underfunded amount of $201 billion based on funded status.

Pension expense includes (roughly) actual costs and adjustments less expected return on plan assets. The expected return is the assumed long-term rate of return. It is always a positive percent of plan assets and usually not close to the actual on a year-to-year basis. Market returns are volatile and should average out long term. It could be assumed that using expected return, pension expense should be close to zero in most years. For the Dow 26 (excluding the 4 with no defined benefit plans) the pension expense averaged $481 million. Pension expense averaged 13.1% of net income (before tax), including a whopping 88% for GM.

Pension expense was $2.5 billion for GM, while net income was $2.8 billion. For what it is worth, the expected return used by GM was $8.5 billion for 2004, while actual return was $11.9 billion—a difference of $3.4 billion. Based on financial reality, GM's net income should have been $3.4 billion higher (before tax). How should these numbers be evaluated for GM? One alternative would be to report pension expense as other comprehensive income (or just the investment return portion as other comprehensive income). This is not GAAP, but an alternative that may better reflect financial reality.

Three actuarial assumption rates are disclosed in the pension note: the discount rate, expected return on plan assets, and rate of compensation increases. These defined are described in Exhibit 7.4.

These rates are necessary for performance calculations but have the effect of smoothing the income statement results. Particularly important is the return on plan assets, because the actual return represents economic reality and is easily determined.

Companies have almost complete control of the assumption rates used but have to disclose those rates. Based on a 2001 survey, the most common return on plan assets was between 9% and 10%. Most companies used discount rates between 7% and 8%, and most used compensation increases of 5% or less (White et al. 2003, pp. 406, 413). Return on plan asset rates for the Dow 30 were in the range of 7% to 9% for 2004.

Discount Rate	Interest rate used to compute the present value of benefit obligations, which should be based on current (market) interest rates.
Expected Return on Plan Assets	Projected long-term return on plan assets, used to eliminate market volatility when calculating net pension expense.
Rate of Compensation Increase	Assumption of average annual expected compensation increases.

EXHIBIT 7.4   DEFINITIONS OF THREE ACTUARIAL ASSUMPTION RATES

	2004	2003	2002	2001	2000	1999
Discount Rate	5.75%	6.0%	6.75%	7.25%	7.5%	7.75%
Return on Plan Assets	8.5	8.5	8.5	9.5	9.5	9.5
Compensation Increases	5.0	5.0	5.0	5.0	5.0	5.0

EXHIBIT 7.5   GE RATES FOR LAST SIX YEARS

Blankley and Swanson (1995) found that firms do not change discount rates as often as should be done to use current market interest rates. This was particularly true when market rates were declining (based on their sample years). By avoiding lowering discount rates, firms could report lower PBO and pension costs. Blankley and Swanson also found that expected rates of return changed infrequently, but this is consistent with the SFAS No. 87 requirement that they reflect long-run expectations. Their findings showed substantial volatility in the actual rate of return experienced by firms.

The rates used by GE for the last six years are shown in Exhibit 7.5.

Rates used by GE stayed within the "average range" over the last six years. The discount rate has been dropping, while return on plan assets dropped 100 basis points in 2002 to 8.5%.

General Motors is used for comparison, because it has both manufacturing and financial components. The rates for GM are shown in Exhibit 7.6.

The rates for GM were within the ranges of the average firm but on the aggressive end. The rates used by the rest of the Dow 30 were similar to GE and GM.

OTHER POSTEMPLOYMENT BENEFITS

Companies often provided early retirees and other former employees certain benefits. Historically, these costs were recognized on a cash (or pay-as-you-go) basis. The most common benefits were health and other forms

	2004	2003	2002	2001	2000	1999
Discount Rate	6.0%	6.75%	7.25%	7.3%	7.3%	7.8%
Return on Plan Assets	9.0	9.0	10.0	10.0	10.0	10.0
Compensation Increases	5.0	5.0	5.0	5.0	5.0	5.0

EXHIBIT 7.6   GM RATES

of insurance. Particularly as healthcare costs rose, these obligations have increased. The accounting rules were changed with SFAS No. 106, which requires OPEB obligations to be recognized as liabilities, with accounting and reporting similar to pensions. SFAS No. 132 added additional disclosure requirements. OPEB can be funded (with invested assets, just like pensions), but tend to be underfunded because the contributions to OPEB plans are not deductible for tax purposes and accrued OPEB costs also are not tax deductible. (Only payments for actual benefits paid are deductible.) OPEB accounting procedures parallel those of pension plans, meaning a lot of complicated assumptions and extensive disclosures.

GE's OPEB note 5 was similar to the pension presentation and had the same basic composition, including the asset portfolio valuation, calculation of the major obligation called accumulated postretirement benefit obligation (APBO), the calculation of the net liability position, and calculation of OPEB cost for the year. APBO is the actuarial present value of benefits earned and represents a "real economic obligation" (or at least an estimate). APBO has the same basic components as PBO, with service cost and interest cost the most significant items.

Similar to pensions, the real economic net liability position (a net asset position is uncommon because of the tax requirements) is APBO less the fair value of plan assets. For GE in 2004, that was $9,250 − $1,652, or $7,598 million. This is the funded status. To arrive at the liability recognized on the balance sheet, smoothing adjustments are added, as shown in the next table.

December 31 (in $ Millions)	2004	2003
Funded Status	$(7,598)	$(8,075)
Unrecognized Prior Service Cost	2,747	3,045
Unrecognized Net Actuarial Loss	1,004	1,584
Net Liability Recognized	$(3,847)	$(3,446)

Unlike GE's pension plan, both funded status and the net reported amount are underfunded. The differences between the two are the annual amortized amounts for prior service cost and net actuarial loss being smoothed over several years. The difference between funded status and net liability recognized ($7,598 − $3,847 = $3,751) is the off–balance sheet liability.

The income statement reconciliation is similar to pensions, with service cost and interest cost the major expenses. This is partially offset by expected return on plant assets (if provided—not all companies bother to provide any investment portfolio for OPEB). GE's table to calculate the net expense was:

(in $ Millions)	2004	2003	2002
Expected Return on Plan Assets	$(149)	$ (159)	$(170)
Service Cost for Benefits Earned	210	307	277
Interest Cost on Benefit Obligation	518	535	469
Prior Service Cost	298	191	96
Net Actuarial Loss Recognized	60	127	78
Retiree Benefit Plans Cost	$ 937	$1,001	$ 750

GE recognized a net $937 million expense for 2004, with expected return on plan assets only a small offset.

Earnings Magic and the Dow 30

OPEB has an "off–balance sheet" focus and similar concerns as pensions. Given current tax laws, underfunding is expected. Consequently, the focus is on the magnitude of underfunding and OPEB expense, plus actuarial assumptions, which include anticipated healthcare cost increases. Twenty-six of the Dow 30 had OPEB obligations (see Appendix 7.2). All but 2 reported a net liability position (underfunded) and negative funded status. The average Dow firm's net liability position was over $3.4 billion (totaling $81.7 billion), while funded status averaged $6.1 billion underfunded (total $146.6 billion). The difference of $64.9 billion ($146.6 − $81.7, an average $2.7 billion) is the off–balance sheet obligation component. The funded status for 6 of the companies was greater than 10% of total assets. GM had an underfunded OPEB funded status of $61.5 billion (about 13% of total assets).

The SEC report on off–balance sheet items included OPEB. The SEC found that 74 of the largest 100 firms had OPEB plans in 2003 and estimated that about 15% of all traded corporations report OPEB plans. OPEB under-funding is based on funded status of $216 billion for the largest 100 firms (that is $302 billion for both pension and OPEB) and estimated total under-funding for all traded firms of $337 billion ($538 billion for both pension and OPEB). The combined pension/OPEB off–balance sheet obligations for the Dow 30 were $231 billion ($64.9 for OPEB + $166.1 for pension).

Given that plan assets are usually small for OPEB, relatively large OPEB expenses are expected. The OPEB expense averaged $491 million for the Dow 26, a total $12.7 billion. The OPEB expense was greater than 10% of net income (before tax) for 7 companies. GM's 2004 OPEB expense of $4.6 bil-lion was 63% greater than net income of $2.8 billion. GM's pension expense was $2.5 billion. Add it up. GM's pension and OPEB expenses were $7.0 billion; in addition, pension and OPEB funded status was underfunded by

$69 billion. That is why GM has been making the business headlines about labor costs and the company's inability to make autos profitably.

In summary, pension and OPEB represent areas of possibly extreme differences between what is reported and economic reality. GM has made the business headlines for exactly this issue, and the reality is as bad as the headlines suggest. GM may be the extreme, but this is a significant problem for the majority of the Dow 30 and a large percentage of America's major corporations.

APPENDIX 7.1

DOW 30 PENSIONS

Company	Net Asset Position*	Funded Status*	Total Assets*	Pension Expense*	Pension Expense/Net Income
3M (MMM)	$ 2,041	$ −1,118	$ 20,708	$ 325	10.9%
Alcoa (AA)	34	−1,951	32,609	202	15.4
Altria (MO)	3,393	−2,052	101,648	332	3.5
American Express (AXP)	350	−246	192,638	118	3.4
American International Group (AIG)	−131	−1,255	798,660	186	1.9
Boeing (BA)	12,069	−3,804	53,963	451	24.1
Caterpillar (CAT)	2,026	−1,462	43,091	274	13.5
Citigroup (C)	3,451	−61	1,481,101	337	2.0
Coca-Cola (KO)	91	−403	31,327	122	2.5
Du Pont (DD)	1,492	−3,507	35,632	997	56.0
Exxon-Mobil (XOM)	−2,719	−11,502	195,256	1,630	6.4
General Electric (GE)	14,552	4,104	750,330	255	1.5
General Motors (GM)	34,817	−7,531	479,603	2,456	87.6
Hewlett-Packard (HPQ)	131	−2,086	76,138	602	17.2
Home Depot (HD)	DCP		38,907		
Honeywell (HON)	2,890	−517	31,062	386	30.1
IBM (IBM)	19,527	−7,382	109,183	1,072	12.7
Intel (INTC)	−85	−90	48,143	36	0.5
J.P. Morgan (JPM)	3,600	1,963	1,157,248	155	3.5
Johnson & Johnson (JNJ)	288	−1,816	53,317	512	6.0
McDonald's (MCD)	DCP		27,838		
Merck (MRK)	1,901	−399	42,573	397	6.8
Microsoft (MSFT)	DCP		92,389		
Pfizer (PFE)	935	−2,986	123,684	603	5.3
Procter & Gamble (PG)	−1,401	−2,353	57,048	239	3.7
SBC Comm. (SBC)	9,329	1,624	108,844	8	0.1
United Technology (UTX)	1,913	−3,139	40,035	346	12.4
Verizon (VZ)	8,585	1,711	165,958	225	2.9
Wal-Mart (WMT)	DCP		120,223		
Walt Disney (DIS)	90	−630	53,902	229	9.8
Total	119,169	−46,888	6,563,058		
Average	4,583	−1,803	218,768	481	13.1%

* In $ millions.

APPENDIX 7.2

DOW 30 OPEB

Company	Net Asset Position*	Funded Status*	Total Assets*	OPEB Expense*	OPEB/ Net Income
3M (MMM)	$ 67	$ −659	$ 20,708	$ 110	3.7%
Alcoa (AA)	−2,546	−3,672	32,609	279	21.3
Altria (MO)	−4,061	−5,276	101,648	652	6.9
American Express (AXP)	−240	−397	192,638	38	1.1
American International Group (AIG)	−273	−278	798,660	34	0.3
Boeing (BA)	−6,014	−8,063	53,963	734	39.2
Caterpillar (CAT)	2,889	3,932	43,091	356	17.5
Citigroup (C)	−810	−979	1,481,101	56	0.3
Coca-Cola (KO)	−610	−791	31,327	73	1.5
Du Pont (DD)	−4,825	−4,807	35,632	−241	−13.5
Exxon-Mobil (XOM)	−2,681	−4,944	195,256	512	2.0
General Electric (GE)	−3,847	−7,598	750,330	937	5.6
General Motors (GM)	−28,111	−61,458	479,603	4,567	162.8
Hewlett-Packard (HPQ)	−973	−1,485	76,138	144	4.1
Home Depot (HD)	No		38,907		
Honeywell (HON)	−1,870	−2,353	31,062	219	17.1
IBM (IBM)	−5,299	−5,844	109,183	372	4.4
Intel (INTC)	−134	−173	48,143	31	0.4
J.P. Morgan (JPM)	23	−275	1,157,248	20	0.4
Johnson & Johnson (JNJ)	−1,071	−1,556	53,317	512	6.0
McDonald's (MCD)	No		27,838		
Merck (MRK)	−173	−727	42,573	124	2.1
Microsoft (MSFT)	No		92,389		
Pfizer (PFE)	935	2,980	123,684	147	1.3
Procter & Gamble (PG)	−160	443	57,048	−141	−2.2
SBC Comm. (SBC)	−9,271	−16,422	108,844	1,279	21.7
United Technology (UTX)	−1,046	−942	40,035	36	1.3
Verizon (VZ)	−10,982	−22,528	165,958	1,774	22.7
Wal-Mart (WMT)	No		120,223		
Walt Disney (DIS)	−450	−739	53,902	145	6.2
Average	−3,402	−6,109	218,769	491	12.9

* In $ millions.

8

REVENUES

*It was Enron's tragedy to be filled with people smart enough to
know how to maneuver around the rules, but not wise enough to
understand why the rules had been written in the first place.*
—Kurt Eichenwald

*MicroStrategy was cooking the books by repeatedly violating
accounting rules on when to recognize revenue on its software and
service contracts. Altogether, MicroStrategy had wrongly
recognized revenues of $66 million on $365 million in revenues
from 1997 to 1999. Instead of positive earnings, MicroStrategy
should have reported net losses all three years.*
—Arthur Levitt with Paula Dwyer

Giant corporations can claim billions of dollars of revenue each year without
giving much detailed information. This is the most likely area of earnings
magic and, from the cash flows from operations (CFO) perspective, relatively
easy to conceal. A manufacturing company records sales of manufactured
products. Other revenue items may include additional services provided and
warranty protection, which might be combined or reported separately. Net sales
usually include discounts and other adjustments to sales numbers. Excluded
adjustments may be reported in cost of sales, elsewhere on the income statement, or not at all. What is specifically included or excluded often is based on
industry norms.

Revenue is recognized when (1) realized or realizable and (2) earned.
Well, maybe. The standard definition of *realizable* means assets are received
that are convertible into cash. Revenue is earned when exchange transactions
(the earnings process) are substantially complete, usually by the time the
product is delivered or service rendered. These definitions are the norm, but
they can lose their meaning in a mark-to-market (fair value) environment—
an Enron claim to fame. More on mark-to-market later.

In a complex business environment, judgment is necessary to determine revenue timing. In addition, corporate executives often have earnings magic incentives to recognize revenues as soon as possible to increase earnings in the current period. If opportunistic behavior is involved, this is referred to as aggressive recognition.

Revenue recognition is primarily a timing issue. Will specific revenue be recognized this year or sometime in the future? Possible sales alternatives include recognition when the sale is made, when the product is shipped, when the product is received and accepted by the customer, or when the cash payment is received. Important exceptions exist to sales-based revenue, including commodities with liquid markets where revenues can be recognized when production is complete and the use of percentage-of-completion method on long-term construction contracts. To insure that earnings targets were made every quarter, software company MicroStrategy did not sign or date sales contracts. These were dated only when management decided, after the fact, in which quarter to assign revenue.

The Securities and Exchange Commission (SEC) tightened revenue recognition criteria with Staff Accounting Bulletin (SAB) No. 101, *Revenue Recognition in Financial Statements*. As pointed out in the SAB: "The accounting literature on revenue recognition includes both broad conceptual discussions as well as certain industry-specific guidance. . . . The staff believes that revenue generally is realized or realizable and earned when all of the following criteria are met: persuasive evidence of an arrangement exists, delivery has occurred or services have been rendered, the seller's price to the buyer is fixed or determinable, and collectibility is reasonably assured." Because of SAB No. 101, recognition policies are more standardized by industry than in the past—good news for analysis. Many companies included an accounting change around 2001 based on implementing SAB No. 101, a likely sign of earlier earnings magic.

REVENUE RECOGNITION CONCERNS

Revenue recognition issues are vast, given accounting creativity to meet earnings targets. External detection by evaluating public documents is unlikely, but discovering the potential for revenue manipulation is possible. The first objective is to determine the basic recognition policies of the company, which are expected to be conservative. Revenue recognition policies are found in note 1. The policy should be reasonable, conservative, and consistent with industry norms.

A basic technique to evaluate potential manipulation is reviewing quarterly and annual trends in revenue, relative to accounts receivable and other factors. A summary of some of the specific concerns are listed in Exhibit 8.1.

Topic	Concern	Detection Strategy
Sales—Trends	Changes in sales, especially unexpected increases, and related items such as receivables and inventory.	Review quarterly and annual changes, including information on specific segments.
Combined Product and Service Sales	Revenues on long-term services recognized immediately as revenue rather than over the life of the service contract.	Review accounting policies and breakout of revenues for products and services (if available in note disclosure).
Recognizing Revenues on Service Contracts before Service Is Performed	Another form of aggressive recognition, more difficult to justify since SAB 101.	Review policy descriptions, notes, and MD&A for evidence.
Leases Recorded as Sales	Long-term leases recorded immediately as revenue rather than recognized over the life of the lease.	Evaluate companies that use long-term leases to sell their products; consider accounting policies, specific notes, and unusual sale trends.
Sales—Installment Sales Method	Long-term credit terms; immediate recognition as revenue and other problematic procedures.	Usually industry specific (e.g., durable goods, land sales); evaluate sales methods and related notes.
Shipping, Handling, and Other Sales-Related Items	Aggressive policies for shipping and handling charges, insurance, set-up costs. Are these treated as revenue items? When should they be recorded?	Review policy descriptions and revenue footnotes; compare to how related costs are treated; compare to competitors.
Bill-and-Hold Sales	Product sold with the stipulation that delivery will occur in a later period; could represent blatant manipulation.	Difficult to evaluate based on annual reports; generally rely on media or SEC coverage.
Reporting Out-of-Period Sales	Timing is everything. In this case essentially reporting sales from early the next fiscal year in the current period.	Difficult to evaluate based on annual reports; rely on external sources and media.
Channel Stuffing	Deep discounts to wholesalers to encourage end-of-period sales, another blatant manipulation scheme.	Unless specifically stated in the notes or MD&A, can be detected only by auditors, regulators, etc.
Round-Trip Transaction	Transaction with related parties for the sole purpose of	Another method to inflate revenue; unlikely to be

(continues)

EXHIBIT 8.1 SUMMARY OF SPECIFIC CONCERNS

Topic	Concern	Detection Strategy
Round-Trip Transaction (Continued)	meeting sales and earnings targets.	detectible; evaluate for fraud environment, review related-party notes.
Excessive Sales Incentives, i.e., Deep Discounts	Given for the sole purpose of boosting end-of-period sales to achieve sales targets.	Review accounting policies, MD&A, and notes, but difficult to detect.
Disclosure of Affiliated and Related-Party Sales	Do these, in fact, represent revenues or simply exchanges? Potential for transactions to boost sales, but without economic substance.	Review notes on related-party transactions and other disclosures that suggest suspect sales.
Prepaid Revenue Items	Is revenue recognized immediately for multiyear commitments?	Review policy descriptions, MD&A, and notes.
Long-Term Construction Contracts	Percent-of-completion method allows considerable judgment on estimating revenue; aggressive (early) recognition.	Determine which method is used. If percent-of-completion, review notes and quarterly and annual reporting trends.
Other Front-End Recognition of Revenues	Any number of aggressive recognition strategies, before revenue is earned.	Review recognition policies and notes for evidence of front-ending.
Fraud, Including Fictitious Sales	The most infamous cases of revenue abuse are fraud and other criminal acts.	Fraud is usually detected by the auditors, the SEC, or whistle-blowers; evaluate for fraud environment.
Back-Pocket Sales	Fictitious sales recorded only if needed to make earnings targets.	Detected only after the fact, usually as the results of a regulatory action or lawsuit.

Adapted from Giroux (2004), pp. 116–117.

EXHIBIT 8.1   SUMMARY OF SPECIFIC CONCERNS (CONTINUED)

Sea View Video, a maker of underwater video equipment, recognized revenue before items were shipped. According to a General Accounting Office (the name was changed to Government Accountability Office in 2004, GAO) report, SeaView and the former chief financial officer "misstated the company's sales and revenue figures; improperly recognized revenues; misrepresented the nature and extent of the company's dealer network; falsely touted purported contracts and agreements with large retailers; misrepresented the company's ability to manufacture, or to have manufactured, its products; and misrepresented SeaView's likelihood of achieving certain publicly announced sales targets" (GAO 2002, p. 196).

Some companies sell products, services, and other items as a package, with service contracts over a long-term period. The product should be recognized after shipment and customer acceptance of the product; the service revenue should be recognized over the life of the contract. Manipulation is problematic if services and related long-term items are recognized immediately or too early. Somewhat related is the use of lease contracts for products sold (often with a significant training and long-term service component). Revenue recognition should be over the life of the lease. Immediate recognition is manipulation. Xerox did exactly that on the lease-sale of copiers and was forced to restate earnings. Sales of real estate and various durable goods may be sold under long-term installment sales agreements, where revenue should be spread over the payment period when collectibility is uncertain. In these circumstances, early recognition can be considered manipulation.

Different circumstances exist for revenue recognition. As with warranties and service contracts, prepaid items such as insurance policies are deferred and revenue recognized over the prepaid period covered. Engineering and construction companies build major capital and infrastructure projects over several years. Two revenue recognition alternatives are allowed: completed contracts (no revenue is recognized until the project is completed) and percentage of completion (where revenue is recognized based on the estimated completion of the project). For example, Boeing uses both for aircraft construction. For commercial aircraft, revenues generally are recognized when deliveries are made (completed contracts). For government cost-reimbursement contracts, revenue is recognized based on scheduled milestones (percentage of completion). Both methods are used for government fixed-price contracts. The completed contracts method is more conservative, but usually is used only when the percentage-of-completion method is not appropriate.

A number of sales-related issues may be a concern in some industries, such as mail order businesses. Shipping and handling, insurance, and other charges may be included as part of revenue (in which case the actual costs would be picked up in cost of sales). Amazon.com recorded shipping charges as revenues, then recorded shipping and handling expenses to selling, general and administrative (SG&A) rather than cost of sales. As of 2001, Amazon has been recording these expenses as cost of sales. How these items are treated can be important to evaluate earnings management and the comparability to competitors.

Several manipulation techniques have interesting names, such as bill-and-hold, channel stuffing, and reporting out-of-period sales. All are essentially mechanisms to meet sales and earnings targets for the current period, blatant manipulation techniques. Bill-and-hold means a sales agreement has been reached, but goods will not be shipped in the current period unless needed to meet earnings targets. This was one of many techniques used by Sunbeam during the regime of "Chainsaw Al" Dunlap to meet aggressive earnings targets in the mid-1990s.

Channel stuffing is the shipment of products at deep discounts to get customers to accept these goods. Bristol-Myers Squibb boosted 2001 earnings using deep discounts to encourage wholesalers to buy more drugs. In the late 1990s, Lucent Technologies overestimated telecom equipment demand and simultaneously lost market share. Channel stuffing was the short-term answer, using deep discounts and easy credit. The company soon collapsed with the rest of the telecom industry. Out-of-period sales is a more generic term to describe all the means to record sales this period, when legitimately the sales should be recognized in another period. All are manipulation methods; discovery usually has meant earnings restatements and lawsuits charging fraud.

Vendor financing can be used to inflate sales, a favorite technique of the telecom companies. Motorola lent almost $3 billion to customers to purchase wireless gear—$2 billion of which was later written off. Cisco gave one customer 135% vendor financing—hard to pass up this largesse.

Another method is the round-trip transaction, the simultaneous purchase and sale between colluding companies. Global Crossing and other telecommunications companies practiced a version of this technique called capacity swaps, essentially swapping (usually using leases) fiber optics capacity in different geographic areas under long-term contracts. Global Crossing immediately recognized the "sale" as revenue and recorded the "purchase" as a capital expenditure. To make the transactions "revenue items" and operating cash flow, Global exchanged identical sums of cash. This was allowed by the auditor—you guessed it, Arthur Andersen.

Various discounts, zero-interest loans, and other sales incentives are common in the auto industry. They represent an industry practice and increase sales but reduce margins. Because they are widely publicized, they do not easily fit the earnings magic tag. This practice represents part of the industry's business; however, the purpose is to boost revenues relative to competitors, and the result is an earnings management concern.

Fictitious sales are outright fraud and a criminal act, and include some of the most infamous accounting scandals. Examples include Equity Funding and ZZZZ Best. Equity Funding was a massive computer fraud from the 1970s. Bogus insurance policies and related bogus data were entered into the computer system, suggesting a booming company. ZZZZ Best was in the insurance restoration business in the 1980s. However, most of the restoration projects recorded did not exist.

Critical Path, an Internet company providing outsource services such as messaging, used a version of back-pocket deals of $4 million (fictitious sales recorded only if needed to meet earnings targets, to be later charged to bad debts reserve), a $7 million sale to a group of big shareholders as resellers (disallowed by auditor PricewaterhouseCoopers), and recognizing revenue before meeting generally accepted accounting principles (GAAP) criteria. The SEC and U.S. Attorney charged several managers with fraudulent acts and insider trading.

Particularly difficult to evaluate is the use of mark-to-market (fair value) related to revenue recognition. Over the last couple of decades, the Financial Accounting Standards Board has been moving to mark-to-market for most financial items. This is reasonable for securities like stock, bonds, and standardized derivatives that trade on specific markets and have a "public price." The downside of mark-to-market is that gains and losses are recorded each period as market values rise and fall. No exchange transaction exists for these gains and losses, and there is no impact on cash flows.

Enron got permission from the SEC to use mark-to-market for long-term gas trading contracts in 1992. This procedure can be defended as an extension of fair value for financing contracts, but it seems a perversion of revenue recognition criteria. The contract had been signed but no revenue had been earned or cash generated over many years. Enron controlled much of the market and essentially used "mark-to-model" to generate virtually any amount of revenue it wanted (or needed to make earnings targets). Enron extended mark-to-market over much of its business to increase revenue and earnings. Market value gains would be booked, while losses were avoided by "selling" assets to Enron's infamous special-purpose entities (SPEs). When earnings targets had to be met, Enron would "sell" assets (to an SPE or other complex transaction using banks) to book a "gain on sale."

REVENUE REPORTING AT INTEL AND IBM

Intel recognized net revenues of $34.2 billion in 2004, up from $30.1 billion the previous year. For a manufacturing company like Intel, key sales events include the initial sale, shipment to the customer, customer billing, receipt and approval of the product by the customer, and cash payment. Intel's revenue recognition policy for product sales (Note 2 on Accounting Policies) was:

> The company recognizes net revenue when the earnings process is complete, as evidenced by an agreement with the customer, transfer of title and acceptance, if applicable, as well as fixed pricing and probable collectibility. Because of frequent sales price reductions and rapid technology obsolescence in the industry, sales made to distributors under agreements allowing price protection and/or right of return are deferred until the distributors sell the merchandise. Shipping charges

billed to customers are included in net revenue, and the related shipping costs are included in cost of sales.

Intel's position of revenue recognition is defensible, because the product has been manufactured, the sale has been made, the product was delivered, and payment is reasonably assured. Having said that, there is little additional information on revenues. Segment reporting provides revenues by operating segment (Intel Architecture Business, Intel Communications Group, and All Other) and by geographic region.

IBM has a broader revenue base that includes both manufacturing and service. Revenue includes Global Services ($46.2 billion), Hardware ($31.2 billion), Software ($15.1 billion), Global Financing ($2.6 billion), and Enterprise Investment ($1.2 billion), for total revenue of $96.3 billion in 2004. This is reflected in a more detailed description of revenue recognition policies (Note a: Significant Accounting Policies):

> The company recognizes revenue when it is realized or realizable and earned. The company considers revenue realized or realizable and earned when it has persuasive evidence of an arrangement, delivery has occurred, the sales price is fixed or determinable, and collectibility is reasonably assured. Delivery does not occur until products have been shipped or services have been provided to the client, risk of loss has transferred to the client and client acceptance has been obtained, client acceptance provisions have lapsed, or the company has objective evidence that the criteria specified in the client acceptance provisions have been satisfied. The sales price is not considered to be fixed or determinable until all contingencies related to the sale have been resolved.
>
> The company reduces revenue for estimated client returns, stock rotation, price protection, rebates and other similar allowances. Revenue is recognized only if these estimates can be reliably determined and if the client has economic substance apart from the company. The company bases its estimates on historical results taking into consideration the type of client, the type of transaction and the specifics of each arrangement. Payments made under cooperative marketing programs are recognized as an expense only if the company receives from the client an identifiable benefit sufficiently separable from the product sale whose fair value can be reasonably estimated. If the company does not receive an identifiable benefit sufficiently separable from the product sale whose fair value can be reasonably estimated, such payments are recorded as a reduction of revenue.
>
> In addition to the aforementioned general policies, the following are the specific revenue recognition policies for multiple-element

arrangements and for each major category of revenue. . . . The company enters into multiple-element revenue arrangements, which may include any combination of services, software, hardware and/or financing.

The "Multi-element Arrangements" discussion is detailed and provides additional information on recognition criteria.

A couple of key points. First, the level of disclosures varies by company. Some companies, such as IBM (GE is another good example), provide quite detailed information, while others seem to provide the minimum possible. Second, recognition policies should be relatively conservative and similar to industry standards. Both Intel and IBM do not recognize revenue until delivery has taken place and collectibility is probable.

Pharmaceutical giant Pfizer states (Note 1 of the 2004 report):

> We record revenue from product sales when the goods are shipped and title passes to the customer. At the time of sale, we also record estimates for a variety of sales deductions, such as sales rebates, discounts and incentives, and product returns.
>
> We generally record sales incentives as a reduction of revenues at the time the related revenues are recorded or when the incentives is offered, whichever is later. We estimate the cost of our sales incentives based on our historical experience with similar incentive programs. . . .
>
> We have agreements to copromote pharmaceutical products discovered by other companies. Revenue is earned when our copromotion partners ship the related product and title passes to their customer. . . .

This policy seems unusual; earnings magic perhaps? What are sales deductions, incentive recognition, and copromotion? It turns out these are standard procedures for drug companies. The only way to check this is comparing the policies to direct competitors. Merck has a similar policy: "Revenues are recorded net of provisions for sales discounts and returns, which are established at the time of sale." Generally, a different policy from competitors is a possible earnings magic signal.

EARNINGS RESTATEMENT AND OTHER SOURCES OF MANIPULATION AND FRAUD INFORMATION

The Treadway Commission report, which reviewed alleged fraud of 200 companies from 1987 to 1997 based on SEC enforcement actions, found over 50% of the frauds involved overstating revenues or recording revenues prematurely or fictitiously (COSO 1999). The GAO report on restatement of financial statements (GAO 2002) found that 38% of the 919 restatements investigated for the period 1997 to 2002 involved revenue recognition, the most important category by far. Many of these restatements were later identified as fraud based on SEC investigations and enforcement actions and various lawsuits. The most common reasons were earlier recognition than allowed by GAAP or recognizing questionable or fictitious revenue.

According to the GAO report, 72 Standard & Poor's 500 companies restated earnings over the five-year period analyzed. Of these, 31 (43%) involved revenue recognition issues. (Note that several restatements included multiple violations.) Exhibit 8.2 summarizes the nature of the revenue recognition issues for some of these restaters.

The violations ranged from minor to severe. More serious examples include many of the listed concerns, such as round-trip sales (CMS Energy), recognition of vendor rebates (ConAgra), revenue based on sales incentives (Harrah's Entertainment), and bill-and-hold sales (Raytheon). A key question is to what extent the existence of restatements signals an earnings manipulation environment.

MARKET REACTION TO "MANIPULATION ANNOUNCEMENTS"

How are restatements and other indicators of manipulation announced to the public? How do investors react to the "bad news"? The GAO found that of the 689 publicly traded companies (all restaters) analyzed, stock prices fell an average 10%, with revenue recognition restatements (39% of these companies) associated with higher declines. The stock price drop was based on the three trading days surrounding the public announcements (called a "short window" analysis). The unadjusted market losses totaled about $100 billion, with $56 billion in losses associated with revenue recognition restatements (GAO 2002).

A major insurance company, and part of the Dow 30, American International Group (AIG) restated earnings in 2005 (an 8-K was issued on May 2, 2005, that AIG would restate financial statements for 2000 to 2003) after a long process of bad news. In February, AIG disclosed that the company was subpoenaed by the New York Attorney General (investor pal Eliot Spitzer) and the SEC for investments in nontraditional insurance products and reinsurance transactions. AIG used phony reinsurance contracts with General Reinsurance to increase revenues and claims reserves. Hank Greenberg resigned as chief executive officer in March. The 2004 10-K was finally filed on May 31, 2005 (two months late). A six-month stock chart in Exhibit 8.3 shows the market reaction to this series of events.

Corporation	Year	Findings
AOL	1997	Reversed $7 million in revenue on long-term contract recognized immediately.
Campbell Soup	2001	Shipping and handling costs reclassified from net sales to cost of sales.
Centex	2001	Net revenues restated to include freight and delivery costs billed to customers.
Clorox	2001	Coupon cost included in advertising expense (now deducted from sales).
CMS Energy	2002	Round-trip trades.
ConAgra Foods	2001	Immediate recognition of deferred delivery sales and vendor rebates and advance vendor rebates (also, related understated bad debts reserve).
Concord Camera	2001	Immediate recognition on shipments to a customer, when payments were expected over an extended period; deferring revenue of $1.7 million resulted in a larger net loss.
Dillard's	2001	Reclassified shipping and handling reimbursements to other income.
Harrah's Entertainment	2001	Recognition of sales incentives and "free products and services" to be delivered in the future—now reported as contra-asset items rather than expenses.
Hewlett-Packard	2001	Delayed recognition from date of shipment to date of delivery, plus restatement of costs previously recorded to SG&A and now charged directly against revenue, based on SAB 101.
Raytheon	2000	Bill and hold sales, ownership passed to buyer but before modifications made and delivery.
TJX	2000	Immediate recognition of layaway sales, now deferred based on SAB 101.
Xerox	2002	Immediate recognition associated with bundled leases, to be reallocated to equipment, service, supplies, and financing.
Xilinx	1999	Immediate recognition for shipments to international distributors, now deferred until products are sold to end customer.

Adapted from Giroux 2004, pp. 125–126.

EXHIBIT 8.2 SUMMARY OF THE REVENUE RECOGNITION ISSUES

The market reaction was quick and devastating to the company. On February 11, 2005, the stock price rose about 10% to almost 73, then dropped below 51 (down 30% in two months) by April 15, then rose a bit to around 55 (which was off about 20% from the February 11 peak). This level of bad news seldom hits a Dow 30 company, but when it does, the reaction is the same: Sell! (Preferably before the bad news hits.)

AMER INTL GROUP INC

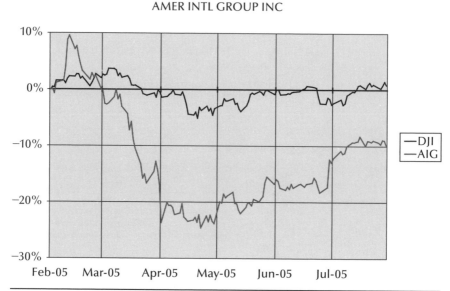

EXHIBIT 8.3   SIX-MONTH STOCK CHART

Shortly before this book went to press, Dow 30 member General Motors issued an 8-K stating that it would restate earnings, possibly for the years 2000–2005. Why? Revenue recognition. As stated in the 8-K (November 9, 2005): "GM erroneously recognized some supplier credits as income in the year in which they were received rather than in the future periods to which they were attributable." Earnings were overstated some $300–$400 million in 2001 (some 25% to 35% of net income). GM stock price dropped about 5% on the news.

9

EARNINGS, EXPENSES, AND EXPECTATIONS

Bad terminology is the enemy of good thinking. When companies or investment professionals use terms such as "EBITDA" and "pro forma," they want you to unthinkingly accept concepts that are dangerously flawed.

—Warren Buffett

GE's earnings from continuing operations rose a phenomenal one hundred quarters in a row. Of course, the businesses that GE managed had plenty of surprises. But you wouldn't know it from GE's smoothly rising bottom line. GE was said to enter every quarter with a specific profit goal in mind.

—Roger Lowenstein

Net income and earnings per share (EPS) usually are considered the premier "bottom-line" numbers, the most appropriate measures of earnings. Net income is a relatively complete measure of all business activity (close to what is called all-inclusive income), because it includes nonrecurring items in addition to normal operating income. Meeting earnings targets specified in terms of net income or EPS suggests the potential for earnings magic in some set of revenue or expense categories.

EPS is a performance measure presented in two formats: (1) basic [(net income − preferred dividends) / weighted average number of common shares outstanding] and (2) diluted, which adjusts for the potential for additional shares associated with stock options, convertible securities, and related factors. Berenson (2003) describes EPS as *The Number,* with the primary executives' goal of meeting the consensus analysts' forecast each quarter.

Institutional Brokers Estimates System (I/B/E/S) and Zacks Investment Research started publishing consensus forecasts in the 1970s. The consensus forecasts became the standard benchmark to measure "earnings surprise," the difference between the consensus forecast and actual EPS. A downside of this information is the short-term focus rather than long-term trends; that mind-set became pervasive in the 1990s.

Financial Web sites have considerable information on EPS, including consensus forecasts. Go to Yahoo!, for example (finance.yahoo.com), put in the ticker for any traded company, and click on "Analysts Estimates." Here we can get earnings and revenue forecasts for the current and future quarters, EPS for the last four quarters (actual to estimate and the difference—surprise!). Get this year, next-year, and five-year (past and future) earnings growth, with relevant industry and market comparisons. The forecasts may not be that accurate, but damn, there are plenty of them.

American International Group (AIG) issued its 2004 10-K over two months late (i.e., five months after the end of the fiscal year) and restated earnings from 2000 onward. But there is a consensus forecast (as of June 9, 2005) for the year 2005 (12.8%), 2006 (12.2%), and 13.0% for the next five years. Because AIG got caught red-handed conducting earnings magic, the company's current net income and EPS are suspect. Question: How much credibility should be assigned to the forecast?

The key point is that the most relevant number available is future earnings. Those year-ahead and five-year EPS forecasts are extremely important. The problem is reliability. If that five-year forecast for AIG of 13% annual growth in EPS is correct, with the big stock price drop and AIG selling at a price earnings ratio of about 11, then BUY!

BOTTOM-LINE ALTERNATIVES

As important as the bottom line is, there is no universal agreement on what that measure is. In addition to net income, there is operating income; earnings before interest and taxes (EBIT); earnings before interest, taxes, depreciation, and amortization (EBITDA); income from continuing operations (usually after tax); net income adjusted for various things (i.e., dividends or eliminating certain nonrecurring or special charges); comprehensive income; and any number of pro forma calculations of earnings. There is Amazon's use of EBIT-DAM (EBITDA plus marketing costs added back) and former Securities and Exchange Commission Chief Accountant Lynn Turner's EBBS: earnings before the bad stuff.

Each measure provides a different perspective. Corporations have considerable flexibility, and focusing on other measures may provide significant earnings magic insight. A summary of bottom-line issues is shown in Exhibit 9.1.

Measure	Concern	Calculations
Operating Margin (OM)	Declining or erratic OM, suggesting serious problems with basic operations.	Calculate OM% for several periods and compare to competitors'.
EBIT and EBITDA	Large differences, suggesting big expenses associated with interest expense, taxes, depreciation, or amortization.	Calculate and evaluate component parts; compare across periods and to competitors.
Income from Continuing Operations versus Net Income	ICO substantially different from net income, because of non-recurring items and related earnings manipulation potential.	Compare and calculate alternative return ratios.
Net Income versus Comprehensive Income	Other comprehensive income items represent large losses, especially if these continue year after year.	Compare and calculate alternative return ratios; evaluate each other comprehensive income item.

EXHIBIT 9.1 SUMMARY OF BOTTOM-LINE ISSUES

Operating margin is sales less cost of sales (COS). COS has a direct relationship to sales and this relationship normally is fairly constant. If margin is rising, it may signal increased efficiency (e.g., strategic outsourcing) and be a positive signal of future performance. A declining or erratic margin may indicate any number of problems.

Operating income is sales minus operating expenses, which include cost of sales, selling, general and administrative expenses (SG&A), research and development (R&D), and special charges. Operating income differs by industry. Pharmaceuticals, for example, have low cost of sales but high R&D and marketing costs. Retailers tend to have high cost of sales and zero or low R&D.

EBIT (also called operating earnings) excludes the impact of interest and taxes from operating earnings and can be used as an indicator of a firm's ability to service its debt. EBITDA (also called cash earnings) somewhat resembles cash flows from operations and can be used for an alternative analysis of cash flows. Depreciation and amortization are noncash expenses and major expense categories at many large corporations. Particularly when EBIT and EBITDA differ substantially from net income, profitability ratios should be recalculated using EBIT and EBITDA.

Income from continuing operations (ICO) is a current operations bottom line. ICO may be a better measure than net income, because it excludes nonrecurring items. ICO, EBIT, EBITDA, and operating margin are "above-the-line" measures, basically a focus on current operations. Net income is a "below-the-line" earnings measure that includes nonrecurring items, which are not part of ongoing operations. Nonrecurring items are erratic, should be rare, and presumably provide no information about the fundamental performance of a corporation. It follows from this argument that nonrecurring items should be analyzed separately, especially for earnings manipulation potential.

Net income is a relatively complete bottom-line measure but does not include all gains and losses. A number of items, called other comprehensive income, are recorded directly to the balance sheet, affectionately known as dirty surplus. Comprehensive income (CI) includes all revenues, expenses, gains, and losses, consistent with an "all-inclusive" concept of earnings.

The alternative measures are summarized in Exhibit 9.2 for four tech companies for 2004.

IBM had the largest sales by far, almost $100 billion for 2004. IBM was also the most profitable, with net income of $8.4 billion, but only slightly larger than Microsoft. How can that be? The major part of that answer is the operating margin, over $60 billion less for IBM. In other words, IBM has substantially larger costs of sales than Microsoft. Hewlett-Packard has almost $80 billion in sales but the lowest net income of the bunch at $3.5 billion; again, the major reason is the relatively high cost of sales. Intel had relatively high EBITDA compared to operating margin (77.8%); the others had an EBITDA of 50% or less than operating margin. Net income was also income from continuing operations for three of the firms, as expected; that is, no nonrecurring items. The exception was IBM, which had a small net loss from discontinued operations (for the sale of the Personal Computing Division). Comprehensive income was similar to net income for the companies, with only Intel having comprehensive income greater than net income; in other words, it had a net gain on "dirty surplus" items.

	Microsoft*	Intel*	IBM*	Hewlett-Packard*
Revenue	$36,835	$34,209	$96,293	$79,905
Operating Margin	30,119	19,746	36,032	19,755
EBITDA	13,282	15,356	17,082	6,896
EBIT	12,196	10,467	12,167	4,501
Income from Continuing Operations	8,168	7,516	8,448	3,497
Net Income	8,168	7,516	8,430	3,497
Comprehensive Income	7,447	7,572	8,265	3,457

* In millions.

EXHIBIT 9.2   SUMMARY OF ALTERNATIVE MEASURES FOR FOUR TECH COMPANIES FOR 2004

	Microsoft	Intel	IBM	Hewlett-Packard
Operating Margin	81.8%	57.7%	37.4%	24.7%
EBITDA	36.1	48.9	17.7	8.6
EBIT	33.1	30.6	12.6	5.6
Income from Continuing Operations	22.2	22.0	8.8	4.4
Net Income	22.2	22.0	8.8	4.4
Comprehensive Income	20.2	22.1	8.6	4.3

EXHIBIT 9.3   BOTTOM-LINE NUMBERS CONVERTED TO A PERCENTAGE OF REVENUE

Converting the dollars to percentages often provides more useful information for analysis. In Exhibit 9.3, the bottom-line numbers are converted to a percentage of revenue, essentially a common-size calculation. For net income this is return on sales.

Using standardized return measures shows how similar Microsoft and Intel are in terms of bottom-line measures. Both have large gross margins and almost identical returns on sales of about 22%. IBM and H-P are much less profitable, with H-P bringing up the rear. In terms of areas for future analysis, the likely focus would be on H-P's lackluster performance on virtually all measures and how Microsoft and Intel can be so damn profitable. H-P's poor performance in part is based on the acquisition of Compaq Computer in 2002; H-P has a net loss of $903 million in 2002.

Note that new ratios can be calculated for any combination of numbers. For example, all standard performance ratios can be recalculated using EBIT and EBITDA. Doing this provides more information on profit from operations before taxes, interest expense, depreciation, and amortization—alternative perspectives on what is important to earn a buck.

Revenues and bottom line ratios are presented in Appendix 9.1 for the Dow 30 for 2004. The operating margin percentage [(revenues − operating margin) / revenues] averaged 47.9%, with a substantial range (14.8% for Boeing to 85.6% for Pfizer). The ratio is best evaluated compared to competitors and to other bottom-line measures. Pfizer's margin was higher than Johnson & Johnson (71.7%) and Merck (78.4%). Return on sales (net income/ revenues) for Pfizer was actually lower than Merck (21.6% versus 25.3%, respectively). EBIT to revenue averaged 18.4%, ranging from 5.0% for Boeing to 42.7% for Citigroup. Citi's ratio was higher than competitor J.P. Morgan (27.1%), as was return on sales (15.7% versus 7.8%). Income from continuing operations (ICO) and net income (NI) averaged about the same, 11.2% versus 11.3%. The difference between the two represents nonrecurring items to the year, most substantial for GM (1.5% versus 2.1%). Large differences between EBIT and ICO usually are explained by high interest expenses, as in Citigroup or GM.

EXPENSE MAGIC

Expenses are the costs recognized with generating revenues. The key concept is the matching principle, with operating expenses matched to revenues during the accounting period. Companies specializing in earnings magic are likely to use both revenue and expense strategies simultaneously, such as recognizing revenues early and operating expenses late (a perverse use of the matching principle). Several of the expense categories will be covered in additional detail as part of the Dirty 30.

A summary of operating expense concerns is shown in Exhibit 9.4.

Cost of sales includes cost of goods sold and other direct costs, such as shipping and handling, service costs, and so on. The primary analysis of cost of sales is to compare the dollar amounts and percentages to sales over time and to direct competitors. Between 1997 and 1999, Rite Aid, a retail drugstore chain with about 3,400 drugstores, made a number of adjustments to COS to understate COS and increase earnings. These included recording vendor allowances as reductions to COS and using other methods to keep costs in inventory rather than COS.

A tempting target for manipulation is capitalizing operating costs. This process reduces expenses, thereby boosting earnings. WorldCom capitalized about $11 billion in operating expenses before filing for bankruptcy in 2002. Reserves associated with expense categories are commonplace and subject to abuse. Reserves include allowance for doubtful accounts and inventory reserves (e.g., for future obsolescence and value declines). The theoretical argument for reserve accounts is to ensure that costs are recorded in the correct period. For example, bad debts expensed this year should be based on receivables associated with credit sales this year. Reserves are accounts that promote income smoothing (amounts charged usually are based on long-term averages); because the amounts are based on judgment, they are subject to considerable abuse. Sunbeam used reserves for product liability and warranty expenses, among many techniques, to increase earnings beginning in 1997. Enron used reserves to sock away excess earnings on energy trades in "good years." Microsoft was overly conservative and established excess reserves in several categories. General Motors has been letting its loan-loss reserves dwindle since 2002; despite this effort to increase the bottom line, GM still lost $1.3 billion in the third quarter of 2005.

Topic	Concern	Calculations
Cost of Sales	Measure of operating efficiency, directly related to sales; is it reasonable and steady over time?	Compare over time and to direct competitors using standard measures (especially operating margin %).
Capitalizing Operating Costs	Generic problem to understate current expenses, thus increasing earnings.	Compare expense ratios over time and look for unexpected drops; review operating policies and relevant notes.
Reserves Accounting	Reserves can be overstated in "good years," to be reduced in "bad years" to boost income (income smoothing).	Review ratio levels over time, with particular concern during down periods.
Selling, General and Administrative	"Overhead" measure with considerable flexibility; is the amount reasonable? Is it changing over time?	Compare over time and to competitors using standard measures (e.g., % of sales, % change).
Research and Development	Short-term cuts can improve current earnings but reduce long-term results; capitalizing R&D.	Compare current period to earlier periods and as a % of sales; evaluate to business strategy.
Provision for Tax	Deferred tax asset and liability accounts, short- vs. long-term; reasonableness of effective rates; procedures that appear unethical.	Start with effective tax rate (provision for tax/income before tax) and review of tax notes; evaluate specific tax items.
Goodwill	Goodwill can be a big number for a firm making aggressive acquisitions; large goodwill allocations may suggest over-paying for specific acquisitions.	Evaluate goodwill allocations of recent acquisitions, goodwill to total assets, and impairment write-downs.
Interest Expense	High leverage often associated with large interest expense.	Review income statement and related notes on interest and debt; calculate interest coverage and other ratios.
Other Expenses	Various expenses "dumped" into the "other" category; little disclosure presented but the amount is large.	Evaluate notes on "other assets and expenses" and scour report for additional information.

EXHIBIT 9.4   SUMMARY OF OPERATING EXPENSE CONCERNS

Selling, general and administrative (SG&A) expenses are "overhead" items with considerable operating flexibility and potential for manipulation. Lots of unrelated costs can be "dumped" into SG&A, and the process is not standardized. For example, the distinction of how overhead items should be allocated to COS, SG&A, and other income statement line items is not obvious. Aurora Foods misstated various trade promotion and marketing activities, which understated SG&A and increased earnings to meet earnings targets. AOL capitalized advertising costs as acquisition costs in the mid-1990s; AOL would have reported losses if these items were expensed. The SEC objected and required AOL to reverse the practice.

Research and development costs are expensed as incurred according to GAAP, with a few exceptions. Because of immediate expensing, companies can reduce expenses by reducing R&D, boosting short-term performance but probably detrimental in the long term. Some R&D costs can be legitimately capitalized, such as software development costs (once technological feasibility has occurred). Based in part on determining feasibility, tech companies capitalize between zero (Microsoft) and close to 100% of all development costs. The amortization period can vary from 18 months or so to about 5 years. The capitalization alternative and differences in relative amounts capitalized and amortization periods make comparability difficult.

Tax is a major expense category. Tax accounting includes the potential to manage both the provision for tax (tax expense based on GAAP and reported in the income statement) and the amount of tax paid to the federal government. Tax policies can be aggressive and appear unethical, such as moving the home office to a tax haven like Bermuda. Big companies have large tax departments and consultants to minimize taxes and, perhaps, perform a little tax magic.

Goodwill is a major asset category of corporations making acquisitions under the purchase method. Companies that are perpetual acquirers can have huge goodwill balances. This might be an indication of overpaying for specific acquisitions. Notes provide details on how the acquisition price is allocated to real assets and liabilities, goodwill, and other intangibles for current mergers. Until 2001, goodwill was amortized over a maximum of 40 years. Companies used vastly different amortization periods, resulting in a lack of comparability. Beginning in 2002, goodwill is no longer amortized, but subject to testing for impairment. Based on certain tests, write-downs should be made. In the first quarter of 2002, AOL Time Warner wrote off over $50 billion in goodwill associated with lost market valuation. WorldCom wrote off all its goodwill when it reemerged from bankruptcy as MCI.

Sunbeam, mentioned under revenue recognition, also used a variety of expense manipulations, including sales returns, advertising, warranty expenses, and product liability reserves. Some operating costs were charged to restructuring or asset impairment (for which reserves were established in 1996). Sunbeam restated earnings for fiscal years 1996 to 1998, resulting in a stock price drop from a high of $52 to under $10 by July 1998. The company declared bankruptcy in 2001, to reemerge as American Household at the end of 2002.

Rite Aid recorded many expense manipulations, including misstated cost of sales (unearned vendor allowances recorded as a reduction in COS, failure to write-down slow-moving and obsolete inventory); failure to expense stock appreciation rights; capitalizing maintenance costs and repairs to property, plant, and equipment; misstating lease obligations; failing to expense costs of store closures; and failure to recognize compensation costs, such as vacation pay and incentive compensation. Rite Aid restated in 1999 for fiscal years 1997 and 1998. The SEC required further restatements and auditor KPMG resigned late in 1999. A class-action lawsuit charged the company, directors, executives, and auditor KPMG with false and misleading statements, and the SEC began a formal investigation (settled in 2002), charging the company with financial fraud.

Aurora Foods produced such well-known brands as Duncan Hines, Mrs. Butterworth, Log Cabin, Van de Kamp's, and Aunt Jemima, with about $1 billion in sales. The company misstated expenses, liabilities, and assets. As stated by the GAO (2002, p. 130):

> Aurora was not accurately reporting trade marketing expense, which is the expense Aurora incurs to induce grocery stores to purchase its products. Instead of properly booking the expense [managers] allegedly tried to conceal it from the auditors by directing division level officers and employees to make false entries in various accounts on the company's books. The effect was to falsely and substantially inflate Aurora's financial results. . . . The object of the scheme was to conceal from the investing public the fact that the company had not met its earnings targets from quarter to quarter.

In 2000 the company restated earnings for fiscal years 1998 and 1999. The U.S. Attorney filed charges in 2001. Various managers were convicted of accounting fraud, and the chief financial officer was sentenced to almost five years in jail. Class-action lawsuits followed, which were settled out of court.

Waste Management (WM) provided waste management services, the result of several business combinations, and had a long history of earnings magic (primarily between 1992 and 1997). The most blatant expense misstatement was the manipulation of depreciation expense and other accounts associated with property, plant, and equipment. The main techniques were to lengthen the useful lives and overstate the salvage value of vehicles, containers, and equipment; and to incorrectly calculate interest capitalization on landfill construction projects. SEC charges stated: "defendants' improper accounting practices were centralized at corporate headquarters. . . . They monitored the company's actual operating results and compared them to the quarterly targets set in the budget" (GAO 2002, p. 221). WM restated in 1998 (for fiscal years 1992 to 1997) a total of $1.3 billion in overstated earnings. WM settled a stockholder lawsuit in 2001, and the SEC filed suit against several managers and auditor Arthur Andersen.

APPENDIX 9.1

BOTTOM-LINE MEASURES COMPARED TO REVENUES FOR THE DOW 30

Company	Revenue*	Ops Margin %	EBIT / Revenue	ICO / Revenue	NI / Revenue
3M (MMM)	$ 20,011	50%	23%	15%	15%
Alcoa (AA)	23,478	21%	11%	6%	6%
Altria (MO)	81,832	35%	20%	11%	11%
American Express (AXP)	29,115	66%	20%	12%	12%
American International Group (AIG)	97,987	NM	15%	10%	10%
Boeing (BA)	52,457	15%	5%	3%	4%
Caterpillar (CAT)	30,251	26%	11%	7%	7%
Citigroup (C)	108,276	NM	43%	16%	16%
Coca-Cola (KO)	21,962	65%	29%	22%	22%
Du Pont (DD)	27,995	27%	6%	6%	6%
Exxon-Mobil (XOM)	298,035	45%	14%	8%	8%
General Electric (GE)	152,866	60%	21%	11%	11%
General Motors (GM)	185,524	18%	7%	2%	2%
Hewlett-Packard (HPQ)	79,905	25%	5%	4%	4%
Home Depot (HD)	73,094	33%	11%	7%	7%
Honeywell (HON)	25,601	20%	8%	5%	5%
IBM (IBM)	96,293	37%	13%	9%	9%
Intel (INTC)	34,209	58%	31%	22%	22%
J.P. Morgan (JPM)	56,931	92%	27%	8%	8%
Johnson & Johnson (JNJ)	47,348	72%	28%	18%	18%
McDonald's (MCD)	19,065	55%	19%	12%	12%
Merck (MRK)	22,939	78%	35%	25%	25%
Microsoft (MSFT)	36,835	82%	33%	22%	22%
Pfizer (PFE)	52,516	86%	27%	22%	22%
Procter & Gamble (PG)	51,407	51%	19%	13%	13%
SBC Comm. (SBC)	40,787	57%	20%	12%	14%
United Technology (UTX)	37,445	27%	12%	7%	7%
Verizon (VZ)	71,283	67%	18%	10%	11%
Wal-Mart (WMT)	287,989	24%	6%	4%	4%
Walt Disney (DIS)	30,752	NM	14%	8%	8%
Average	$ 73,140	48%	18%	11%	11%

* In millions.

10

STRANGE SPECIAL ITEMS AND OTHER THINGS THAT SHOULD NOT BE ON THE INCOME STATEMENT

Lucent said it would take a one-time charge of $1.2 billion to $1.6 billion. By April 2001, the write-off had climbed to $2.7 billion worth of unusual charges. The mushrooming of the charge alone should have warned investors that Lucent was putting everything but the kitchen sink into the write-downs.
— Arthur Levitt with Paula Dwyer

Sometimes, a company would mislabel one-time (and nonrecurring) revenue as operating revenue—as if it had sold products. This is precisely what IBM did in 1999 when it used a one-time $4 billion gain from its sale of its global network business to offset that year's normal expenses.
— Maggie Mahar

Revenues, cost of sales, and most period costs are part of income from continuing operations, consistent with the concept of current operating performance (also called above-the-line earnings). Various special items such as restructuring charges are typically above the line. Nonrecurring items are gains and losses that are unusual and called below-the-line earnings. Nonrecurring and other special items do not provide much information about normal operations, but are likely earnings magic signals.

Companies have wide latitude for when and how to classify strange stuff. Depending on the circumstance, these items can be recorded as part of continuing operations, a special or unusual item, or a specific type of nonrecurring item. Earnings magic concerns include likely income smoothing issues, the potential for "big bath" write-offs, and how "good news" or "bad

Category	Description	Concern
Extraordinary Items	Unusual in nature and infrequent in occurrence.	Is it bad luck or real manipulation?
Discontinued Operations	The discontinuance or sale of a business component.	Either a gain or loss can be recorded; company has flexibility on how and when to record these items. Is there a good reason for the discontinuance? What is the impact on business strategy?
Accounting Change	Various changes include accounting estimate, accounting principle, or reporting entity. Change in principle can be mandatory (usually based on a new pronouncement) or discretionary (where alternatives are allowed by GAAP).	Discretionary accounting changes are a concern: Why was the change necessary? Earnings manipulation is a likely explanation. Relative magnitude is important.

EXHIBIT 10.1   LIST OF CONCERNS RELATED TO NONRECURRING ITEMS

news" is reported (e.g., "buried," separate line item, above or below the line). A list of concerns related to nonrecurring items is shown in Exhibit 10.1.

Other unusual or special items show up in various places on the income statement and should be explained in a note. Examples are included in Exhibit 10.2.

Nonrecurring items are reported separately after continuing operations, net of tax. Examples could be unexpected weather damage, such as tornadoes, or expropriation of assets by foreign governments. Selling or abandoning a business component can be recorded as a discontinued operation. Non-operating income is reported from the discontinued operations and any

Category	Description	Concern
Restructuring Charge	Some operations are restructured; usually associated with layoffs and inventory and other write-offs.	Potential to reclassify operating activity to nonrecurring items; likely impact on business strategy.
Special Charges	Term lacks specificity; could be for restructuring or any number of other items, such as marketing.	Same as above, operations potentially treated as nonrecurring; what is impact on business strategy?
Other Unusual or Special Items	These can be virtually any write-off, from fixed asset write-downs or abandonment to inventory or investments.	Many of these are seemingly part of operations. The use of a separate charge, especially as a nonrecurring item, suggests manipulation.

EXHIBIT 10.2   EXAMPLES OF OTHER UNUSUAL OR SPECIAL ITEMS

gains or losses on sales reported separately (net of tax). Accounting changes can be changes in principle or changes in estimate.

Special charges and other unusual items can be problematic. They typically have characteristics of both current operations and "abnormal" circumstances. Generally they are treated as part of continuing operations, often "buried" and occasionally recorded as a separate line item on the income statement, if material. Losses are more likely to be recorded as separate items to emphasize that they are not really "current operations." Where these items actually show up and how they are disclosed is based largely on management judgment. Thus, the potential for manipulation is high.

The use of the various nonrecurring items and other "special" charges should be rare, but 57% of New York Stock Exchange and American Stock Exchange firms reported at least one in 1998 (up from 44% in 1989). The majority of these were "special or unusual items" (49% of the firms reported at least one of these in 1998), compared to 12% for extraordinary items and 10% for discontinued operations (Revsine et al., 2002, 55–58).

Nineteen of the Dow 30 (63%) reported nonrecurring items on the 2004 income statement (see Appendix 10.1). Discontinued operations followed by accounting changes were the most common. Only SBC Communications had the trifecta of all three categories, including discontinued operations all three years presented. The gain from selling directory advertising businesses in 2004 increased SBC's net income $900 million (15.4% of net income). Even with the gain, net income was down 30.8% from 2003.

Various special items were even more common for the Dow 30 in 2004, with 21 corporations represented. These were all reported in continuing operations (above the line) and usually buried in the notes. The most common categories were restructuring and asset impairment, including interesting terminology: "streamlining costs," "sale of nonstrategic business," and "litigation reserve charge." There is nothing inherently evil in special items, but they hint at previous business strategies that went awry. Coca-Cola, for example, recorded goodwill impairment, franchise impairment, and streamlining costs in 2004 (and 2003).

Only four Dow 30 companies had neither nonrecurring nor special items: Caterpillar, Johnson & Johnson, Microsoft, and Wal-Mart. Thus, only 13% of the Dow 30 represents what should be the standard practice for all firms.

EXAMPLES OF NONRECURRING ITEMS

Examples of nonrecurring items worth analyzing in some detail are included in Exhibit 10.3.

AOL Time Warner	Wrote off $54 billion in goodwill as a nonrecurring item in 2002, a huge "big-bath" write-off.
Du Pont	Disposed of Conoco in 1999 and Du Pont Pharmaceuticals in 2001.
Goodyear	Change in accounting principle from LIFO to FIFO in 2000.
Sunbeam	Special charges recorded for restructuring, marketing, and other items after new CEO was hired in 1996; related reserves later used to boost earnings in future years.
Sun Trust Banks	Extraordinary gain on sale of credit card portfolio in 1999.
TWA	Recorded losses for discontinued operations during period when substantial operating losses generated, a "big-bath" write-off.
WorldCom/MCI	WorldCom emerged from bankruptcy in 2004 as MCI, with much reduced assets; however, the $87 billion decline was not mentioned; only a discontinued gain of $26 million was reported for the year.

EXHIBIT 10.3   EXAMPLES OF NONRECURRING ITEMS WORTH ANALYZING IN DETAIL

Goodyear changed accounting principles for inventory valuation from last in, first out (LIFO) to first in, first out (FIFO) in the fourth quarter of 2000, citing a better match of revenues to expenses. This would seem normal enough, except that net income after the change for 2000 was $40.3 million (a poor 0.3% return on sales). Instead of a loss of $4.1 million, the accounting change conveniently increased net income $44.4 million. Thus, it seems an example of blatant manipulation to ensure a positive net income. Particularly irksome is that this was explained in note 7 on inventory rather than on the income statement—where no accounting change was reported.

Du Pont recorded income from discontinued operations for 1997 and 1998, a gain on disposal of discontinued business in 1999 and 1998, and an extraordinary loss from early extinguishments of debt in 1998, all net of tax. The discontinued operation in 1999 was the divestiture of Conoco. What makes this especially problematic is that nonrecurring item amounts were larger than income from continuing operations (ICO). In 1999, ICO was $219 million, but net income was $7,690 million, thanks to the $7.5 billion gain on disposal. Net income showed healthy annual gains from 1997 ($2,407 million) through 1998 ($4,480 million) to 1999. But how useful is this big rise in earnings when analyzing Du Pont? ICO dropped from 1997 ($1,432 million) to 1999 ($219 million). Du Pont's return on sales for 1999 was a healthy 28.6% ($7,690 / $26,918), but when ICO is substituted for net income, the return on sales was only 0.8%. Du Pont's ICO increased from $219 million in 1999 to $2,314 million in 2000. However, net income for 2000 also was $2,314 million, because no nonrecurring items were recorded. Consequently, for 1997 to 2000, ICO increased by $2,095 million (957%), but net income decreased by $5,376 million (70%).

In 2001 Du Pont sold Du Pont Pharmaceuticals to Bristol-Myers Squibb for a total price $7.8 billion, booking a $6.1 billion pretax gain. Du Pont treated this sale as part of continuing operations (the after-tax gain on the sale was $3.9 billion) rather than a nonrecurring item. The result was 2001 net income of $4.3 billion rather than a minuscule income of $0.4 billion (before the gain). This transaction seems similar to the earlier Conoco sale but was treated in a different manner.

Nonrecurring items require additional analysis, because they are unexpected and do not contribute to the understanding of normal operations. They may relate to troubled companies and poor management decisions in earlier periods. Management may have "big-bath" incentives to write off large amounts of losses in poor-performing periods when cash bonuses are not expected anyway. TWA reported an operating loss for 1999 of $92.7 million, then reported nonrecurring write-offs for discontinued European operations, leasehold improvements, special charges, and other items to arrive at a net loss of $353 million for the year. By taking large write-offs, earnings in future periods should be higher than without the write-offs. In the case of TWA, the write-offs were ineffective; the company filed for Chapter 11 bankruptcy in January 2001.

AOL Time Warner wrote off $54.2 billion in the March 2002 quarter, turning a small loss of $1 million (income before the accounting change on the income statement) to a $54.2 billion net loss (roughly the gross domestic product of New Zealand). Consequently, equity fell from $157 billion to $98 billion. Was this a big-bath write-off based on earnings management incentives or a required adjustment based on the application of a new pronouncement? Both chief architects of the mergers (Gerald Levin and Steven Case) resigned, so whatever the reason for the write-off, the merger did not work well.

Al Dunlap had a reputation for restructuring companies and turning them around, partly through slashing expenditures and employees (figuratively— he just fired them). He took over Sunbeam in 1996 and, almost immediately, recorded a massive restructuring as a special charge of some $340 million. He established corresponding reserves as the credit. These reserves were released to increase earnings in 1997 and later. This was part of the pattern of massive earnings magic across the company. The later profitability was wiped out by restatements mandated by the Securities and Exchange Commission, not to mention extensive legal actions by regulators and investors.

Extraordinary items appear to be recorded more often than expected and many seem "ordinary," that is, far from the unusual and infrequent requirements of generally accepted accounting principles. An example is Sun Trust Bank's extraordinary gain of $203 million (net of tax) for the sales of its

| 2001 | Accounting change in 2001 (adapting to SAB 101 on revenue recognition); sale of Du Pont Pharmaceuticals, part of continuing operations |
| 1999 | Discontinued operations in 1999, sale of Conoco |

Financial statement numbers included:

	Du Pont, 2001*	Du Pont, 1999*
Revenues	$25,370	$27,892
Du Pont Pharmaceuticals	6,136**	
Income from Continuing Operations (ICO)	6,844	219
Discontinued Operations (Sale of Conoco)		7,471
Accounting Change	11	
Net Income (NI)	$ 4,339	$ 7,690

* In millions.
** Part of continuing operations (therefore, before tax).

Du Pont ratios are:

	Du Pont, 2001	Du Pont, 1999
ICO / Revenues	27.0%	0.8%
NI / Revenues	17.1	27.6
Special/Nonrecurring Items / Revenues	24.2	26.8

EXHIBIT 10.4   DU PONT'S FINANCIAL NUMBERS

consumer credit card portfolio to MBNA American Bank. This transaction increased net income 15%.

WorldCom became the largest U.S. bankruptcy in July 2002. Assets were $103.9 billion and equity was $57.9 billion; MCI emerged from bankruptcy in 2004 (using "fresh-start" reporting), with assets of $17.1 billion and equity of $4.2 billion. Goodwill (previously $49.8 billion) and other intangibles (previously $8.1 billion) were long gone. There was no mention in the financial statements or notes about the asset and equity decreases of $86.8 billion and $53.7 billion, respectively. The only nonrecurring item reported was income from discontinued operations of $26 million.

It is useful to conduct a quantitative analysis of strange items if the amounts are substantial. A first step would be to calculate the ratio of the individual item and totals by net income and sales. Further analysis would depend on the individual items under analysis, the relative magnitude, and the likely manipulation potential. For example, the financial numbers for the Du Pont example are shown in Exhibit 10.4.

The impact of the special/nonrecurring items was substantial, roughly 25% of revenues in both years. Consequently, they dominated performance measures. In 1999 it is obvious that operating performance is poor; ICO/ Revenues is less than 1%. However, when the focus is on net income (which includes the huge gain on sale of Conoco), then performance is excellent, with a return on sales of 27.6%. The sale of Du Pont Pharmaceuticals seems virtually the same as Conoco, except it was recorded as part of operating income. Without this item, operating performance again would be poor. These disposals of business units give the appearance of manipulation, with the presumption that sales of major segments were timed to offset poor performance. The alternative explanation is a major shift in business strategy, which also has merit as an explanation for both discontinued operations.

APPENDIX 10.1

DOW 30: NONRECURRING AND SPECIAL ITEMS, 2004

Company	Nonrecurring Items	Strange/Special Items
3M (MMM)	None	Corporate restructuring program (note 4)
Alcoa (AA)	Discontinued operations (2002–2004); accounting change	Asset retirement, restructuring (p. 48)
Altria (MO)	Discontinued operations (2002–2004)	Asset impairment (note 3)
American Express (AXP)	Accounting change (2003–2004)	none
American International Group (AIG)	Accounting change (2003–2004)	**Restated earnings (2002–2004)**
Boeing (BA)	Discontinued operations (2002)	Impairment charges (p. 104) plus goodwill and receivables impairment (p. 121)
Caterpillar (CAT)	None	None
Citigroup (C)	Discontinued operations, accounting change (2002)	Restructuring (note 17); **restated earnings**
Coca-Cola (KO)	Accounting change (2004)	Goodwill impairment (p. 80); franchise impairment (p. 107); "streamlining costs" (p. 108)
Du Pont (DD)	Accounting change (2002–2003)	Employee separation and asset impairment (note 4)
Exxon-Mobil (XOM)	Discontinued operations; accounting change	None
General Electric (GE)	Accounting change (2002–2003)	Restructuring derivatives (note 1); **restated earnings**
General Motors (GM)	Discontinued operations (2002)	Asset impairment (note 3)
Hewlett-Packard (HPQ)	None	Restructuring charges (note 7)
Home Depot (HD)	Accounting change (2003)	None

(continues)

146

Company	Nonrecurring Items	Strange/Special Items
Honeywell (HON)	None	"Repositioning and other charges" (note 3); sale of nonstrategic business (p. 57)
IBM (IBM)	Discontinued operations (2002–2004)	None
Intel (INTC)	None	Goodwill impairment (2003)
J.P. Morgan (JPM)	None	Litigation reserve charge
Johnson & Johnson (JNJ)	None	None
McDonald's (MCD)	Accounting change (2002–2003)	Restructuring/restaurant closing, impairment (p. 74)
Merck (MRK)	Discontinued operations (2002–2003)	Restructuring (note 4)
Microsoft (MSFT)	None	None
Pfizer (PFE)	Discontinued operations; accounting change	Merger-related costs (note 3); restructuring
Procter & Gamble (PG)	None	Restructuring program (note 2)
SBC Communications (SBC)	Discontinued operations (2002–2004); accounting change; extraordinary item	Restructuring
United Technology (UTX)	None	Restructuring (p. 65)
Verizon (VZ)	Discontinued operations, accounting change (2002–2004)	Special charges (note 5)
Wal-Mart (WMT)	None	None
Walt Disney (DIS)	Accounting change (2003)	Restructuring; impairment (note 14)

11

TREASURY STOCK AND DIVIDENDS

*Before the 1990s, dividends were the primary means that
firms had to show that earnings were real.*

—Alex Berenson

*[Hank] Greenberg [former chairman and chief executive
officer of AIG] continually pressed his equity traders to buy
back AIG stock to keep the price from falling.*

—Devin Leonard and Peter Elkind

*Time Warner announced yesterday it will buy back up to
$5 billion of its stock during the next two years, in the hopes
of boosting its lagging stock price.*

—Wall Street Journal

Equity represents the ownership interests of the corporation, but complexity
has increased. Treasury stock is the company's outstanding shares that are
repurchased in the market and usually treated as a separate, "negative equity"
line item on the balance sheet. Profitable companies can buy outstanding
shares rather than pay dividends, often using treasury stock to pay future stock
options outstanding.

The evaluation of treasury stock must be in the context of the overall
equity strategy of the firm. Many successful companies in the 1990s bought
treasury securities at inflated prices, presumably for future options payouts.
The joint impact was a further increase of share prices and zero or reduced
dividend payment. Then stock prices collapsed. The result has been expensive treasury stock reducing the equity of nondividend-paying companies,
with limited operating prospects.

RELATIONSHIP OF STOCK OPTIONS TO
TREASURY STOCK AND DIVIDENDS

What is the relationship among options, treasury stock, and dividends? Historically, companies have paid out lots of dividends. That is how companies

demonstrated superior performance—generating cash and paying a large share as dividends. As companies switched to stock options, they issued fewer dividends and used more cash to buy back outstanding shares. The typical rationale was to use the accumulated treasury stock to limit the dilution effect of options. Consequently, options, treasury stock, and dividends should be evaluated together. In terms of cash flows, the use of stock options can be considered to have "inverse incentives," that is, the focus on option incentives, which leads to purchasing treasury stock and limiting or avoiding the payment of dividends. This is a beneficial strategy for executives (especially for those who do not actually own much stock) but detrimental to investors who prefer dividends.

The practice of buying back outstanding stock has a number of earnings management problems and can have a dramatic effect on the financial position of corporations. Acquiring treasury stock is problematic for four reasons:

1. Acquisition reduces both cash and stockholders' equity. If substantial, this can have a sizable effect on standard quantitative financial analysis.

2. Buying back stock is antidilutive: It decreases number of shares outstanding, which increases earnings per share (EPS).

3. Stock repurchasing can be used as a rationale for not paying dividends. The argument is that this is the best use of available cash and investors can "cash in" their shares if they disagree.

4. Large purchases can be used to prop up share prices (possibly when executives are exercising and cashing out their options). The buybacks may make sense if the stock price is low, but even so: Is it the best use of cash for investment?

An extreme case was Maytag. At the end of 2001, options outstanding were 1.4 million, or 1.9% of outstanding shares. Accumulated treasury stock was 40.3 million shares, at a total cost of $1.5 billion. This was the major item that resulted in stockholders' equity of only $23.5 million. When compared to total liabilities of $3.1 billion, Maytag had almost no equity (less than 1% of total assets). On top of that, Maytag paid out $55.1 million in dividends, more than net income for the year. Treasury stock was rising at a good clip over the previous three years, and it seems difficult to explain why, except Maytag's actions to maintain stock price. Maytag recorded a net loss for the 2004 fiscal year and had negative equity of $75 million. It looks like the company will be gobbled up by chief rival Whirlpool. A merger agreement was signed between Whirlpool and Maytag in August 2005.

What about the Dow 30? All of them buy back their own shares and all use stock options—presumably the rationale for treasury stock. The first problem is that not all of them report the amount. Treasury stock should be reported on the balance sheet as a separate line item under stockholders' equity, giving the amount and number of shares repurchased. Seven of the Dow 30 do not report this. Of the remaining 23 firms, the amounts range from $142 million for Verizon to $36 billion for Pfizer.

As an initial rule of thumb, a substantial amount could be equivalent to 10% or more of stockholders' equity. Using this criterion, 15 firms have substantial amounts. IBM, Coca-Cola, and Merck had treasury stock greater than total stockholders' equity. As acquiring treasury stock reduces equity, it increases the relative leverage. IBM had equity of $29.7 billion at the end of 2004 (treasury stock was $31.1 billion), compared to total liabilities of $79.3 billion, resulting in a total debt to equity ratio of 2.7.

Interestingly, the amount of treasury stock does not correlate that well to the amount of options outstanding for the Dow 30. IBM had lots of options (equal to 15% of shares outstanding), but Coca-Cola has a relatively low amount of options (equal to 7.6% of shares outstanding). In other words, there must be additional reasons for Dow 30 firms to buy back stock than for options—increasing earnings per share or stock price perhaps.

WHAT IF TREASURY STOCK IS NOT REPORTED?

Seven Dow 30 companies did not report treasury stock on the 2004 balance sheet: American Express, GM, H-P, Intel, Microsoft, Procter & Gamble, and Wal-Mart. That does not mean they had zero treasury stock; more likely it means a violation of transparency and more work is needed. Companies must show annual treasury stock acquisitions on both the statement of stockholders' equity and the statement of cash flows. Exhibit 11.1 shows Wal-Mart's numbers listed as "Purchase of treasury stock" on the statement of shareholders' equity for the last six years, in millions. (Because three years of data are shown, the last six years of data are available on the 2005 and 2002 reports.)

That is not zero! During the last six years, Wal-Mart bought back 266 million shares for $14,486 million. That represents the equivalent of 32% of net income over the period, 48% of net income in the last three years. Wal-Mart also exercised 41 million options over this period as well for $1.6 billion, a fraction of treasury stock purchased. The net increase of treasury stock was 225 million shares at $12.9 billion. This is not the total amount of treasury stock, but it still represents 26.1% of total equity ($12.9/$49.4).

	2000	2001	2002	2003	2004	2005
Shares*	2	4	24	63	92	81
Amount*	$ 101	$ 193	$1,214	$3,383	$5,046	$ 4,549
Net Income*	$5,377	$6,295	$6,671	$7,955	$9,054	$10,267

* In millions.

EXHIBIT 11.1   WAL-MART'S PURCHASE OF TREASURY STOCK

Are the results for the remaining nonreporting Dow 7 similar to those of Wal-Mart? Exhibit 11.2 shows the purchases of treasury stock compared to net income for the last six years (1999–2004) for the remaining six (in millions).

These numbers are in the same category as Wal-Mart, with companies spending an average $13.2 billion on treasury stock over the last six years, equivalent to almost two-thirds of net income over the same period. With the exception of Microsoft, nondisclosure means big purchasers of treasury stock—a signal of nontransparency.

DIVIDENDS

For most of American history, dividends were used to demonstrate that earnings were real. Until the 1970s, the dividend yield on the average stock was higher than the interest rate on the average bond. Companies typically paid out more than half their earnings in dividends. Thus, operations had to generate cash as well as accounting earnings. For some reason, investors began to focus on earnings numbers, with much less regard for dividends and cash flows. The Financial Accounting Standards Board was probably

	Treasury Stock*	Net Income*	TS/NI
American Express	$ 9,245	$15,699	58.9%
General Motors	15,891	18,995	83.7
Hewlett-Packard	11,518	12,729	90.5
Intel	28,169	35,414	79.5
Microsoft	2,451	45,606	5.4
Procter & Gamble	11,671	19,330	60.4
Average	$13,158	$24,628	63.1%

* In millions.

EXHIBIT 11.2   PURCHASES OF TREASURY STOCK COMPARED TO NET INCOME FOR THE LAST SIX YEARS

pleased, because this implied that the earnings numbers were believable. Before the 2000 stock crash, the Standard & Poor (S&P) 500 had a dividend yield of less than 1%.

Like treasury stock, dividends reduce both cash and equity. On the down side, dividends do not reduce shares outstanding (increasing EPS). Dividends are supposed to be the reward to investors for successful operations that generate enough cash to pay shareholders and invest in future productive operations. Unless investors put a premium on dividends, executive incentives should favor treasury stock. Note that Warren Buffett's highly successful Berkshire Hathaway (he owns 40% of the company) does not pay dividends, although Berkshire had over $43 billion in cash at the end of 2004. Instead, the company buys back shares. Unfortunately, Berkshire does not report treasury stock as a separate line item. The oracle of Omaha does not get great marks for transparency.

With the stock crash of 2000, including assistance from tax changes that reduced the tax rate on dividends and regulations tightening up on stock option accounting, dividends are coming back into vogue. The average yield on the S&P 500 is over 2%. The Dow 30 are bigger dividend payers, with an average dividend yield of 2.8%. The dividend payout (measured as dividends per share/EPS) is 57.8%, more than half of net income. This is reasonable for giant, mature companies. Only five have a yield below 1%, while four yield more than 5% (note that Microsoft's 13% yield includes a one-time special payout of $3 a share).

Accumulated treasury stock and dividend yields do not correlate that well. IBM has a low yield and a high level of treasury stock (greater than total equity), the expected relationship—using cash for buybacks rather than dividends. However, both AIG and Disney have both low dividends and low treasury stock levels. Altria has lots of treasury stock (81% of equity) and has a whopping 5.4% dividend yield. The treasury stock versus dividends decisions are not either/or, but these are interrelated. Treasury stock has the potential for earnings magic (especially increasing EPS and influencing stock price). Dividends should be the antithesis of manipulation, because the payment requires "real cash." Earnings magic normally requires accrual hanky panky.

When comparing options, dividends, and treasury stock together (see Appendix 11.3), the average Dow 30 has options equal to 9% of outstanding shares, pays a 2.8% yield with a 58% payout, and has treasury stock equal to 41% of stockholders' equity. Earnings magic champ AIG has low amounts in all these categories (2.1% options to shares, .7% yield and 11% payout, and treasury stock equal to 3% of equity), while Merck has big values (options equal to 11.6% of shares, yield of 4.8%, payout of 60.6%, and treasury stock over 1.5 times equity). The relationships have to be evaluated individually and with care.

APPENDIX 11.1

DOW 30 TREASURY STOCK

Company	Treasury Stock*	Equity*	TS/Equity
3M (MMM)	$ 5,503	$ 10,378	53%
Alcoa (AA)	1,926	13,300	14%
Altria (MO)	24,851	30,714	81%
American Express (AXP)	NL	16,020	NM
American International Group (AIG)	2,211	80,607	3%
Boeing (BA)	8,810	53,963	16%
Caterpillar (CAT)	3,277	7,467	44%
Citigroup (C)	10,644	109,291	10%
Coca Cola (KO)	17,625	15,935	111%
Disney, Walt (DIS)	1,862	26,081	7%
Du Pont (DD)	11,377	35,632	32%
Exxon-Mobil (XOM)	38,214	101,756	38%
General Electric (GE)	12,762	110,821	12%
General Motors (GM)	NL	565,000	NM
Hewlett-Packard (HPQ)	NL	37,564	NM
Home Depot (HD)	6,692	24,158	28%
Honeywell (HON)	4,185	11,252	37%
IBM (IBM)	NL	38,579	NM
Intel (INTC)	31,072	29,747	104%
J.P. Morgan (JPM)	1,073	105,653	1%
Johnson & Johnson (JNJ)	6,004	31,813	19%
McDonald's (MCD)	9,578	14,202	67%
Merck (MRK)	26,192	17,288	152%
Microsoft (MSFT)	NL	74,825	NM
Pfizer (PFE)	35,992	68,278	53%
Procter & Gamble (PG)	NL		NM
SBC Comm. (SBC)	4,535	40,504	11%
United Technology (UTX)	6,312	14,008	45%
Verizon (VZ)	142	37,560	0%
Wal-Mart (WMT)	NL	49,396	NM
	$11,775.6087	$ 61,096.27586	41%

NL = not listed; NM = not meaningful.
* In millions.

155

APPENDIX 11.2

DOW 30 DIVIDENDS

Company	Dividends*	Yield	Payout
3M Co.	$1.56	2%	40.20%
Altria Group Inc.	3.6	5.35%	75.80%
American International Group	0.4	0.71%	10.80%
American Express	0.46	0.84%	16.30%
Boeing Co.	0.9	1.43%	40.90%
Citigroup Inc.	1.68	3.54%	51.10%
Caterpillar Inc.	1.64	1.63%	26.40%
Coca-Cola Co.	1.31	3.02%	67.20%
Du Pont (E. I.) De Nemours	1.42	3.05%	68.90%
Disney (Walt) Co.	0.24	0.90%	19.70%
Exxon-Mobil Corp.	1.1	1.84%	25.70%
General Electric Co.	0.84	2.37%	50.90%
General Motors Corp.	2	5.74%	**229.90%**
Home Depot Inc.	0.26	1.15%	19.70%
Honeywell International Inc.	0.79	2.09%	50.60%
Hewlett-Packard Co.	0.4	1.63%	33.10%
International Business Machines Corp.	0.74	0.96%	14.80%
Intel Corp.	0.24	0.89%	19.40%
Johnson & Johnson	1.19	1.80%	39.90%
J.P. Morgan Chase & Co.	1.36	3.75%	91.90%
McDonald's Corp.	0.55	1.90%	28.20%
Merck & Co.	1.52	4.75%	60.60%
Microsoft Corp.	3.32**	13.24%	**322.30%**
Pfizer Inc.	0.72	2.50%	58.50%
Procter & Gamble Co.	1.03	1.89%	39.60%
SBC Communications Inc.	1.27	5.35%	87%
United Technologies Corp.	0.79	1.49%	27.60%
Verizon Communications	1.56	4.45%	52.20%
Wal-Mart Stores	0.56	1.15%	22.50%
Average	$1.135	2.79%	57.84%

* $ per share.
** Includes a $3 special dividend.

APPENDIX 11.3

DOW 30 OPTIONS, DIVIDENDS, TREASURY STOCK COMPARISON

Company	Options to Shares	Yield	Payout	TS/Equity
3M (MMM)	10%	2%	40.20%	53.00%
Alcoa (AA)	5%	2.17%	43.50%	14.50%
Altria (MO)	4%	5.35%	75.80%	80.90%
American Express (AXP)	11%	0.84%	16.30%	NL
American International Group (AIG)	2%	0.71%	10.80%	2.70%
Boeing (BA)	3%	1.43%	40.90%	16.30%
Caterpillar (CAT)	12%	1.63%	26.40%	43.90%
Citigroup (C)	6%	3.54%	51.10%	9.70%
Coca Cola (KO)	8%	3.02%	67.20%	110.60%
Disney, Walt (DIS)	11%	0.90%	19.70%	7.10%
Du Pont (DD)	10%	3.05%	68.90%	31.90%
Exxon-Mobil (XOM)	3%	1.84%	25.70%	37.60%
General Electric (GE)	3%	2.37%	50.90%	11.50%
General Motors (GM)	19%	5.74%	229.90%	NL
Hewlett-Packard (HPQ)	19%	1.63%	33.10%	NL
Home Depot (HD)	4%	1.15%	19.70%	27.70%
Honeywell (HON)	7%	2.09%	50.60%	37.20%
IBM (IBM)	14%	0.89%	19.40%	104.50%
Intel (INTC)	15%	0.96%	14.80%	NL
J.P. Morgan (JPM)	11%	3.75%	91.90%	1.00%
Johnson & Johnson (JNJ)	8%	1.80%	39.90%	18.90%
McDonald's (MCD)	13%	1.90%	28.20%	67.40%
Merck (MRK)	12%	4.75%	60.60%	151.50%
Microsoft (MSFT)	9%	13.24%	322.30%	NL
Pfizer (PFE)		2.50%	58.50%	52.70%
Procter & Gamble (PG)	11%	1.89%	39.60%	NL
SBC Comm. (SBC)	6%	5.35%	87%	11.20%
United Technology (UTX)	9%	1.49%	27.60%	45.10%
Verizon (VZ)		4.45%	52.20%	0.40%
Wal-Mart (WMT)	2%	1.15%	22.50%	NL
Average	9%	3%	57.84%	40.75%

NL = not listed.

12

OFF–BALANCE SHEET ITEMS: OPERATING LEASES AND SPECIAL-PURPOSE ENTITIES

The "all-or-nothing" nature of the [lease accounting]
guidance means that economically similar arrangements
may receive different accounting—if they are just to
one side or the other of the bright line test.
— SEC report on off–balance sheet arrangements

In three transactions reminiscent of Enron, AIG had
formed special-purpose entities to let [PNC Financial Services]
tidy up its financial statements by removing bad assets from
its balance sheet. The work had been lucrative for AIG,
generating $40 million in fees.
— Devin Leonard and Peter Elkind

The most infamous of the off–balance sheet items are operating leases and, thanks to Enron, special-purpose entities. Both are fundamental financing items that are common for corporations large and small. The problem is that they can be abused. As demonstrated in Chapter 7, these are not the only off–balance sheet items. In addition to other postemployment benefits (OPEB) and pensions associated with defined benefit plans, other items include contingencies and commitments, lines of credit and other loan commitments, and the equity method for stock investments—all to be discussed in the next couple of chapters.

Why are off–balance sheet items important? The basic answer is that the financial position of a company should be apparent from the balance sheet. Items that are missing mainly represent liabilities, which indicate greater credit risk than shown. They also may suggest possible risks, such as big outstanding lawsuits or large derivative positions that may go bad if the bet is wrong. There could be one single big item that spells potential disaster, such as massive operating leases at major airlines, or a series of items, such as the accumulated debacle that hit Enron.

OPERATING LEASES

Leases usually are considered a financing arrangement, an alternative to buying fixed assets. Because these generally are long-term leases, there should be no problem—capital leases show up on the balance sheet as both fixed assets and long-term liabilities. Conceptually, these are leases that transfer the benefits and risks of property ownership. The problem is the use of operating leases that are recorded as rental contracts and never show up on the balance sheet. The operating leases issue is the clearest example of "rules-based" rather than "principles-based" accounting. The determination of an operating lease rather than a capital lease is based strictly on what are now called bright-line tests (the old term was *cookbook accounting*), such as the present value of minimum lease payments must be at least 90% of the fair value of the leased property. Thus, if the lease is set equal to 89% of the fair value, it is an operating lease—economic substance is irrelevant. Corporations seem to have mastered the technique.

Operating leases are summarized in a separate note to the financial statements. They tend to be large in certain industries, such as airlines (which lease most of their airplanes) and various retail concerns (which lease retail space). Of particular importance is the relative magnitude of the operating leases and the impact on the overall debt structure of the company. If the magnitude is large (say greater than 10% of total assets), then restating total liabilities as if the operating leases were capitalized and recalculating leverage ratios is useful.

The Securities and Exchange Commission report on off–balance sheet arrangements (SEC 2005) found that 91 of the 100 largest firms used operating leases, compared to 39 using capital leases. The report estimated that about 63% of all listed companies used operating leases and 22% used capital leases. The large companies had operating lease commitments of $196 billion, and the estimate for all listed companies was $1.25 trillion—that is right, trillion! When you get to a trillion bucks not on the balance sheet, you are talking real earnings magic.

Nineteen of the Dow 30 reported operating leases, averaging $4.8 billion ($71.4 billion in total). Only 2 had operating leases greater than 10% of total assets: McDonald's at 45.6% ($12.7 billion in operating leases) and Home Depot at 22.1% ($8.6 billion). Wal-Mart had $10.3 billion in operating leases, but this was less than 9% of total assets. This means further analysis for Home Depot and Mcdonald's, possibly Wal-Mart.

Home Depot's note 5 for the 2004 annual report shows capital leases (total future minimum lease payments; i.e., before discounting) of $1.1 billion and operating leases of $8.6 billion. The balance sheet amount for the capital leases was $351 million, representing the net present value of the leases. That means that the company is reporting 31.7% of total lease payments as net present value ($351/$1,108). The equivalent amount of operating leases can be added to assets and liabilities to recalculate leverage ratios. Assuming the same relationship of present value to total minimum payments (31.7%), then the estimated present value of minimum lease payments of operating leases was 0.317 × $8,614 = $2,731 million. (Note that this value is overstated if operating lease terms are shorter than capital leases.) The adjusted calculations for debt-to-equity ratios for Home Depot are shown in Exhibit 12.1 (in millions).

Higher liabilities are recognized, but equity remains unchanged (because leases involve only assets and liabilities). In this case, liabilities increased by 18.5%, which increase the debt-to-equity ratio to 72.4%. This is not particularly high, but it represents a more realistic evaluation of leverage.

Mcdonald's reports a higher proportion of operating leases than Home Depot. According to the leasing arrangements note: "At December 31, 2004, the Company was the lessee at 15,235 restaurant locations through ground leases (the Company leases the land and the Company or franchise owns the building) and through improved leases (the Company leases the land and buildings). Lease terms for most restaurants are generally for 20 years." This resulted in operating lease commitments of $12.7 billion, but no capital leases. Operating leases for 20-year terms suggests earnings magic. The problem is that without capital leases, there is no obvious basis for determining a discount rate. For simplicity, a 50% rate is used. (Another alternative would be to use an average capital lease discount rate for Mcdonald's competitors.) The 50% rate results in discounted lease commitments of $6,348 (50% ×

	Balance Sheet*	Operating Leases*	Adjusted*
Total Liabilities	$14,749	$2,731	$17,480
Total Stockholders' Equity	24,158	—	24,158
Debt to Equity	14,749 / 24,158 = 61.1%		17,480 / 24,158 = 72.4%

* In millions.

EXHIBIT 12.1   HOME DEPOT'S ADJUSTED CALCULATIONS FOR DEBT-TO-EQUITY RATIOS

	Balance Sheet	Operating Leases	Adjusted
Total Liabilities*	$13,636	$6,348	$19,984
Total Stockholders' Equity*	14,202	—	14,202
Debt to Equity	96.0%		140.7%

* In millions.

EXHIBIT 12.2   MCDONALD'S ADJUSTED CALCULATIONS FOR DEBT-TO-EQUITY RATIOS

$12,696). The adjusted calculations for debt-to-equity ratios (in millions) are shown in Exhibit 12.2.

The "adjusted" operating leases increased liabilities by nearly 47%, resulting in the much higher debt-to-equity ratio of 1.4. Note that the discount rate used has a significant effect. The undiscounted operating lease amount for McDonald's was almost as large as the company's total liabilities.

SPECIAL-PURPOSE AND OTHER OFF–BALANCE SHEET ENTITIES

The business world heard about special-purpose entities (SPEs) with the financial collapse of Enron. In its October 2001 quarter 10-Q, Enron consolidated three SPEs in its financial statements, and income (a net loss of $569 million) and equity (a net reduction of $1.2 billion) were restated. Then Enron filed for bankruptcy. Enron's long-term fraud and financial collapse revolved around SPEs. Enron had several partnerships using hundreds, perhaps thousands, of SPEs, which were off–balance sheet and unreported by the company prior to the third-quarter 10-Q. What are SPEs? Can they be used to manipulate earnings on a massive scale? Are they common among America's largest corporations?

According to Financial Executives International, a special-purpose entity is a separate legal entity established by asset transfer to carry out some specific purpose. This entity could be a partnership, trust, or corporation. SPEs are a form of structured financing, to achieve a specific purpose based on some set of financing or operating needs. These can be used to access capital or manage risk. Examples include leasing, sales, and transfer of assets to an SPE, which then issues debt obligations or equity for these assets, financing arrangements with third-party financial institutions, or various project development activities.

General Motors created SPEs to redevelop closed factories with environmental problems. Airlines created SPEs to hold airplane leases (called synthetic leases), keeping the liabilities off the balance sheet or even in the lease notes. AOL Time Warner and Microsoft also used SPEs to create synthetic leases (using sales and leasebacks through the SPEs) to borrow funds from financial institutions to finance fixed assets or other asset acquisitions. Mortgage companies used them to consolidate and sell mortgages to investors. Dell dabbled in SPEs, creating a joint venture with Tyco International for computer financing of customers.

SPE accounting is difficult because the contracts and rules are complex and cover extremely diverse transactions. A key component is determining when they have to be consolidated in the financial statements rather than off–balance sheet (and unreported). Generally, a third party has to maintain a 10% equity interest (up from 3% in January 2003) at market value for the SPE to be off–balance sheet. The rules for the similar variable interest entities (VIEs) involve relative risks and rewards rather than ownership percentages.

Specific Types of SPEs and How They Are Used

SPEs got their start in the early 1980s to achieve specific financial benefits. Banks started moving loan receivables and mortgages into SPEs to get them off the books (i.e., to reduce their reported liabilities) and then "securitize" them for resale as bonded debt instruments. Many companies started using synthetic leases primarily for tax advantages and the related off–balance sheet treatment. American Express moved high-interest-cost debt into an SPE and, as a result, removed the liabilities from the balance sheet and recorded a gain of over $150 million on the transaction (using a process called in-substance defeasance).

A summary of the major uses of SPEs is shown in Exhibit 12.3.

SPEs use structured financing, placing assets and corresponding liabilities into a separate legal structure, such as a corporation, partnership, trust, or joint venture. These are all common legal entities, but when used as SPE vehicles, they have a limited life, a unique formal structure, and a specialized purpose. SPEs have relatively high transactions costs. Benefits must be substantial enough to fund these costs. It is hoped that the benefits represent legitimate business "savings," such as lower interest costs or tax savings, rather than hiding excessive debt or camouflaging fraudulent activities.

An SPE has at least one equity investor, a trustee, and a servicer. The SPE must have an outside equity investor contributing assets (usually cash) of at least 10% of the fair value of assets. This is required for the originator (that is the corporation being evaluated) to avoid consolidation (i.e., to keep it off the books). The trustee is an independent third party paid a fee to advocate the interests of the SPE. The servicer provides the basic accounting

Synthetic Leases	An asset such as an office building is "sold" to the SPE and then leased back (sale-and-leaseback for accounting) to the originator. This is then treated as a capital lease for accounting purposes and as a loan for tax purposes. The company gets the tax benefits of interest and depreciation expense and the accounting benefits of off–balance sheet treatment.
Securitize Loans and Mortgages	A bank "sells" outstanding loans or mortgages to the SPE; these receivables serve as collateral. The SPE repackages these and sells them as bonds or notes to investors. The bank remains as servicer and charges a fee to manage the original loans or mortgages, while the receivables are no longer on the books.
"Sell" Receivables	A manufacturing firm making credit sales eliminates some percent of the receivables by "selling" them to an SPE. The SPE uses the receivables as collateral to borrow the cash to fund the receivables, which is paid back to company. The company now has cash and a lower receivables balance (suggesting that credit terms are more stringent than they really are).
Take-or-Pay Contracts	Require the buyer to take some amount of product or pay a specific amount if refused. The contract can be used as collateral to fund a new manufacturing plant using an SPE.
Throughput Arrangements	Similar to take-or-pay, used primarily by gas or oil pipelines and requiring a specific guaranty of acquisition. The throughput contract (similar to a forward contract) can be used as collateral to fund the construction of a pipeline using an SPE.
Asset Construction Projects	An SPE can be set up to finance future construction projects by using a forward contract on the project, which is then used as collateral by the SPE to fund the construction. The construction costs and corresponding debt are off the books of the builder. Upon completion, the company can then lease back the fixed assets as a synthetic lease for additional tax benefits.
In-Substance Defeasance	An existing debt agreement is placed in trust using an SPE against specific assets (e.g., government bonds with essentially equal terms). Usually established to take advantage of lower interest rates than on existing debt.
Research and Development Costs	An SPE can be established to fund R&D, transferring the risk and avoiding recognizing either the expense involved or liabilities used to fund the ongoing R&D.

EXHIBIT 12.3   SUMMARY OF THE MAJOR USES OF SPES

and other administrative requirements, for a fee. The servicer often is the originator, such as a bank servicing the loans or mortgages that have been securitized.

Supporters of SPEs point out their obvious advantages. As stated by Kahn (2002, p. 1):

> Like many complex instruments, SPEs were created to perform a straightforward, necessary task—isolating and containing financial risk. Businesses that wanted to perform a specialized task—an airline buying a fleet of airplanes; a company building a big construction project—would set up an SPE and offload the financing to the new entity.
>
> In theory, SPEs protected both sides of the transaction if something went awry. If the project went bust, the company was responsible only for what it had put into the SPE; conversely, if the company went bankrupt, its creditors couldn't go after the SPE's assets.
>
> Over time, SPEs became essential components of modern finance. Their uses expanded wildly—and legitimately. For example, virtually every bank uses SPEs to issue debt secured by pools of mortgages. And companies as diverse as Target and Xerox use SPEs for factoring—the centuries-old practice of generating cash by selling off receivables.
>
> SPEs are also a good way to keep money away from Uncle Sam. Most tax-avoidance techniques using SPEs cleverly exploit discrepancies between accounting rules and tax laws. Synthetic leases are a good example.

Enron—Extreme Use of SPEs

Enron used SPEs on a vast and fraudulent basis—and made SPEs infamous. Not only were Enron's financial statements misstated, but CFO Andrew Fastow and other executives enriched themselves by acting as the so-called independent third-party trustees. At a minimum, these should have been disclosed as related-party transactions and, in many cases, consolidated in the Enron financial statements. The degree to which the SPEs were mishandled and CFO Fastow was allowed to manipulate these by both the audit committee and auditor Arthur Andersen was remarkable.

The company's reports failed to explain the high-risk nature of the business or how much of the business was funneled through partnerships, joint ventures, and other structured finance contracts using SPEs. Of course, the related-party deals, massive off–balance sheet liabilities (with high-risk compounded by side agreements using, among other things, Enron stock as the asset guaranteeing payment), and fraudulent transactions were not disclosed. Somewhat like utility pyramiding schemes of the 1920s, Enron had created a partnerships-and-SPE pyramiding scheme that collapsed.

Bentson and Hartgraves (2002) pointed out six areas of accounting and auditing concerns with Enron:

(1) The accounting policy of not consolidating SPEs that appear to have permitted Enron to hide losses and debt from investors. (2) The accounting treatment of sales of Enron's merchant investments to unconsolidated (though actually controlled) SPEs as if these were arm's length transactions. (3) Enron's income recognition practice of recording as current income fees for services rendered in future periods and recording revenue from sales of forward contracts, which were, in effect, disguised loans. (4) Fair-value accounting resulting in restatements of merchant investments that were not based on trustworthy numbers. (5) Enron's accounting for its stock that was issued to and held by SPEs. (6) Inadequate disclosure of related party transactions and conflicts of interest, and their costs to stockholders. (pp. 106–107)

The New Rules

SPE use is widespread and justified as a viable approach for various financial and operating procedures. SPEs raise substantial concerns because of their ability to hide liabilities and certain types of operations. Even with substantial disclosure, it can be difficult to determine the true impact of structured financing activity on the balance sheet and other implications to earnings and cash flows. As demonstrated by Enron, the potential for blatant manipulation is present and can be hard to detect beyond basic signals of questionable activities. Specific issues are shown in Exhibit 12.4.

The SEC and Financial Accounting Standards Board (FASB) have been studying and issuing new standards to attempt to deal with SPE issues. The SEC's Final Rule FR-67 requires the disclosure of contracts involving unconsolidated entities. The FASB's Interpretation 46R (FIN 46R) on variable interest entities (VIEs, legal entities often holding financial assets with specific characteristics defined by the FASB) requires consolidation of an entity if exposed to a majority of the risk and reward, rather than voting majority control. Statement of Financial Accounting Standards (SFAS) 140 on transfers of financial assets, with securitization particularly important, focuses on whether a transfer should be considered a sale (involving recognizing gains and losses as well as the "derecognition" of the financial assets). Entities that are not qualified SPEs (QSPEs) or VIEs are subject to SFAS 94 to determine whether or not to consolidate.

To date, the new rules have been modestly effective. Problems for standard setting include the sheer complexity of the topic and SPE users that stay

Topic	Issue
Fit to Business Strategy	Why are the SPEs being used? The reasons should be obvious.
Relative Magnitude of Off–Balance-Sheet SPEs	SPEs can result in substantial reduction in liabilities, understating the true financial position of the corporation.
Ambiguous Disclosures	Thanks to new SEC rules, at least minimum disclosures are necessary; but are they adequate?
Impact on Financial Ratios	There can be a substantial negative effect on debt to equity, return on assets, performance, and financing costs.
SPE Use Relative to Credit Rating and Other Credit-Risk Characteristics	Firms with operating problems, declining bond ratings, and rising credit risk might resort to SPE use.
Accounts Receivable	SPEs can be used to move substantial receivables off the balance sheet, making it difficult to determine credit terms and impact on sales.

EXHIBIT 12.4 SPECIFIC ISSUES REGARDING SPEs

a step or two ahead of new standards. A fundamental problem is the flexibility to structure an off–balance sheet entity to achieve particular earnings magic objectives: report or avoid a sale, recognize or avoid a gain or a loss, or apply particular assumptions. The standards will continue to change, but this is expected to be a perpetual earnings magic haven.

Most large corporations use SPEs for a limited number of peripheral operations. They should have legitimate purposes and be fully explained in the annual report, so that investors can evaluate the real impact of these operations and underlying obligations. Because the primary purpose of SPEs is to keep these items off–balance sheet, they should be viewed skeptically. The question is to what extent their use signals an environment of potential manipulation.

SPE (and related-entity) disclosure should be in both the Management Discussion and Analysis (MD&A) and appropriate notes. This disclosure tended to be limited or nonexistent in the past, with Enron the most notable example. Therefore, the first step is to find the disclosure (do not expect a separate category called special-purpose entities). There are two prominent categories: QSPEs associated with SFAS No. 140 and VIEs associated with FIN 46R. The key question is the fit of SPE use to the overall business strategy. The QSPE's are usually associated with securitization; that is, "selling" financial assets such as a pool of credit card debt to the QSPE. As long as the transactions meet the definition of a sale, the financial assets are removed from the books of the corporation and a gain or loss recorded. A VIE is usually a securitization entity that is not a QSPE and may have to be consolidated with the corporation, if the company maintains a majority of the risks and rewards of ownership (the primary beneficiary). QSPEs and VIEs are usually reported in separate notes if material.

SPE Use among the Dow 30

Most SPEs relate to financial services, so banks, other financial institutions, and firms with substantial financial operations are likely users. Among the Dow 30, Citigroup, J.P. Morgan, American Express, and insurer American International Group are expected to be big users, as are GE and GM, which both have large financial operations (see Appendix 12.2). All five had substantial SPE transactions; however, the extent and understandability of the disclosures differed for each company. The 2004 annual reports of Citigroup and J.P. Morgan had extensive and relatively understandable notes and MD&A analysis. AIG's report was especially opaque.

Securitizing financial assets is a major banking activity and the primary use of SPEs. Citigroup had securitized transactions of $1,698 billion in 2004—that is right, $1.7 trillion! These were mainly credit card receivables and mortgages, also auto loans, student loans, and corporate debt. Citi sells these receivables to trusts but maintains the customer accounts. The securitization is revolving; as customers pay the balances, the cash is used to "purchase" new receivables for the trusts. Citi reported delinquencies on credit card receivables (at least 90 days past due) of $2.9 billion (54.9% on balance sheet) and credit losses of $9.2 billion (44.9% on balance sheet) for 2004. VIEs were used for several commercial purposes, with total assets of $500 million in 2004 ($36 billion consolidated by Citi; i.e., reported on the balance sheet). Typical uses included commercial paper conduits, structured finance, collateralized debt obligations, and investment vehicles. Citi securitizes financial assets purchased or from clients to create "new financing opportunities."

A key issue is that these entities are reported at fair value, but market value often is not available. Then Citi used financial models or sales of similar assets. Remember Enron's use of "mark-to-model" as a major earnings magic tool. Citi states that fair value is estimated "by determining the present value of expected future cash flows using modeling techniques that incorporate management's best estimates of key assumptions."

Securitized financial assets were similar at the other four corporations with financing operations. J.P. Morgan uses QSPEs for residential and commercial mortgages, credit card receivables, and auto loans. VIEs include synthetic leases and asset-backed securities, including multiseller conduits for access to commercial paper. AIG uses SPEs for securitized collateralized bond and loan obligation trusts and VIEs for various real estate partnerships. American Express securitizes credit card receivables through a lending trust (transferring $3.9 billion in 2004) and uses VIEs for structured investments including collateralized debt obligations and secured loan trusts. GE uses securitization entities for commercial and residential real estate, credit card receivables, and GE trade receivables, which totaled $61 billion in 2004 (43.7% on balance sheet). GM uses synthetic leases, consumer finance receivables, wholesale lines of credit, mortgage funding, and construction and real estate lending. Caterpillar also has a major financial subsidiary and used QSPEs for securitizing receivables and other purposes.

Most of the remaining companies of the Dow 30 mention VIEs. Coca-Cola uses VIEs for some of the bottling companies; SBC uses them for real estate leases; Disney uses VIEs for foreign interest in Euro Disney and other theme parks. Most of the rest say they have VIEs but they are not material. Consequently, there is no mention of how they are being used or whether they're consolidated. In addition, there was no mention of SPEs of any kind in a few of the annual reports.

The SEC report on off–balance sheet arrangements indicated that off–balance-sheet entities are a big-firm issue. Thirty of the largest 100 firms used securitization of financial assets, but the SEC estimated that only 4.3% of all traded firms securitize. They estimated that the population securitizes some $950 billion in financial assets; however, because Citigroup reported securitizing $1.7 trillion, the SEC calculation is suspect. It suggests the difficulty of correctly analyzing the information presented on off–balance-sheet entities.

APPENDIX 12.1

DOW 30: OPERATING LEASES, 2004

Company	Operating Leases*	Total Assets*	Operating Leases/Total Assets
3M (MMM)	$ 521	$ 20,708	2.5%
American International Group (AIG)	3,250	798,660	0.4%
Caterpillar (CAT)	1,168	43,091	2.7%
Citigroup (C)	9,182	1,481,101	0.6%
Du Pont (DD)	957	35,632	2.7%
Exxon-Mobil (XOM)	8,482	195,256	4.3%
General Motors (GM)	4,898	479,603	1.0%
Hewlett-Packard (HPQ)	5,328	76,138	7.0%
Home Depot (HD)	8,614	38,907	**22.1%**
Honeywell (HON)	1,349	31,062	22.1%
IBM (IBM)	6,607	109,183	6.1%
Johnson & Johnson (JNJ)	979	53,317	1.8%
McDonald's (MCD)	12,696	27,838	**45.6%**
Merck (MRK)	520	42,573	1.2%
Pfizer (PFE)	2,307	123,684	1.9%
Procter & Gamble (PG)	920	57,048	1.6%
Verizon (VZ)	4,748	165,958	2.9%
Wal-Mart (WMT)	10,300	120,223	8.6%
Walt Disney (DIS)	2,690	53,902	5.0%
Average	$ 4,759	$ 199,261	6.1%

* In millions.

APPENDIX 12.2

DOW 30: SPECIAL-PURPOSE AND RELATED ENTITIES, 2004

Company	Special-Purpose Entity Type and Description
3M (MMM)	None.
Alcoa (AA)	No material VIEs.
Altria (MO)	None specified.
American Express (AXP)	Securitized credit card receivables through trust; VIEs for CDOs and securitized loan trusts.
American International Group (AIG)	SPEs for collateralized bonds and loan obligation trusts; VIEs for real estate partnerships.
Boeing (BA)	Various VIEs.
Caterpillar (CAT)	Cat Financial: securitized trade receivables, originally QSPE for collateralized trust obligations; VIE consolidated $2.6 billion in 2004.
Citigroup (C)	QSPEs for securitized credit card receivables, mortgages, auto loans, student loans, and corporate debt. VIEs for commercial paper conduits, structured finance, collateralized debt obligations, and investment vehicles.
Coca-Cola (KO)	Some bottlers now considered VIEs, some consolidated.
Du Pont (DD)	Minor use of VIEs.
Exxon-Mobil (XOM)	VIEs mentioned.
General Electric (GE)	SPEs for securitizing commercial and residential real estate, credit card receivables, and GE trade receivables.
General Motors (GM)	Synthetic leases, consumer finance receivables, wholesale lines of credit, mortgage funding, construction and real estate lending.
Hewlett-Packard (HPQ)	No material VIEs.
Home Depot (HD)	Synthetic leases.
Honeywell (HON)	No material VIEs.
IBM (IBM)	No material VIEs.
Intel (INTC)	No material VIEs.

(continues)

Company	Special-Purpose Entity Type and Description
J.P. Morgan (JPM) (Continued)	QSPEs for residential and commercial mortgages, credit card receivables, and auto loans. VIEs used for synthetic leases and asset-backed securities.
Johnson & Johnson (JNJ)	No material VIEs.
McDonald's (MCD)	None listed.
Merck (MRK)	None listed.
Microsoft (MSFT)	No material VIEs.
Pfizer (PFE)	No material VIEs.
Procter & Gamble (PG)	No material VIEs.
SBC Communications (SBC)	VIE for real estate leases.
United Technology (UTX)	Only states that controlled entities are consolidated.
Verizon (VZ)	No material VIEs.
Wal-Mart (WMT)	No material VIEs.
Walt Disney (DIS)	VIEs for foreign minority interest in Euro Disney and Hong Kong International Theme Park.

VIE: variable interest entity; QSPE: qualified SPE; CDO: collateralized debt obligation.

13

ACQUISITIONS AND ALL THAT GOODWILL

*The highest-risk [audit] clients seemed to be those that did
massive acquisitions in fairly short time periods (thereby
acquiring enormous debt).*

— Barbara Toffler with Jennifer Reingold

*Tyco specialized in buying low-margin companies and magically
increasing their profits. The company's growth-by-acquisition
had been proven a failure a generation earlier, and its financial
statements were filled with red flags.*

— Alex Berenson

American industry is Big Business primarily as a result of major acquisition
activity over the last century and a half. Significant public policy issues are
associated with business combinations, such as the elimination of competition. A host of problems develop when attempting to evaluate the financial
consequences of these transactions. Once a merger happens, a new company
exists that is not the same as just adding the accounts of the two old companies
together. The opportunities for earnings magic are magnified and the ability
to evaluate acquisition activity difficult.

Mergers can be used in three ways:

1. To increase economies of scale and reduce competition (horizontal mergers, i.e., Standard Oil)
2. To expand activities into related areas (vertical mergers)
3. To diversify (conglomerate mergers)

John D. Rockefeller, Andrew Carnegie, and other nineteenth-century robber
barons moved from horizontal mergers to eliminate competitors to vertical
mergers to obtain raw materials, ensure distribution channels, and reduce
overall costs. Henry Ford was the premier entrepreneur in the first half of the
twentieth century. He introduced the moving assembly line (although meat

packers used similar methods long before) and the cheap, standardized Model T a century ago. Ford Motor grew using retained earnings and then used a vertical merger strategy to acquire related firms: parts suppliers, ships and railroads for distribution, mines, and basic metal manufacturers. Ford owned most business components of auto manufacturing from mines to transportation to dealerships.

The strategies for conglomerate mergers developed during the 1950s. The advantages for diversification are well known. In theory, a manager can run a company in any industry effectively. The practice of owning a "portfolio" of unrelated businesses became particularly popular in the 1960s. James Ling formed a holding company, Ling-Temco-Vought (LTV), and proceeded to build an empire across multiple industries with borrowed money. Major acquisitions included Braniff Airlines, Wilson Sporting Goods, National Car Rental, and Jones and Laughlin Steel. The acquisitions brought in additional revenues and accounting magic resulted in increasing earnings. (Generally accepted accounting principles [GAAP] had little to say about accounting for business combinations at the time.) Other well-known conglomerates active in this period included Litton, ITT, and Gulf and Western.

Difficult economic times for LTV (including recessions and the "stagflation" of the 1970s and early 1980s) and the problems of controlling the complex and diverse empire led to huge losses, massive sell-offs of segments, and bankruptcy in 1986. LTV would emerge from bankruptcy primarily as a steel company. There is less enthusiasm for the concept of conglomerate management (Tyco was the latest example of a conglomerate going belly up), but conglomerates exist and many are successful. General Electric is one of the largest and most successful companies in the United States, and it is a conglomerate.

Buyer	Target	Year	Value*
Bell Atlantic	GTE	2000	$52.0
Exxon	Mobil	1999	77.2
Hewlett-Packard	Compaq	2002	24.0
J.P. Morgan	Chase Manhattan	2001	30.0
J.P. Morgan	Bank One	2004	58.5
Pfizer	Warner-Lambert	2000	93.9
Procter & Gamble	Gillette	2005	53.2
Pfizer	Pharmacia	2003	56.0
SBC	Ameritech	1998	61.4
SBC	AT&T Wireless	2004	41.0
SBC	AT&T	2005	16.0
Travelers Group	Citicorp	1998	70.0

* In billions.

EXHIBIT 13.1 EXAMPLES OF ACQUISITIONS

Acquisitions are every bit as common today as 50 or 100 years ago, and many big ones directly relate to the Dow 30 (see Exhibit 13.1). For size and impact, current mergers match any period in American history. The merger of Travelers with Citicorp created the first American trillion-dollar bank, Citigroup—and busted the Depression-era Glass-Steagall Act that separated commercial and investment banking. The Bell Atlantic-GTE merger created SBC, which later acquired AT&T Wireless and then got AT&T to boot. The effects on concentration and business strategies across industries are enormous. Given the leeway in accounting practices, the earnings magic potential also is huge.

SFAS NOS. 141 AND 142

The Financial Accounting Standards Board (FASB) passed Statement of Financial Accounting Standards (SFAS) No. 141, *Business Combinations,* and SFAS. No. 142, *Goodwill and Other Intangible Assets,* in June 2001. The major change is the purchase method is required for all business combinations. Under SFAS No. 142, goodwill is no longer amortized. Instead, goodwill is tested for impairment at least annually. An impairment loss is recognized if the carrying value is not recoverable and if the carrying value exceeds fair value. Impairment write-offs can be expected, and they might be big. AOL Time Warner recorded a $54 billion loss for first quarter of 2002. The write-off of goodwill turned a $1 million operating loss to a $54 billion loss.

The elimination of the pooling of interest method makes financial analysis of business combinations somewhat easier, because mergers now use the same method. However, the impairment charges to goodwill under SFAS No. 142 are problematic. It is not at all clear how fair value of goodwill can be determined or under what circumstances goodwill should be written off. The AOL Time Warner write-off suggests a big-bath earnings management strategy in a quarter that was losing money (although only a small $1 million loss for AOL). Further write-offs are likely from any number of firms. From an analyst's perspective, these write-offs will be hard to predict and may be difficult to evaluate even after the fact.

EARNINGS MANAGEMENT ISSUES AT ACQUISITION DATE

A business combination is consummated on a specific date, usually during the middle of the fiscal year of both companies (and they may have different year-end dates). On that date, the acquired company is essentially consolidated into the parent. Key questions exist on recognition strategies and the specific amounts recorded. The acquired company has to be recorded at acquisition price (the purchase method must be used). Valuing assets is not an exact science, and considerable leeway is allowed.

Alternative price allocation strategies exist, including these three:

1. Allocate as much of the value to depreciable or amortizable assets as possible. Restate property, plant, and equipment and intangibles, such as patents, to the highest possible values. The results will be lower future net income because of increased expenses and lower future tax expense because depreciation and amortization are tax deductible. This makes the most economic sense, because it saves cash.

2. Allocate as much as possible to in-process research and development (IPRD). Because the R&D results have not been finalized, valuing IPRD is particularly difficult. In other words, flexibility abounds. IPRD has to be written off soon after the acquisition, potentially a big loss. However, it is essentially a nonoperating item and may be ignored by analysts. In its 1998 acquisition of MCI, WorldCom tried to write-off $6 billion in IPRD (15% of the acquisition price—the Securities and Exchange Commission [SEC] allowed only $3 billion).

3. Allocate as much as possible to goodwill—the major earnings magic alternative. Under SFAS No. 142, goodwill is not expensed, and this method should yield the highest earnings after the acquisition. The downsides of this strategy are the lack of depreciable/amortizable assets as well as the potential for write-downs of goodwill in future years, such as AOL Time Warner.

Evaluating acquisition allocation strategies is dependent on the corporate disclosures for the acquisition year, which may be less than thorough. Pfizer disclosed the acquisition of Pharmacia (fiscal year 2003, Note 2), summarized as shown in Exhibit 13.2.

The total acquisition cost was almost $56 billion, with $21 billion (38.3%) allocated to goodwill. The major asset category is intangible assets, consistent with the R&D of a major drug company. In-process R&D of $5.1 billion was recognized and written off within the year. The earnings magic strategy seems to be to allocate substantial costs to goodwill, reducing expenses in future years (assuming no goodwill write-offs will occur). Pfizer's 2004 balance sheet showed $23.8 billion in goodwill, 19.2% of total assets.

The maximizing goodwill strategy seems prevalent among the Dow 30. J.P. Morgan's acquisition of Bank One in 2004 for $58.5 billion included

	Pharmacia Acquisition*
Net Tangible Assets — at Book Value	$ 7,236
Intangible Assets	37,066
In-Process R&D	5,052
Restructuring Costs and Tax Adjustments	(15,129)
Other Adjustments to Fair Value	344
Goodwill	21,403
Total	$55,972

* In millions.

EXHIBIT 13.2   SUMMARY OF PFIZER ACQUISITION OF PHARMACIA

goodwill of $34.1 billion (58.1%). IBM made 14 acquisitions in 2004 for $2.1 billion, recording $1.4 billion in goodwill, or 67.8%. 3M has the record with four acquisitions in 2004, costing $116 million, but recording $128 million in goodwill (110.3%). Essentially, 3M paid a premium over $100 million for net liability positions.

If specific acquisitions are considered immaterial, virtually no disclosures may be included. The conglomerate Tyco made a vast number of relatively small acquisitions under Dennis Kozlowski. Tyco spent some $8 billion on over 700 acquisitions over a three-year period and disclosed not a one. The disclosure decisions were based on the individual acquisitions, allowable under GAAP, but the net effect was deceptive.

ACQUISITION ISSUES

Acquisitions can be brilliant transactions that fit into the business strategy of the corporation, but several have proven to be real disasters. Key questions are whether these were based on business strategy considerations or the increased potential for earnings magic. This is an area for skepticism, including poor disclosure.

Some of the issues are shown in Exhibit 13.3.

In 2001 Tyco acquired CIT Group, a financial services company renamed Tyco Capital. Before the acquisition date, CIT disposed of $5 billion in poorly performing loans, made downward adjustments of $221.6 million, increased the credit-loss provisions, and took a $54 million charge to acquisition costs ("pushed down" from Tyco). Revenues for CIT were extremely low and dramatically increased after the deal. The result was a net loss reported by CIT just before the acquisition date. After the acquisition, CIT reported net income of $71.2 million. This is a technique called "spring loading," where the acquired

Topic	Issue
	At Acquisition Announcement Date
Why the Acquisition	Does the specific acquisition make sense?
Acquisition Cost	Is an excessive premium paid?
Long-Term Acquisition Strategy	What are the recent acquisition (and divestiture) trends? Are there disasters in the making?
Quantity and Magnitude of Acquisitions	If acquisitions are common (and especially if large), the earnings magic potential increases.
	After Acquisition Date
How Were Asset Values Allocated?	Allocation decisions signal earnings magic strategies.
Depreciable/Amortizable Assets	These will increase future operating expenses but are tax deductible. Do these seem to be inflated or too small?
In-Process R&D	Must be written off. Does the amount seem reasonable?
Goodwill	No longer amortized, but subject to impairment write-offs. Can be overstated to reduce future expenses associated with the acquisition.

Exhibit 13.3   Acquisition Issues

company is mandated to make various write-offs and adjustments to immediately benefit the parent. That increased Tyco's earnings for the September 2001 quarter, but luck ran out. Tyco Capital had extreme problems with credit, because it was now tied to Tyco. Ultimately, this new business segment was sold as an initial public offering in 2002. Tyco recorded this as a discontinued operation (recording an after-tax loss of $6.3 billion). Tyco had a total net loss of $9.4 billion in 2002. Chief executive officer Kozlowski and chief financial officer Swartz resigned and shortly thereafter were indicted for various illegal acts.

The information for CIT and Tyco was available only because CIT continued to file reports to the SEC for the first few months after the merger. This was necessary to maintain a high credit standing with the debt markets. In most cases, analysts must rely on the quarterly reports of the two companies just before the acquisition date and then the parent company for the quarter after the acquisition. The acquired firm has "disappeared" from the financial statements, with only the limited note disclosure provided.

The usual arguments for acquisitions are economies of scale and restructuring to increase efficiencies. Specific decisions on acquisition issues also are made. Four key issues are:

1. Write-offs based on the acquisition
2. The nature of the restructuring in progress
3. In-process research and development
4. Goodwill

The major problem to the external analyst is to understand what the corporation did and why. The earnings magic potential is substantial—what is capitalized or expensed, how are charges against earnings made, how is the profitability from the acquisition firm incorporated?

Companies with a history of acquisitions often quickly restructure the new subsidiaries. GE gobbles up more firms than anyone else but seems to do it very successfully. The GE team seems ruthless in slimming down acquisitions with substantial layoffs and other cost-cutting measures. The financial results make the GE strategy seem successful, but the direct impact of earnings magic is difficult to detect. Specific notes on restructuring in the annual report almost always appear, sometimes continuing for years after the acquisition, if major. Pfizer's acquisition of Pharmacia included both integration and restructuring costs as merger-related costs. Some $2.2 billion of the first-year restructuring costs (terminations and exiting some businesses) were capitalized and included in goodwill (on the theory they are really part of the purchase price). An additional $881 million was expensed in 2003–2004.

In-process research and development seems straightforward. The acquiring firm will write off the amount recognized in the acquisition. However, the value of IPRD is difficult to determine because at the development stage, the potential value is unknown. Consequently, a case can be made that the value is near zero or worth millions. Near zero is a swell answer to limit the write-off cost. Millions works if a big write-off is desired. This can be recorded as a nonoperating expense and justified specifically as an acquisition cost. Lucent acquired Octel in 1997 and Yurie in 1999. Both were billion-dollar acquisitions and large amounts were recorded as IPRD and expensed as nonoperating costs. This "saved" later amortization expenses, which would have been recognized as operating expenses.

GOODWILL

Goodwill can be considered a plug figure in a purchase acquisition. The assets and liabilities are revalued to fair value (not an exact science), then the difference between the purchase price and revalued net assets is goodwill. From this perspective, goodwill represents nothing except the premium paid for net assets. (Note that the common way to identify premium is the difference in the acquisition price announced and the stock price before the announcement.) Goodwill is on the books as an asset but has no obvious meaning except to measure the total premium paid for past acquisitions (plus it is deductible for tax purposes). It is particularly meaningless in bankruptcy. WorldCom had over $50 billion in goodwill and other intangibles (48.6% of total assets) just before bankruptcy.

The Dow 30 has more than its fair share of goodwill. All had goodwill, and 29 of the 30 had goodwill over $1 billion in 2004, with GE leading the way at $71.2 billion (see Appendix 13.2). Goodwill averaged $11.5 billion, or just over 10% of total assets. Nine of the Dow 30 had goodwill greater than 10% of total assets, with Procter and Gamble the goodwill champ at 34.4%. This amount will increase because PG completed the acquisition of Gillette on October 1, 2005. Why are these companies part of the Dow 30? A history of major acquisitions seems an obvious answer. The goodwill does not represent the purchase price—it is only the premium paid over revalued net assets. And that is based on the purchase method. Prior to SFAS No. 141, the majority of acquisitions used the pooling method, which did not recognize goodwill. Even Microsoft, renowned for its internal growth, had over $3 billion in goodwill (but only a fraction of 1% of total assets).

Goodwill is tested for impairment at least annually. Now the strategy is under what circumstances should an impairment loss be taken and how much. If a loss cannot be avoided, key issues are timing and amount. A few Dow 30 firms had goodwill impairments, but usually for relatively small amounts. Du Pont had a goodwill impairment charge in 2003 associated with the sale of the textiles and interiors segment of $295 million, in addition to "separation charges" of $1.6 billion associated with the sale. Both were recorded as separate line items on the income statement and can be considered major since Du Pont's net income was only $973 million in 2003. Intel had goodwill impairments of $611 million for divestitures in its Intel Communications Group. McDonald's 2004 impairment was part of a $130 million charge associated with poor performance in South Korea.

IMPACT ON FINANCIAL STATEMENTS AND RATIOS

When an acquisition is made, the acquiring company is expanded in size and operations. How this affects specific balance sheet and income statement items as well as cash flows depends on the specific characteristics of the agreement: the exchange of voting common stock versus cash, debt instruments, or a combination.

When the acquisition is cash (some or all the cash involved may be borrowed), the net asset (equity) position does not go up. Acquired assets (and liabilities) are recorded at fair values, which are offset by the cash paid. Balance sheet totals rise only to the extent that external financing is used, either debt or equity. But asset and liability composition can change substantially. Acquired patents, goodwill, and other intangibles are recorded. Cash ratios will drop for the acquiring firm (unless the acquisition was funded by new debt or equity), with liquidity ratios partially offset by the working capital position (at fair value) of the acquisition. Fixed assets and intangibles can rise substantially because fair values are used and goodwill recognized. Liabilities rise because of the acquisition's obligations and any debt used to finance the acquisition. Equity is unchanged in a cash or debt transaction. Consequently, leverage ratios can rise, often substantially.

The income statement of the combined firm includes the acquisition's operations only after the effective date of the merger. Revenues rise because of the acquired firm's operations. Several negative results occur. Operating expenses usually are relatively larger because of write-ups of inventory to fair value at the acquisition (particularly if the acquired firms used last in, first out [LIFO]), higher depreciation, and other allocations because fixed and other assets generally are written up, plus the potential write-down of goodwill and other intangibles. Also, if the cash paid is from borrowed funds, additional interest expense is recorded. Investment banking and other transaction costs are substantial. Restructuring charges can be large. Consequently, profitability and activity ratios can suffer. That is, earnings for the combined entity should be higher because of the acquired firm's operations, but performance ratios may decline because of increased expenses.

Substantial cash flow effects result. The acquisition price paid in cash (less preacquisition cash held by the acquired firm) is recorded as cash used for investing. (If there was any borrowing, cash received is recorded as cash flows from financing.)

The impact on financial statements is considerably different if equity is exchanged. Assets and liabilities of the acquisition are restated to fair value, and equity used also is recorded at fair value. Liquidity usually would be higher because cash is not used. Inventory is generally restated upward. Property, plant, and equipment, intangibles, and other items are recorded the same whether cash or equity is used. Leverage ratios are lower when equity is used. (Note that the acquirer assumes the debt of the acquisition.) There should be little difference under the alternative purchase method circumstances for the income statement. Interest expense would be higher if borrowed cash is used rather than equity, but equity dilution occurs when stock is used.

ACQUISITION DISASTERS

A relatively high proportion of acquisitions turn out to be mistakes—perhaps a majority. The rationale for merger usually sounds great. As stated by Henry (2002, p. 60):

> The spring of 1998 was a fast and furious time for dealmakers. . . . These deals were solid undertakings—purchases of long-established companies with proven business models, tangible assets, and thousands of workers. . . . On April 6, Travelers Group announced a $70 billion merger with Citigroup . . . The next day, insurer Conseco announced it was paying $7.1 billion and a huge 86% premium to buy mobile-home lender Green Tree Financial. The following Monday, Bank One offered $28.8 billion for First Chicago, and NationsBank bid $509.3 billion for BankAmerica. Three weeks later, Germany's Daimler Benz snapped up Chrysler for $38.6 billion.

Henry (2002) analyzed 302 big mergers from mid-1995 to mid-2001, which included the monster deal, AOL's acquisition of Time Warner for $166 billion. A key point was that about two-thirds were losing deals. Four major reasons were suggested: (1) overpaying by offering a big premium over market value, (2) inflating the possible cost savings and synergies, (3) delayed integration of operations, and (4) cutting costs beyond reason and damaging operations and customer relations.

Then there were mergers that were complete disasters. Perhaps the biggest disaster, because of the fraud involved, was the acquisition of CUC (formerly Comp-U-Card) by HFS to form Cendant in 1997. Unfortunately for HFS, CUC had been reporting fraudulent earnings for years. CUC sold consumer products using long credit terms. To meet analysts' expectations, long-term revenues (which should have been deferred) often were recognized immediately and related marketing and other costs capitalized. Some "other revenues" were entirely fictitious. The fraud scheme was initially developed in the early 1980s, essentially a "menu" of revenue, cost, reserves, and write-offs specifically to meet earnings targets.

Acquisitions became necessary to keep up the gimmicks, because of the new fraud opportunities. With acquisitions, large reserves could be created with charges lost in the shuffle, through a combination of spring-loading results to the acquisition before the merger and netting costs to the balance sheet in the consolidation. The reserves would then be used to increase earnings after the acquisitions, by charging expenses against the reserves. The HFS acquisition was big and made essential to CUC when the schemes were falling apart—the real losses were increasingly hard to camouflage. The fraud was reported shortly after the merger, and financials were restated. Restatements for 1995 to 1997 reduced net income by $440 million, including a net loss of $217.2 million in 1997 instead of the $55.4 million gain initially reported. Investor suits against Cendant and auditor Ernst & Young followed, as did criminal indictments against several former CUC executives. Cendant paid out $2.85 billion to settle investor lawsuits.

MARKET REACTION TO ACQUISITION ANNOUNCEMENTS

An acquiring firm typically pays a substantial premium over current stock price to complete a merger. This is needed to persuade the target company's board of directors to accept the offer and to fend off other potential acquiring firms. This market premium can top 50% of current price, resulting in an immediate market reaction for both acquiring and target firms. Almost always, the stock price of the target approaches the announced acquisition. The price of the acquiring firm can go up or down, depending on how investors view the benefits of the acquisition relative to the premium paid.

Consider the announcement of the SBC acquisition of AT&T on January 31, 2005. The merger was approved by AT&T stockholders on June 30. A stock chart is presented in Exhibit 13.4 for both firms below (AT&T ticker is T).

As expected, AT&T got an immediate bump in price of over 10% around the end of January. However, SBC's stock price dropped over 5%. The February 22 formal merger process announcement resulted in a rise in price for AT&T. Over the next few months those relationships stayed relatively stable, with AT&T generally up about 5% and SCB down about 5%. The Dow Jones average was in between. Both firms seemed to get a small bump up at the AT&T stockholders' okay. Reviewing the stock price reaction for a merger announcement is a useful first step for analysis. The market tends to take a sophisticated but skeptical view on mergers.

REGULATORY ISSUES

Mergers by big business can have a major impact on economic activity. One aspect is increasing market share and reducing competition, which can involve potential antitrust violations. Declining competition also may reduce new innovation. Therefore, the Department of Justice, the Federal Trade Commission, and other federal regulators review mergers by major corporations.

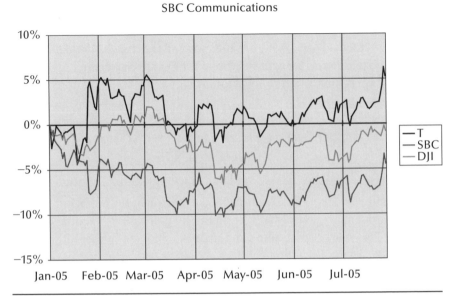

EXHIBIT 13.4   STOCK CHART FOR SBC AND AT&T

The regulators may disallow the merger or require certain structural changes (e.g., selling off of certain market segments) to meet antitrust criteria.

An interesting case was the merger of Travelers with Citicorp to form Citigroup in 1998. Citigroup became the first American bank with over $1 trillion in assets—a really big bank. The problem was it violated federal law, the Depression era Glass-Steagall Act, which separated commercial from investment banking. Citigroup was one of the largest commercial banks, and Travelers included Salomon Smith Barney, a big investment bank. As a policy matter, regulators were approving mergers. Shortly after the merger, the Gramm-Leach-Bliley Act of 1999 allowed combinations of commercial and investment banks.

More brutal was the busy acquisition activity of telecoms following the Telecommunications Act of 1996. This was a deregulation bill, with the goal of allowing anyone into any part of telecom (especially local and long distance, cable programming, video services, and broadcasting). AT&T tried to be an integrated player as its long-distance market dried up and botched it badly; AT&T was acquired by SBC. The combined company assumed the AT&T brand name on December 1, 2005. Bell Atlantic bought GTE in 2000 in a $52 billion deal to become the number one telecom Verizon. Global Crossing and WorldCom were major telecom acquisition players and seemed to specialize in acquisition fraud. Enron made strange acquisitions to dominate broadband and then hide the disasters in SPEs.

APPENDIX 13.1

MAJOR RECENT DOW ACQUISITIONS

Company	Acquisitions
Citigroup (C)	First American Bank in 2005; 2004: KorAm Bank and Washington Mutual Financial; 1998 Citicorp/Travelers merger ($70 billion) busted Glass-Steagall.
Exxon-Mobil (XOM)	Mobil in 1999.
General Electric (GE)	Amercham ($11.3 billion, goodwill, $2.7 billion); completed VUE (Universal).
Hewlett-Packard (HPQ)	Compaq in 2002 ($24 billion, $14.5 billion in goodwill); minor in 2004.
IBM (IBM)	14 acquisitions, total $2.1 billion, goodwill $1.4 billion (67.8%); acquired PWC Consulting in 2002, $3.9 billion.
J.P. Morgan (JPM)	Chase Manhattan in 2001; Bank One in 2004, $58.5 billion, goodwill, $34.1 billion.
Pfizer (PFE)	Pharmacia, 2003, $56 billion, $21.4 billion in goodwill; Warner-Lambert in 2002; minor in 2004.
Procter & Gamble (PG)	PG announced the acquisition of major competitor Gillette in January, 2005 for about $57 billion; the acquisition was completed in late 2005.
SBC Communications (SBC)	AT&T Wireless, $41 billion; AT&T completed in 2005, about $16 billion (2005). Combined company called AT&T beginning December 1, 2005.
United Technology (UTX)	2004 acquisitions, $1.3 billion.
Verizon (VZ)	Bell Atlantic acquired GTE in 2000 to form Verizon, $52 billion.

Appendix 13.2

Dow 30 Goodwill

Company	Goodwill*	Total Assets*	Goodwill/ Total Assets
3M Co.	$ 2,655	$ 20,708	12.8%
Alcoa Inc.	6,541	33,609	19.5%
Altria Group Inc.	28,056	101,648	27.6%
American Express	2,192	192,638	1.1%
American International Group	8,601	798,660	1.1%
Boeing Co.	1,948	53,963	3.6%
Caterpillar Inc.	1,450	43,091	3.4%
Coca-Cola Co.	1,097	31,327	3.5%
Citigroup Inc.	31,992	1,484,101	2.2%
Disney (Walt) Co.	16,966	53,902	31.5%
Du Pont (E.I.) De Nemours	2,082	35,632	5.8%
Exxon-Mobil Corp.	7,836	195,256	4.0%
General Electric Co.	71,191	750,507	9.5%
General Motors Corp.	3,874	479,603	0.8%
Hewlett-Packard Co.	15,828	76,138	20.8%
Home Depot Inc.	1,394	38,907	3.6%
Honeywell International Inc.	6,013	31,062	19.4%
Intel Corp.	3,719	48,143	7.7%
International Business Machines Corp.	8,437	109,183	7.7%
Johnson & Johnson	5,863	53,317	11.9%
J.P. Morgan Chase & Co.	$43,203	$1,157,248	3.7%
McDonald's Corp.	1,828	27,838	6.6%
Merck & Co.	1,086	42,573	2.6%
Microsoft Corp.	3,115	92,389	3.4%
Pfizer Inc.	23,756	123,684	19.2%
Procter & Gamble Co.	19,610	57,048	34.4%
SBC Communications Inc.	1,625	108,844	1.5%
United Technologies Corp.	10,111	40,035	25.3%
Verizon Communications	837	165,958	0.5%
Wal-Mart Stores	10,803	120,223	9.0%
Average	$11,457	$6,567,235	10.1%

* In millions.

14

Dishonorable Mention: The Rest of the Dirty 30

We view [derivatives] as time bombs, both for the parties that deal in them and the economic system.
—Warren Buffett

The business pages of American newspapers should not resemble a scandal sheet.
—George W. Bush

The issues keep coming. Manipulative genius can turn up anywhere to fudge the numbers or gum up the disclosures. Because public disclosures are limited, discovering the earnings magic signals is an art, not a science. Exhibit 14.1 lists the rest of the Dirty 30 worth considering. It should be pointed out that several of these items did not make the big list only because detection is so difficult, not that they are less important.

Issue	Discussion
	Detailed Ratio Analysis
Working Capital and Liquidity	Reasonable amounts of cash and working capital (current assets minus current liabilities) are needed to pay the bills as they come due. Some companies make a practice of little cash and negative working capital—seemingly a poor liquidity strategy.
Receivables and Inventory	Receivables and inventory both tie into revenue and can be used as a check on revenue recognition behavior. Increasing inventory (beyond increasing sales) may signal obsolete inventory. Big increases in receivables suggest lowering of credit terms to increase sales (and other possible aggressive revenue recognition techniques).

(continues)

EXHIBIT 14.1   SOME DIRTY 30 ISSUES WORTH CONSIDERING

Issue	Discussion
	Detailed Ratio Analysis
Reserve Accounts (Continued)	Reserve for bad debts is the most common reserve account and the only one almost always recorded in the annual report. However, there can be hundreds of reserve accounts, most with the potential for "cookie jar" reserve status made infamous by former SEC chair Arthur Levitt.
Cash from Operations and Free Cash Flow	Earnings can be considered an accounting artifact. Ultimately, cash must be generated to measure performance. Measures of cash from operations and free cash flow are a useful check on real bottom-line performance.
Credit Risk and Leverage	Companies have a real risk of defaulting on debt and declaring bankruptcy, real investment downers. High-leverage companies may be paying big bucks on interest with detrimental consequences to performance and credit risk.
Selling, General and Administrative, Research and Development	SG&A and R&D can be big expense categories in some industries and out of control for certain companies. These are items that should be evaluated, looking for trends over time and relative to competitors.
Comprehensive Income	Dirty surplus gains and losses are not part of net income but reported directly to stockholders' equity. These are real gains and losses and should be part of earnings analysis.
	Complex Accounting Issues
Risk Management and Derivatives	Global companies face all kinds of risk, from economic collapse, to natural disaster, to big legal liabilities. Derivatives are used to hedge for some of these risks. (Currency fluctuations and interest rates are most commonly disclosed.) Derivatives are complex and can be used to speculate rather than hedge.
Contingencies	It seems that all major companies are sued, some quite regularly. They are also subject to extensive regulations. The current state of outstanding contingencies is reported in a note, which can be long. This is from the company's perspective and is not expected to be particularly unbiased, but it suggests possible big problems. Contingencies are especially severe for some industries, including tobacco, chemicals, and pharmaceuticals.
Equity Method and Joint Ventures	Less than 50% ownership of a subsidiary changes everything for accounting. The "49%" solution means the equity method—not consolidation. Spin-offs of something over half a sub suggest this earnings magic solution. A 50-50 joint venture also requires the equity method—great for sharing risks and magic tricks.
Divestitures	Big corporations may simultaneously be acquiring companies and divesting of other operations. This suggests a changing business strategy that may result from changing circumstances but suggests bad decisions in the past.

(continues)

EXHIBIT 14.1   SOME DIRTY 30 ISSUES WORTH CONSIDERING (CONTINUED)

Issue	Discussion
Complex Accounting Issues	
Taxes	Companies pay big bucks to minimize taxes, and most are good at it. Tax accounting also can be deceptive and occasionally illegal. It is worth checking the effective tax rate and other indicators of unusual amounts.
Pro Forma Earnings	These are non-GAAP earnings measures and could be anything the company is creative enough to come up with. The only logical reason for using pro forma earnings is to present earnings numbers that are much better than GAAP and therefore not very meaningful.
Segment Reporting	Limited information is presented by major operating and geographic segments. Look for poor segment performance (especially return on sales) and what it may mean—perhaps bad acquisitions or bad business strategy.
Auditing and Corporate Governance	
Audit Report and Timely Reporting	The auditor's report is likely signed by a Big Four firm to be a clean opinion (no qualifications), and have a report date shortly after the end of the fiscal year—a late date may suggest disputes with the auditor. Companies have to report 10-Ks within 60 days and 10-Qs within 30 days (2006). Companies that do not make the dates deserve a red flag; companies that barely make the dates may be having problems.
Audit Fees	Total audit fees include audit-related, tax, and other fees. Lack of auditor independence is more likely when nonaudit fees are particularly high.
Board Composition	Thanks to Sarbanes-Oxley, the majority of board members must be independent. Lack of independence has been a problem in the past but should be a nonissue today; is still worth checking.
Executive Compensation and Role of the CEO	Companies must report top executive compensation in the proxy statement. Is the compensation reasonable, given the performance of the firm? Most CEOs of the giant corporations also chair the board. This suggests too much power and greater potential for abuse.
Related-Party Transactions and Insider Trading	Sweetheart deals with executives, directors, and other insiders may indicate other potential problems. Companies must report the buying and selling of stock by executives, directors, and other insiders (reported to the SEC and available from various Web sites, including Yahoo!). Big sell-offs may signal impending disaster.
Internal Control Reports	Thanks to Sarbanes-Oxley, both senior executives and auditors must sign off on internal control. Weak controls may signal current or future problems.
Other Issues	
Restated Earnings and Regulatory Investigations	Restating earnings (and other financial statement information) is a likely red flag signaling blatant earnings

(continues)

EXHIBIT 14.1   SOME DIRTY 30 ISSUES WORTH CONSIDERING (CONTINUED)

Issue	Discussion
	Other Issues
Restated Earnings and Regulatory Investigations (Continued)	magic. Unfortunately, restatements are now more common than in the past. When the SEC and other government regulators start an investigation, it is bad news. Regulatory responses suggest evidence of earnings magic and the potential for financial fiascos.
Stock Prices: What Does the Market Tell Us?	The market goes up and down but responds to specific events. When a big event happens, how does the market react? Euphoria means a run-up; catastrophe means losses. Stock price changes can provide important information.

EXHIBIT 14.1   SOME DIRTY 30 ISSUES WORTH CONSIDERING (CONTINUED)

DETAILED RATIO ANALYSIS

Specific areas can be analyzed in more quantitative detail, looking for indicators of relative earnings quality and magic. Basic data usually are available from a combination of financial statement and notes, and analysis may be combined in several ways. For example, revenue recognition should also include reviewing receivables, inventory, and bad debts reserves. When issues exist, there are often multiple signals.

Working Capital and Liquidity

Working capital is net current assets (total current assets – total current liabilities), one measure of liquidity. Because cash and other current assets are needed to pay current obligations, negative working capital can be an issue. Cash is important, partly because of the economic focus on cash flows. Cash equivalents usually are defined as high-quality debt-marketable securities due within 90 days. Managing cash is easier if there is a large sum. The alternative to the big pile of cash theory is that better investment alternatives should be available.

The Dow 30 should have great liquidity, which was generally true in 2004. The average current ratio (current assets / current liabilities) was 1.4, with a substantial variance. Microsoft had a current ratio of 4.7, but 12 of the Dow had negative working capital, including whopping negative balances by the two big banks. However, the banks do not separate short-term from long-term assets and liabilities, and the amounts are estimates. GM had negative working capital of $13 billion (current ratio, 86.8%), while SBC was negative $10 billion (current ratio, 45.1%). Other nonfinancial firms with negative working capital were Boeing, McDonald's, Procter & Gamble, Verizon, Wal-Mart, and Disney.

Most of the Dow had large amounts of cash, with an average cash ratio (cash including cash equivalents / current liabilities) of 59%. Three had ratios greater than 100% (AIG, Intel, and Microsoft), while three had ratios less than 10% (Alcoa, Caterpillar, SBC); the range was 2.7% for Caterpillar to Microsoft at 405%. SBC was the only Dow 30 firm with both negative working capital and a cash ratio below 10%. Liquidity also is part of credit risk, and low-liquidity firms should be evaluated carefully for other credit risk characteristics, especially high leverage.

Receivables and Inventory

Accounts and notes receivable are the amounts due on credit sales, reported on the balance sheet net of allowance for doubtful accounts. The relative magnitude of receivables and their relationship to sales are the first consideration. The expected balances and ratios depend on competitor and industry characteristics as well as comparisons over time. What is not apparent are the relative credit terms given by the corporations. Relaxing credit standards can increase sales. However, bad debts would increase. The optimum level of credit sales is difficult to estimate, but extreme changes in credit terms can be determined. Large and growing receivables suggest declining credit terms. Corporations that use aggressive revenue recognition have relatively higher receivables. Receivables will tend to grow faster than sales, and the average days receivable will increase. The key indicator is a receivables balance growing at a much higher rate than sales. The bad debts percent, when compared over time and to direct competitors, indicates the relative level of credit terms and changes in credit terms.

Companies can dispose of their receivables. The most common method is factoring, essentially selling a portfolio of receivables to a financial intermediary specializing in factoring. Doing this has the advantage of removing some percent of the receivables from the balance sheet, but it is a relatively expensive form of financing. A more recent alternative is to transfer the receivables to an SPE. It has essentially the same effect as factoring for removing the receivables from the balance sheet, but at a lower cost. Banks and financial firms securitize substantial amounts of receivables using SPEs. This information may or may not be well disclosed in the annual report.

In some industries, inventory is the most critical asset for analysis. Retail firms can have large inventory levels on store shelves and in warehouses. Wal-Mart is considered one of the most efficient retailers, but inventory was 76.5% of current assets and 24.5% of total assets for 2004. The relative level of inventory is a sign of efficiency in manufacturing (the lower the better), and inventory levels vary by company and industry. Microsoft was the efficiency champ among the high-tech firms, with inventory at 0.6% of current assets (compared to 7.1% at IBM, 10.9% at Intel, and 16.5% at Hewlett-Packard).

A key area of concern is obsolete inventory items and goods that are slow sellers. Certain fashionable items are vulnerable to slow selling and potential write-downs, such as toys and apparel. Hot items can make a bundle for the manufacturers and retailers. Mistakes can mean large losses and massive write-offs. High-tech hardware and software are subject to quick obsolescence. Generally accepted accounting principles (GAAP) require write-downs to market value. Companies have considerable flexibility here, especially before year-end. Corporations may not be quick to write these off and take the losses, especially if the lower income affects bonuses and other compensation rewards. Once the auditors arrive, flexibility diminishes. Unless specifically discussed in the annual report, determining overstated inventory is difficult but can be attempted by looking at inventory levels over time.

Inventory and receivables changes should be proportional to sales changes. If sales go up 10% a year, it is reasonable to expect receivables and inventory also to rise about 10% a year. Unusually large inventory or receivables changes without comparable sales growth may indicate problems. With luck, additional inventory information may be available from the Management Discussion and Analysis (MD&A) or notes. The business media and SEC investigations also may indicate inventory problems. The four high-tech firms had sales increases between 2003 and 2004 of 8.0% to 14.1%, with inventory and receivables increases roughly proportional. The one exception was Microsoft, which had the 14.1% increase in sales (and 13.4% increase in receivables) but a 34.2% decrease in inventory, probably due to increased efficiency.

Receivables averaged almost $14 billion for the Dow 30 in 2004, up 18% from the previous year, while revenues increased 12%. Receivables were particularly big for the financials, because they included loan portfolios: $53 billion for J.P. Morgan and $51 billion for GE. Nonfinancials with large receivables included IBM at $30 billion and H-P at $22 billion. Particularly important as potential earnings magic signals were receivables increases much bigger than revenue gains. Du Pont had revenue increases of only 1% for 2004, but receivables increased 20%; GM saw a decline in revenues of about 1%, while receivables increased almost 13%. GM announced in an 8-K issued on November 9, 2005 that it had incorrectly recorded supplier credits as revenue and would restate financial statements from 2001–2005. At the other extreme, AIG had revenue growth of 20.5%, while receivables declined over 50%. This change could be from securitizing receivables, but this was not obvious from the annual report.

Inventory averaged $4.7 billion for the Dow 30, up 2% for the year and about 6% of revenues. Given revenue growth averaging 12%, this average suggests greater inventory efficiency. Boeing, Du Pont, GM, and Merck had large drops in inventory. CAT and Verizon had large increases in inventory, 53.4% at CAT and 93.7% at Verizon. The increase at CAT is partially explained because of a 33% increase in revenues, but revenues grew only 5% at Verizon. This is a signal of possible obsolete inventory at Verizon; however, the inventory amount is relatively small at $2.5 billion (3% of revenues).

Reserve Accounts

Reserve accounts exist for most asset categories. These accounts include allowance for doubtful accounts for receivables, reserves for overstated inventory (reduced value, obsolescence, or other measures of impaired value), investment impairments, and so on. Concerns exist on the relative value of the reserves, changes in reserves (e.g., reduced reserves to increase income in the current quarter to meet earnings targets), and the existence of impaired assets that have not been written down.

Arthur Levitt (Levitt and Dwyer 2002) railed against "cookie jar" reserves, essentially excess reserves that can be tapped in "bad years" to smooth earnings. Microsoft was overstating multiple reserve accounts, according to a 2002 SEC Accounting Proceeding, and a cease-and-desist order was issued. Sun Trust Banks restated earnings for 1994 to 1997 because it overstated its provision for loan losses. Similarly, National City Bancorp (a bank holding company) restated earnings in 1999 after identifying a "special reserve" that reduced loans receivable at subsidiary Diversified Business Credit.

The only reserve account likely to be presented in an annual report is the allowance for doubtful accounts. The allowance should be a reasonable percent of sales and stay relatively constant (roughly increasing with sales). Intel had an allowance of $43 million in 2004 (only 1.4% of receivables), down from 1.9% in 2003. Revenues for 2004 increased 13.5%, while receivables increased 1.3%. Perhaps this represents more efficient credit policies, but it is a signal of possible earnings magic to meet earnings targets. By comparison, IBM's allowance was 2.6% in 2004, down from 3.5% in the previous year. The allowance account would not be expected to decrease.

Twenty-four of the Dow 30 presented bad debts reserve information. Reserves averaged $1.5 billion (or 2% of receivables), but were particularly big at financial firms that included loan portfolios. Citigroup had reserves of $11.3 billion, but this was only 2.1% of receivables. Nineteen of the Dow (79% of 24 reporting) recorded decreases in reserve percentages in 2004, 8 over a 20% decrease (Alcoa, Citigroup, H-P, Intel, Microsoft, United Technology, and Verizon). This is a potential warning of earnings magic. Microsoft headed the list, with a drop of over 31%; the bad debts reserve was 2.7% of receivables but about 0.5% of revenues. All four high-tech companies had a double-digit drop in reserve percentage. Did they fudge the numbers to meet analyst's forecasts, or were they just more confident of higher collection rates?

The Wall Street Journal reported that both General Motors and Ford were dipping into cookie-jar funds to offset bad debts (McCracken 2005). The companies were putting less money into the reserves each quarter in 2005 (by reducing bad debts expense) to prop up earnings—actually reducing quarterly losses in 2005. Consequently, GM's loan-loss provisions (for General Motors Acceptance Corp.) at the end of the third quarter 2005 dropped to $915 million, down 36% from 2004.

Cash from Operations and Free Cash Flow

Essentially the cash flow statement is restated information with a different perspective: cash. The statement provides additional information on the liquidity of the company and its ability to finance operations and growth from internal funds. It can highlight certain problems, such as lagging cash collections or the relative need for operating capital. Cash from operations (CFO) is an alternative definition of performance, roughly equivalent to removing the impact of accruals. CFO tends to parallel net income. When the trends between these two numbers change, earnings magic is a possible cause. Most often, CFO is positive because net income is normally positive, and noncash expenses such as depreciation increase CFO. Cash flows from investing (CFI) include capital expenditures and investments. Generally CFI is negative because investments are uses of cash. Cash flow from financing (CFF) includes the acquisition or disposal of equity or debt and the payment of dividends. The Dow 30 had an average CFO of $9.9 billion, 47% above net income. However, three (Caterpillar, Citigroup, and J.P. Morgan) had negative CFO, while net incomes were positive—a possible signal of earnings hanky panky. The basic reason for negative CFO for these three was increases in other current asset accounts. Citi had an increase in trading accounts receivable of $43 billion and a decrease in federal funds sold of $28 billion. Morgan had an increase in trading accounts receivable of $49 billion. CAT had increases in both receivables and inventory.

Free cash flow (FCF) is a measure of cash available for discretionary uses after making required cash outlays. Although there are several potential calculations, the basic concept is cash from operations less capital expenditures. Presumably, this measures available cash net of maintaining existing productive capacity. An alternative calculation is cash from operations less cash from investments (CFO − CFI). Only three firms had a negative FCF as defined as CFO less capital expenditures, the same three as had negative CFO: CAT, Citi, and Morgan. When defined as CFO less CFI, nine had negative CFI. GM had a FCF (defined as CFO − CFI) of almost $48 billion, but this is explained by increasing investments of $49 billion. Both CFO and FCF can be used as reality checks on performance. "Real earnings" should result in cash.

Credit Risk and Leverage

Credit risk is associated with possible default on debt or the probability of bankruptcy. Leverage is the relative mix of debt and equity. As leverage increases, credit risk rises. Most liabilities require a specified cash payment at a stated due date. If not paid, the company is in default. Standard financial analysis techniques are used to evaluate default risk. Red flags associated with increasing risk include low liquidity, high leverage, poor or erratic earnings, declining sales, and negative cash flows from operations. When firms have operating or liquidity problems, earnings magic techniques to camouflage existing problems are more likely. In most cases, multiple red flags are expected.

Generally the higher the leverage, the greater the credit risk. However, leverage levels vary by industry. Banks and other finance industries rely on deposits and other debt instruments; consequently, they have high leverage. Companies that have substantial financial components, such as GM and GE, also have relatively high leverage. Standard leverage ratios include debt-to-equity, long-term debt-to-equity, debt ratio (total liabilities / total assets), and interest coverage (interest expense / earnings before interest and taxes [EBIT]).

Many of the Dow 30 had high leverage ratios. First of all, this is expected from banks (Citigroup and J.P. Morgan), other financial firms (American Express and AIG), and other firms that have large financial components (GE, GM, and to a lesser extent Caterpillar). As expected, these are the firms with high leverage ratios (e.g., firms with long-term debt-to-equity greater than 1). The banks and financial companies had debt ratios of about 90%, indicating that equity was about 10% of total assets—not unreasonable for these firms. GM had a debt ratio of 94.4%, or equity of 5.6%. Even considering GMAC, this is a low level of equity for a manufacturing firm and a red flag. Nonfinancial firms with debt ratios greater than 70% include Altria (73.9%), Boeing (79.1%), IBM (72.8%), and Verizon (77.4%). Interest coverage measures the impact of interest expense relative to operating earnings as measured by EBIT. Fourteen of the Dow 30 had interest coverage greater than 10% (8 were nonfinancial firms). Particularly striking was GM's 76.0%, over three-quarters of operating earnings.

Several multivariate models have been developed to predict bankruptcy. Basically, a sample of bankrupt firms is matched to a comparable sample of nonbankrupt firms and a set of ratios is used to correctly classify firms as bankrupt or nonbankrupt. The best known of these models was developed by Altman (1983) for industrial firms, including his 1983 model:

$6.56 \times$ (working capital / total assets—a measure of liquidity)

$+ 3.26 \times$ (retained earnings / total assets—a measure of accumulated profit)

$+ 6.72 \times$ (EBIT / total assets—a performance measure)

$+ 1.05 \times$ (book value of equity / book value of debt—leverage)

Under this model the Z-score cutoffs are:

less than 1.1	bankrupt
1.10 − 2.6	gray area
greater than 2.6	healthy

This Z-score model can be used as a general indicator of financial health. A Z-score below 1.1 does not mean the company will go bankrupt, but signals a potential credit risk problem. Three of the industrial firms (it does not work well for financial firms)—GM, Boeing, and Verizon—had failing Z-scores primarily because of low liquidity and high leverage.

Bond ratings are issued by Moody's and Standard & Poor's (S&P), among others. These ratings indicated the agencies' evaluation of the creditworthiness of the firms. Most investors typically consider only investment-grade bonds, those from BBB to AAA. Below that are speculative or junk bonds (with many junk bonds unrated). As the bond rating declines, the interest rate goes up to attract investors when default risk is high. Successful companies according to financial ratios are expected to have healthy Z-scores and high bond ratings. Bond rating agencies can react quickly to changing circumstances, especially bad news.

Most of the Dow 30, among the oldest, biggest, and most prestigious of firms, would have mainly AAA ratings. Right? Alas, such is not the case. Only GE, Exxon-Mobil, Johnson & Johnson, and Pfizer had AAA ratings (S&P ratings). Altria and Disney had the lowest investment-grade ratings at BBB. GM had been barely holding on to investment grade at BBB−, but S&P downgraded GM bonds (Ford also) to BB in May 2005—the humiliation

Company	Debt Ratio	Interest Coverage	Altman's	Bond Rating	Current Ratio
Altria	73.9%	10.9%	3.09	BBB	99.9%
Boeing	79.1	25.9	0.85	A	72.4
Caterpillar	82.7	21.7	2.22	A	128.7
Disney	51.6	14.4	2.27	BBB+	140.6
General Motors	94.4	76.0	0.16	BB	86.8
SBC	62.8	12.5	1.38	A	45.1
Verizon	77.4	19.1	0.92	A+	84.2

EXHIBIT 14.2   SUMMARY INFORMATION ON DOW 30 FIRMS WITH HIGH CREDIT RISK

of a Dow 30 having a junk bond rating! This can be considered a red flag for GM's credit risk.

Summary information on Dow 30 firms with high credit risk is shown in Exhibit 14.2.

These seven companies have high debt ratios, and interest expense was more than 10% of operating earnings. Three have failing Altman Z-scores, five have negative working capital, and three have BBB ratings or below. GM signals credit risk problems on all dimensions. These are the companies most likely to hide additional debt, especially through off–balance sheet schemes, and are expected to have other financial problems.

Selling, General and Administrative; Research and Development

Selling, general and administrative (SG&A) expenses are "overhead" items with considerable operating flexibility. Many unrelated costs can be "dumped" into SG&A, and the process is not standardized. For example, the distinction of how overhead items should be allocated to cost of sales, SG&A, and other income statement line items is not obvious. Research and development (R&D) costs are expensed as incurred; R&D costs can be reduced only by decreasing current R&D.

Both SG&A and R&D vary by industry and business strategy differences. Dell has relatively low R&D costs, while competitor Apple has substantial R&D—a difference in business strategy. Retailers usually have large SG&A (primarily marketing costs) but low R&D. SG&A for 2004 was 22.6% of sales for Home Depot and 17.7% for Wal-Mart, while R&D was essentially zero for both. The pharmaceuticals companies have large expenses in both categories but relatively low cost of sales, as shown for 2004 (in millions) in Exhibit 14.3.

	Pfizer*	% of Sales	J&J*	% of Sales	Merck*	% of Sales
Sales	$52,516	100.0%	$47,348	100.0%	$22,939	100.0%
Cost of Sales	7,541	14.4	13,422	28.3	4,960	21.6
SG&A	16,903	32.2	15,860	33.5	7,346	32.0
R&D	7,684	14.6	5,203	11.0	4,010	17.5

* In millions.

EXHIBIT 14.3   SG&A, R&D, AND COST OF SALES FOR 2004 (PHARMACEUTICALS)

All three have SG&A at about a third of sales and R&D over 10%. Because R&D is central to their business, more spending on R&D and less on SG&A would seem to be the desired strategy.

Across the Dow 30, SG&A average a substantial 29.1% of revenue. Four firms had SG&A greater than 40% of revenues, including Disney (86.8%), J.P. Morgan (49.8%), Citigroup (50.4%), and American Express (46.1%). The two pharmaceuticals firms were among eight firms with SG&A between 30% and 40% of revenues. Alcoa (at 5.5%) and Boeing (7.0%) were the SG&A efficiency champs with SG&A less than 10% of revenues. R&D averaged only 3.7% of revenues, with five firms above 10% of revenues. In addition to the pharmaceutical companies were high-tech firms Microsoft at 21.1% and Intel at 14.0%.

Comprehensive Income

Net income is a relatively complete profitability measure, because it includes nonrecurring items and other unusual items in addition to normal operating income. However, not all gains and losses are included in net income; a number of items are recorded directly to the balance sheet, resulting in the "dirty surplus" previously mentioned.

The advantage of comprehensive income (CI) is that it includes absolutely all revenues, expenses, gains, and losses, consistent with the all-inclusive concept of earnings. A rationale for other comprehensive income (OCI) is that these tend to be items that zero out over time (e.g., foreign currency fluctuates with the changing value of the dollar). Of particular concern is the potential to eliminate important although unrealized gains and losses (particularly losses) from the income statement. GM has struggled to make a buck, with 2004 net income of $2.8 billion, only 1.4% of revenues. However, other comprehensive income for 2004 was a net loss of $2.9 billion. Thus, GM had a negative CI of $80 million, 3% of net income. This was mainly from a $3 billion pension liability adjustment, which followed a comprehensive loss of $3.6 billion in 2003. Boeing also had a negative CI, $53 million compared to net income of $1.9 billion.

Across the Dow 30, the average firm had a net other comprehensive loss of $334 million; average net income was $6.6 billion and CI was $6.3 billion. Twenty had other comprehensive losses, with GE leading the way with a $7.2 billion loss (43% of net income). The primary factor was foreign currency losses associated with the declining dollar. AIG had a $9.6 billion OCI, which would almost double net income on a comprehensive basis. Foreign currency losses were more than offset by unrealized gains on investments and cash flow derivatives. In addition to the two comprehensive loss firms, CI was at least 20% lower for five additional companies: CAT, Coca-Cola, Du Pont, GE, and Pfizer.

COMPLEX ACCOUNTING ISSUES

Complex accounting issues are areas where qualitative analysis usually works best, based on information in the notes and MD&A. The issues often are industry- and company-based. For example, contingencies are especially critical for evaluating chemical, tobacco, and pharmaceutical companies. The equity method is common for some firms (e.g., Coca-Cola), and joint ventures are widely used in industries such as oil and gas.

Risk Management and Derivatives

Risk management attempts to reduce or control the multitude of risks associated with a complex corporation. Some risks are outlined in Exhibit 14.4. (The complete list is essentially endless.)

Corporations can use hedges to manage specific risks. Natural hedges include matching asset and liability interest rates or foreign currencies. Derivatives are the most common form of artificial hedges. Hedges can reduce most of the risks shown in Exhibit 14.4; however, all financial and operating risks cannot be eliminated simultaneously.

Commodity Risk	Changing prices of commodities such as agricultural goods, industrial metals, oil, and other energy products.
Interest Rate Risk	Interest rate fluctuations, complicated by fixed versus variable rates and duration (maturity dates).
Market Value Risk	Price fluctuations for items that trade on a market, including stocks, credit instruments, and currencies.
Foreign Exchange Risk	Currency fluctuations against all other currencies, creating substantial risks for global corporations.

EXHIBIT 14.4 EXAMPLES OF RISKS

A derivative is a financial contract *derived* from another contract, event, or transaction. Complex financial arrangements can be made by using derivatives, always for specific reasons. Common derivatives involve options, futures and forwards, swaps, and collars. The basic derivative strategy expected from major corporations is attempting to reduce or manage various market risks. Reducing risks on financial instruments and currency fluctuations in a complex global market is expected.

Speculating can be the strategy actually used. The problem is to determine to what extent derivatives exist to effectively reduce various financial and other market risks and volatility (and in some cases operating risks) and when a company is doing a poor job hedging or is in fact speculating, which increases financial risks.

Two groups specialize in using derivatives, banks and hedge funds. Derivatives are a major revenue source for banks, which make markets and establish specialized derivatives to meet the needs of customers. Banks use credit derivatives to pass on default risks as part of securitization, often using special-purpose entities (SPEs), such as synthetic collateralized debt obligations. They also trade for their own accounts. It is not clear to what extent the big banks are using derivatives as risk management tools or as revenue generators with built-in extreme risk. Warren Buffett called derivatives "weapons of mass destruction."

Hedge funds can hedge or speculate on virtually anything to make a buck. The infamous Long-Term Capital Management (LTCM) was extremely successful until the markets went awry in 1998. LTCM borrowed to make trillion-dollar bets, about a thousand times its capital. It took a Federal Reserve–sponsored bailout to unload these positions, presumably saving the economies of the western world but not LTCM. It is safe to say that huge bets mean big risks, no matter how smart the investor.

The use of derivatives as part of corporate strategy gets complex quickly, and detecting earnings management strategies that increase risk is difficult. Despite the difficulty, risk management and derivatives use disclosures should be evaluated for relative effectiveness. The typical financial analysis strategy includes the evaluation of objectives of derivatives used, the risk exposure of the corporation, hedging effectiveness, and disclosures that indicate whether derivatives are used for trading or speculation.

As expected, the Dow 30 are big users of derivatives. The banks and other financial institutions make markets in derivative instruments and literally use every derivative category imaginable. Most industrials use interest rate and foreign currency derivatives (e.g., swaps, forward contracts, or options); firms using commodities (including Alcoa and Du Pont) often have commodity futures and other derivatives to price-protect themselves. Only

Alcoa (AA)	Futures contracts for aluminum, fuel, electricity, etc., interest rate swaps (pay floating, receive fixed), cross-currency interest rate swaps, foreign currency exchange contracts, power supply contracts that contain pricing provisions related to the London Metal Exchange (LME) aluminum price. The LME linked pricing features are considered embedded derivatives, Alcoa has also entered into certain derivatives to minimize its price risk related to aluminum purchases. Alcoa has not qualified these contracts for hedge accounting treatment. Therefore, the fair value gains and losses on these contracts are recorded in earnings.
Boeing (BA)	Interest rate swaps, cross-currency swaps, foreign currency forward contracts, and commodity purchase contracts, Boeing also holds certain nonhedging instruments, such as interest exchange agreements, interest rate swaps, warrants, conversion feature of convertible debt, and foreign currency forward contracts. Boeing held forward-starting interest rate swap agreements to fix the cost of funding a firmly committed lease for which payment terms are determined in advance of funding.
General Motors (GM)	Hedge exposure to foreign currency exchange risk, hedge exposure to commodity price changes, hedge exposure to interest rate risk, forward contracts, and options.
Intel (INTC)	Warrants and equity conversion rights, currency forward contracts, currency options, currency interest rate swaps and currency investments and borrowings, equity options swaps, or forward contracts.
McDonald's (MCD)	(1) Interest rate exchange agreements to convert a portion of its fixed-rate debt to floating-rate debt and are designed to reduce the impact of interest rate changes on future interest expense; (2) foreign currency exchange agreements for the exchange of various currencies and interest rates; (3) forward foreign exchange contracts and foreign currency options that are designed to protect against the reduction in value of forecasted foreign currency cash flows such as royalties and other payments denominated in foreign currencies.

Exhibit 14.5   Derivatives Disclosure for Some of the Big Dow 30 Users

a few claim nonhedging derivative usage, such as Boeing. ("We also hold certain non-hedging instruments, such as interest exchange agreements, interest rate swaps, warrants, conversion feature of convertible debt and foreign currency forward contracts.") Exxon-Mobil claimed: "The company's size, geographic diversity and nature of the business mitigate risks, therefore the company makes minimal use of derivative instruments." Disclosure for some of the big users is shown in Exhibit 14.5.

Contingencies

Contingencies and commitments are detailed in the notes, and these should be reviewed carefully, particularly considering the characteristics of the industries involved. Chemical, tobacco, pharmaceutical, and automobile companies are examples of industries where contingencies are likely to be substantial. Generally companies explain the potential obligations but often understate the probability for future claims.

Evaluating contingencies is a qualitative analysis, focusing on note disclosures and other sources. Big new contingencies make the business media headlines, and the results can be stock price disasters. A recent case was Merck's Vioxx recall in September 2004. A stock price drop followed, with class-action lawsuits and government investigations following. Dow's pharmaceutical giants Pfizer and Johnson & Johnson also have substantial contingencies. Pfizer's contingencies include patent infringements, product liability, environmental and tax litigation; government investigations; and personal injury claims for Rezulin, asbestos liabilities, and wholesale price litigation. Johnson & Johnson contingencies include several product liability lawsuits, patent infringement cases, and investigations by the New York State Attorney General, Boston Attorney General, U.S. House of Representatives, Securities and Exchange Commission (SEC), and Inspector General of Personnel Management.

All the companies of the Dow 30 have substantial contingencies, primarily litigation and other legal issues. The biggest factor is industry; in addition to the pharmaceutical firms, Du Pont (chemical) and Altria (tobacco litigation) had substantial concerns. Retailer Home Depot had few concerns, but Wal-Mart had substantial contingencies—unexpected for a retailer. Many of these involved current and former employees, an issue that may impact the future performance of Wal-Mart.

A summary of 2004 contingency disclosures from high-contingency firms is presented in Exhibit 14.6.

AIG	Claims asserting injuries from toxic waste, hazardous substances, and other environmental pollutants and alleged damages to cover the cleanup costs of hazardous waste dump sites and indemnity claims asserting injuries from asbestos ($1.5B). Caremark cases that allege misrepresentation of extent of coverage (class requesting $3.2B), challenging certain insurance brokerage practices related to contingent commissions, shareholder derivative action filed in Delaware Chancery Court alleging breaches of fiduciary duty of loyalty and care against AIG's directors.
Altria	Numerous litigation proceedings relating to smoking-related products. These include a 2000 settlement against Altria for approximately $145B in the Engle class action suit (the judgment has been appealed). Numerous other cases include: smoking and health litigation (failure to warn, gross negligence, design defect, etc.), healthcare cost recovery litigation (brought by insurers and government entities to recover past

(continues)

EXHIBIT 14.6   SUMMARY OF 2004 CONTINGENCY DISCLOSURES FROM HIGH-CONTINGENCY FIRMS

Altria (Continued)	expenditures and cover future expenditures), light/ultralight cigarette cases (deceptive marketing), price discrimination cases, asbestos-related cases (plaintiffs claim that smoking caused the health issue, not asbestos), contraband cases (illegal importation), Italian tax cases (failure to pay), Italian antitrust case.
Boeing	Litigation by U.S. government relating to A-12 aircraft for the U.S. Navy, Evolved Expendable Launch Vehicle program litigation ($2B plus punitive damages) filed by Lockheed Martin (unsure whether unfavorable outcome will occur), shareholder derivative lawsuit claiming that the directors breached their fiduciary duties in failing to put in place adequate internal controls and means of supervision to prevent the EELV incident, Department of Justice and SEC investigations into hiring of an executive, which led to favorable contract awarding to Boeing, BSSI/ICO breach of contract litigation (plaintiffs seeking $2B).
Du Pont	Benlate 50 DF litigation with claims that the product caused crop damage and birth defects, PFOA (perfluorooctanoic acid and its salts) cases (EPA states there could be developmental and other issues associated with exposure to PFOA) and that Du Pont failed to follow administrative regulations relating to the reporting of potential problems. There have been some related lawsuits that were settled for a total of $108M. Synthetic rubber antitrust litigation losses anticipated at $268M; $359M relating to environmental litigation and cleanup programs.
General Motors	Various product defects, employment matters, government regulations relating to safety, emissions, and fuel economy, product warranties, financial services, dealer, supplier, and other contractual relationships, and environmental issues. In management's opinion, these issues are not expected to have a material adverse impact on the company's consolidated financial condition or results of operations.
Merck	Product liability (Vioxx, both in U.S. and abroad), shareholder suits relating to information provided by the company relating to the Vioxx issue, SEC investigation regarding Vioxx, antitrust cases including inflated average wholesale price figures, lawsuits relating to vaccines that caused illness, patent litigation, governmental investigations into revenue recognition issues, environmental cases.
Pfizer	Patent infringement litigation (Lipitor, Celebrex, etc.), product liability (Rezulin, asbestos-related claims, Lipitor, hormone replacement therapy, promotion and sale of certain drugs including Zoloft at inflated average wholesale price figures, shareholder litigation relating to the above-described issues, litigation surrounding the company's effort to prevent importation of drugs from Canada, environmental litigation, etc.

EXHIBIT 14.6   SUMMARY OF 2004 CONTINGENCY DISCLOSURES FROM HIGH-CONTINGENCY FIRMS (CONTINUED)

Equity Method and Joint Ventures

Corporations can invest in other companies without control. For accounting purposes, control means greater than 50% common stock ownership. Accounting control requires consolidation. Investments that are less than 50% change the accounting characteristics and earnings magic strategies. Three categories of ownership are particularly important from an accounting perspective: (1) equity investments below 20% ownership, (2) the equity method, and (3) joint ventures. Equity investments that are acquisitions of less than 20% of outstanding shares presume no significant control, and these shares are treated as marketable securities

The equity method normally is used with ownership between 20% and 50% of shares. The rationale is that the investor has significant influence but not control. Under this method, the acquisition is recorded at cost (purchase price) as a long-term investment. The parent's share of net income is recorded as income and an increase in investment. Cash-dividend payments are recorded as an increase in cash and a decrease in investment.

Coca-Cola Company is the world leader in soft drinks. Despite having over $16 billion in revenue and $11 billion in equity in 2004, Coca-Cola does no bottling. This is left to "bottling partners" around the world. What Coke does is sell the concentrate at a high margin to the bottlers; the bottlers' margins are much lower. The bottlers can be: (1) independent, (2) investments of Coca-Cola using the equity method, or (3) subsidiaries, where Coca-Cola has a controlling interest and full consolidation is used. Investments in the independent bottlers (i.e., Coca-Cola has less than 20% of the equity) are available-for-sale marketable securities recorded at fair value and gains and losses recorded as other comprehensive income. In terms of book value, almost all the bottlers are recorded under the equity method, $6 billion, 19.1% of total assets (with $344 million as marketable securities). Currently, none of the bottlers is consolidated.

Coca-Cola uses the equity method for the major bottling affiliates. The equity investments for 2004 are shown in Exhibit 14.7.

The market value of Coca-Cola Enterprises (CCE) was $10.3 billion in July 2005, making it the largest bottling company in the world. Coca-Cola owned 36% of CCE, plenty for effective control. CCE was created as a 1986 spin-off from Coca-Cola. Bottling has a much lower profit margin, and CCE has a massive amount of debt, which is no longer on the books of Coca-Cola.

Equity Method Investments	2004*	2003*
Coca-Cola Enterprises	$1,569	$1,260
Coca-Cola Amatil Lmt.	1,733	1,697
Coca-Cola HBC	1,528	1,326
Other	1,147	966
Total	$5,977	$5,249

* In millions.

EXHIBIT 14.7   COCA-COLA EQUITY INVESTMENTS FOR 2004

White et al. (2003) list three distortions associated with the equity method: (1) profitability is overstated, (2) liabilities are hidden, and (3) considerable information is lost. The proportionate share of income is included, but most of the assets are excluded; therefore, return on assets is overstated. Because income is reported net, revenues and expenses of the affiliate are excluded and return on sales is overstated. Affiliate liabilities are excluded (another possible form of off–balance sheet accounting), understating leverage. Information loss includes the lack of information on assets, liabilities, commitments, and contingencies of the affiliate.

Joint ventures (JVs) are contractual arrangements with other corporations to form a separate legal entity, usually a corporation or partnership. The JV could be central to the operation of the parent, or represent a financial arrangement or virtually anything else. The JV would keep its own accounting records, and each partner would record its proportionate share. If the ownership is between 20% and 50% (with 50% the most common arrangement), the equity method is used for accounting.

What is potentially different about a JV is the unique contractual arrangements that may be involved. Virtually anything that can be thought up as a partnership can be contracted as a JV. Examples include major global operations in the primary business of the company, financial agreements, and supplier/customer arrangements. JVs are common in oil and gas, particularly the global integrated corporations, as well as banking and financial organizations.

The joint ventures can be defended as risk-sharing relationships. JVs with foreign countries can have significant political implications and corresponding risks. Risk sharing may include operating risks, financial risks, political risks, and other legal risks that may be global in scale. Simultaneously, accounting issues can cloud the risk-reward relationships. Oil giant Exxon-Mobil has major JVs around the world, including oil drilling in Kazakhstan and Abu Dhabi and liquefied natural gas operations in Qatar.

Twenty-three of the Dow 30 indicate the use of the equity method, including 21 using joint ventures. However, only 2 have equity method investments greater than 10% of net assets, Coca-Cola and SBC. The major equity investment for SBC is Cingular, carried on the books of SBC at $33.7 billion, or 95% of SBC's equity method investments. The interesting part is SBC owns 60% of Cingular and uses the equity method: "since we share control equally [with BellSouth, which owns 40%], we have equal voting rights and representation on the Board of Directors that controls Cingular." Wow! Is this earnings magic brilliance or what?

Divestitures

The other side of combining is divesting, potentially part of a successful business strategy or a change in strategies. Also, parts of a major acquisition may be divested. Various methods exist to divest, from selling a subsidiary to another corporation, to a spin-off, to establishing a JV from a wholly owned subsidiary. However, substantial earnings concerns exist with each divestiture.

The most famous divestiture was the 1984 agreement to break up American Telephone and Telegraph (AT&T). This was the result of an agreement with the Justice Department after a decade-long antitrust case. As AT&T put it:

> The United States woke up on January 1, 1984 to discover that its telephones worked just as they had the day before. But AT&T started today a new company. Of the $149.5 billion in assets it had the day before, it retained $34 billion. Gone even was the famous Bell Logo. (www.att.com)

AT&T has been in the acquisition and divestiture business ever since, trying to figure out how to compete in a newly competitive business. This never happened. AT&T divested AT&T Wireless to SBC in 2004 and was acquired by SBC in 2005.

Fourteen of the Dow 30 reported divestitures in 2004 (5 from earlier years). Generally these were relatively small operations and suggest some changes in business strategy. IBM, for example, sold its Personal Computing Division (completed in 2005) and Altria sold its sugar confectionery business (including Lifesavers). SBC has been selling international businesses, a change in business strategy. The focus is to become noninternational and generate the cash to acquire AT&T, moving toward a domestic integrated telecom. Verizon also is selling various businesses to pay for the acquisition of MCI (the former WorldCom).

Taxes

Objectives are different between financial reporting and tax regulations in the United States. Generally managers want to minimize current taxes. Financial reporting objectives are more complex, with user needs of economic reality tempered by earnings magic incentives. Temporary differences between tax and GAAP (called interperiod tax allocation) are recorded as assets and liabilities. For example, most companies use straight-line depreciation for reporting and accelerated methods for tax. The timing differences "wash out" over the life of the depreciating asset but in the meantime are deferred tax liabilities.

U.S. corporations pay federal, state, and local taxes and global companies pay taxes to foreign governments. The current federal income tax rate is 35%, with companies attempting to reduce current taxes by such means as accelerated depreciation illustrated earlier. Simultaneously, there are tax liabilities from the various other governments. Consequently, effective tax rates potentially can be quite high, and analysts must consider the impact of tax requirements as part of the financial analysis. However, corporations have tax departments (and the Big 4 often serve as tax consultants) with minimizing taxes paid to the Internal Revenue Service and other tax collectors as a major objective—and they are very good at it. Usually the effective tax rate (provision for income tax / pretax income) is lower than the 35% federal rate.

The effective tax rates for the high-tech four (2004) are shown in Exhibit 14.8.

The effective tax rate was below the 35% federal rate in each case. The average tax rate for the Dow 30 was 26.1%, with only Home Depot above the 35% rate (36.8%). Du Pont actually had a negative tax rate of minus 22.8%, largely because of tax loss carryforwards.

A fair bit of accounting research suggests that taxes are used as part of the earnings magic strategy; see Bauman et al. (2001). The research suggests that firms actually lower their effective tax rates to meet earnings targets, especially in the fourth quarter of the fiscal year. However, firms may overpay taxes because of earnings magic to inflate earnings. A recent working paper by Erickson et al. (2004) investigates this point. Thus, evidence exists that taxes are central to earnings magic but are difficult to detect. The best plan is to consider effective tax rates, review tax rates over time and to competitors, and look for unusual factors in the tax note.

An interesting case is Marriott International, the nation's largest hotel corporation. Marriott generated net income of $596 million in 2004, a return on sales of 6%. The company's effective rate was only 15%. (Tax expense was negative in 2003.) The major reason for the tax rate was its synthetic

	Hewlett-Packard	IBM	Intel	Microsoft
Effective Tax Rate (Income Tax Expense / Pretax Income)	16.7%	29.8%	27.8%	33.0%

EXHIBIT 14.8   EFFECTIVE TAX RATES FOR THE HIGH TECH FOUR (2004)

fuel business, which is a money loser. However, tax subsidies turn it into a money maker after tax. (The $59 million loss became an $18 million gain after tax for first quarter 2005, because of the tax subsidy, 22% of net income.) Why would a hostelry operate a synthetic fuel business? Only one reason: the tax benefits. Brilliant tax planning perhaps, but blatant earnings magic.

Pro Forma Earnings

In addition to net income and other GAAP bottom-line measures, companies can reestimate earnings in various ways to emphasize certain features or components. Pro forma earnings are "restated earnings," based on another perspective or based on future forecasts. When management prepares pro forma statements, the point is to put the company in a better light than under GAAP—there are no rules for pro forma earnings. However, SEC Regulation G (thanks to Sarbanes-Oxley) requires companies using pro forma numbers to compare them to "the most directly comparable GAAP financial measure."

Fortunately, big companies including the Dow 30 rarely use pro forma numbers. They are usually reported by relatively small companies that have no earnings according to GAAP but want to claim profitability anyway. Amazon.com was a major user of pro forma numbers for virtually all the years the company was losing money. Amazon got GAAP religion only when it became profitable in 2003. I2 Technologies recently reported 2-cent-per-share earnings pro forma, although the company had a GAAP net loss (the difference being an amortization charge). Inktomi disclosed only pro forma earnings in its press release, a 22-cent loss versus a 46-cent loss based on GAAP.

Segment Reporting

Major corporations can have a multitude of business segments and have operations globally. They must disclose reportable segments for components that have 10% of any of three characteristics: total revenues, combined operating profits, or combined identifiable assets. Disclosure requirements include sales, operating profit, and identifiable assets. Foreign operations also require disclosure, based on 10% criteria for sales or identifiable assets. Companies have substantial leeway in defining segments.

Segment reporting represents additional information that can be useful for evaluating performance. It is particularly useful to highlight segment problems, which could relate to earnings management decisions. Segments can be difficult to evaluate because presentation and disclosure levels can

Walt Disney	Revenue*	Operating Income*	Identifiable Assets*
Media Networks	$11,778	$2,169	$26,193
Parks and Resorts	7,750	1,123	15,221
Studio Entertainment	8,637	662	6,954
Consumer Products	2,511	534	1,037
United States and Canada	$24,012	$2,934	46,788
Europe	4,721	892	5,370
Asia Pacific	1,547	566	1,622
Latin America, Other	472	96	122

* In millions.

EXHIBIT 14.9   WALT DISNEY INFORMATION ON INDUSTRY AND GEOGRAPHIC SEGMENTS

vary substantially from one company to another and operations can vary by both operating and geographic segment.

Walt Disney has information on industry and geographic segments (in thousands), as shown in Exhibit 14.9.

These figures can be converted into ratios: return on sales (operating income/revenue), asset turnover (revenue/identifiable assets), and return on assets (operating income/identifiable assets) as shown in Exhibit 14.10.

Now the segments can be compared. Media Networks is the largest revenue generator and also has a substantial return on sales of 18.4% and return on assets of 8.2%. However, it has a low asset turnover of 45%. Although generating the smallest revenue stream, Consumer Products had the higher ratios on all measures. Parks and Resorts and Studio Entertainment are relatively mediocre. The United States and Canada have the largest revenue but the lowest ratios. All other areas are more profitable and efficient. Thus, a business strategy emphasizing foreign operations seems the most viable choice. More important, none of the segments is a money loser.

Walt Disney	Return on Sales	Asset Turnover	Return on Assets
Media Networks	18.4%	45.0%	8.3%
Parks and Resorts	14.5%	50.9%	7.4%
Studio Entertainment	7.7%	124.2%	9.5%
Consumer Products	21.3%	242.1%	51.5%
United States and Canada	12.2%	51.3%	6.3%
Europe	18.9%	87.9%	16.6%
Asia Pacific	36.6%	95.4%	34.9%
Latin America, Other	20.3%	386.9%	78.7%

EXHIBIT 14.10   WALT DISNEY INFORMATION CONVERTED INTO RATIOS

With Disney and other huge companies, reported segment data may be inadequate for a thorough analysis. Media Networks has a swell return on sales of over 18%, but that includes Walt Disney Studios, Miramax, various Buena Vista segments, and so on. Studio Entertainment has a much lower return on sales of 7.7%, but is this because of Disneyland, Disney World in Orlando or Paris, Disney Cruise Line, or various others? If you want to know all about the Mighty Ducks, you're out of luck. They are just a small part of Parks and Resorts.

AUDITING AND CORPORATE GOVERNANCE

Auditing and corporate governance provide the oversight needed to ensure transparency and earnings quality. Scandals are more likely to happen when auditors and directors are accommodating to earnings magic schemes. This analysis looks for signals of diligence and potential problems, such as a late audit report or the reporting of internal control weaknesses.

Audit Report and Timely Reporting

The auditor's report (opinion) is presented in the financial statement section of the annual report. The content indicates whether there is an unqualified ("clean") opinion or if specific problems exist. Almost all opinions are unqualified ("the statements present fairly the financial position and results of operations . . . in accordance with GAAP"). The date of the opinion indicates when the audit was completed; a relatively early date suggests a relatively problem-free audit.

An interesting case is Krispy Kreme Doughnuts, which has not issued financial reports since the August 1, 2004 10-Q. The CEO was canned after a Securities and Exchange Commission probe found padded sales figures and other earnings magic. Earnings restatements, shareholder lawsuits, and federal fines are expected.

Corporations had 75 days to issue the 10-K to the SEC from the end of the fiscal year (reduced to 60 days beginning in 2006). Most Dow 30 companies have no problem beating this deadline. The average filing was done in 68 days, with only restaters AIG, GE, and Caterpillar missing the 75 days. Missing the deadline almost always means significant accounting problems.

The audit firm should be a Big Four (PricewaterhouseCoopers, Ernst & Young, Deloitte & Touche, or KPMG). Despite their involvement in the various corporate scandals, they are considered the best auditors, with both industry and complex systems expertise. With only four to choose from, the selection process is narrowed, and corporations may pick non–Big Four auditors instead. Doing so may signal that the audit was rejected by the Big Four because of high audit risk. (The Big Four firms have sophisticated systems to test audit risk in advance of accepting a client.)

All of the Dow 30 were audited by Big Four firms; 14 by Pricewater-houseCoopers, 8 by Ernst & Young, and 4 each by Deloitte & Touche and KPMG. Each had a clean opinion. The average number of days from the fiscal year-end to the report date was 51 days. Two major delays were noted. AIG had 147 days, two months beyond the SEC deadline for submitting the 10-K. AIG restated earnings from 2000 to 2004, a red flag. GE had two report dates; the first was 42 days, the second 125 days—when GE also restated earnings, another red flag.

Audit Fees

Audit fees are the major revenue source of the Big Four; however, major fees are derived from nonaudit services for audit clients. The perception of the SEC and others is that the nonaudit fees reduce auditor independence and make the auditors more accommodating. Consequently, many nonaudit services have been banned by the Sarbanes-Oxley Act. Across the Dow 30, audit fees averaged $24.3 million and ranged from $4.1 million for Home Depot to $78.2 million at GE. AIG had a large audit fee of $66.7 million, presumably scandal-related. Nonaudit fees averaged $12.9 million, about 53% of audit fees, primarily for audit-related and tax services. Three firms had nonaudit fees greater than audit fees: Caterpillar (audit of $10.2 million, nonaudit $16.9 million), IBM (audit $21.6 million, nonaudit $56 million), and Johnson & Johnson (audit $20.1 million, nonaudit $21.6 million). All had large tax fees and IBM also had large audited-related fees.

Board Composition

The board of directors is responsible for the overall business strategy, long-range planning, hiring and determining compensation terms of executives, and oversight, including audit overviews. The chief executive officer (CEO) and other senior executives are normally responsible for day-to-day operations and developing plans and strategies for board approval. The professional responsibilities of these leaders are extensive, and they are rewarded with substantial compensation. How they function is central to the overall operations and future of the corporation as well as the establishment of the earnings management environment of the firm.

The board of directors has substantial control (limited to some extent by founders and other strong CEOs who are often also chairs of the board). Thus, the composition of the board, the number of board members, and the board's committee structure are major signals of manipulation potential. Key factors could be the relative indifference of the board, ability or willingness to stand up to a strong CEO, and possible collusion of board members in questionable acts. A desirable board is made up primarily of outsiders picked for competence rather than because they are friends of the CEO.

Based on Sarbanes-Oxley and new rules at the major stock exchanges, all traded corporations must have a majority of independent directors. Assuming that the lack of corporate oversight was the major cause of previous scandals, this may be one of the most significant new rules from Sarbanes-Oxley. The average Dow 30 board had 12 to 13 members, with over 10 independent (an average of 81.7% independent). All 11 board members of Boeing were independent; GE had the lowest percentage of independent members, at 67% (10 of 15).

The 2005 scandal at AIG suggests that beefing up director independence is not a complete panacea. AIG had 11 independent directors (73% of the 15 total directors). However, Chairman and CEO (now former chairman and CEO) Hank Greenberg dominated the company, with little if any effective oversight by the board until the regulators were trying to settle the various issues and were being stonewalled by Greenberg. Only then did the directors step in and strip Greenberg of the CEO title.

Executive Compensation and the Role of the CEO

The current operating success of a major corporation rests squarely on the CEO and his or her executive team. The focus is on real economic performance based on the execution of a successful business strategy. In addition, the CEO is central to the basic earnings management environment of the firm. The key issue is whether the company is run solely for the best interests of the investors based on financial reality. Executive compensation may or may not be based exclusively on investor interests. Prior to the scandals at the start of the century, the CEO also was chair at most major corporations. Allowing a single individual to have that level of power is a potential cause of scandal, and more and more corporations are separating these positions. However, only 9 of the 30 Dow companies have separated the two positions. The percentage is expected to rise in the future.

The board of directors must have a compensation committee. The board determines executive compensation and generally approves employee compensation and benefits. The compensation agreements for senior executives are summarized in the annual proxy statement (and this information occasionally is found in the annual report). Employee compensation and benefits are summarized in the notes to the annual financial statements. Detailed notes usually are presented for pension plans and other postemployment benefits, stock options, and other compensation agreements. The qualitative analysis focuses primarily on the executive compensation packages.

Executive compensation has four basic components: (1) base salary; (2) bonuses, which are usually based on current earnings performance; (3) stock options (with restricted stock and stock appreciation rights ownership-based alternatives); and (4) various perquisites. Base salary is normally limited because of IRS regulations on deductibility; however, performance-based salary, including bonuses, is effectively unlimited. Base salary usually is not an earnings management concern.

Bonuses can be important, because executives subject to large bonuses have increased incentives to meet bonus targets. Bonus targets typically are based on a specific definition of earnings, which means that executives would tend to focus on that specific target. Consequently, if the target is based on some definition of income from current operations (above the line), earnings management strategies are expected to dump losses as nonrecurring items (below the line). Stock options became more popular in the 1990s, and with the booming stock market became a huge source of wealth to many executives. Consequently, the executive mind-set seemed to focus on whatever it took to ensure that stock prices continued to ratchet up. Perquisites vary substantially and must be evaluated on a case-by-case basis.

The average CEO base salary from the Dow 30 was $1.4 million, and total compensation (excluding equity compensation) was $5.9 million. Three CEOs received over $10 million in (nonequity) compensation, with Home Depot's CEO Bob Nardelli topping the list at $14.6 million. These CEOs also received massive stock options and other equity-based compensation (mainly restricted stock). On average, each CEO received over 340,000 options, with Procter & Gamble's CEO A. G. Lafley at the top with 706,000 (plus a restricted stock award of $9.9 million). Only six CEOs received no options, and only Microsoft CEO Steve Ballmer got neither options nor other stock compensation.

Shown in Exhibit 14.11 are 2004 salary numbers for some of the better-paid CEOs and equity grants.

A basic point is that stock options are not going away, although they are being supplemented by restricted stock and other long-term incentives.

P&G's Lafley seemed to top the list in total compensation, with a nonequity salary of $5.7 million, restricted stock worth almost $10 million, plus over 700,000 stock options. Did he deserve it? P&G's net income rose 25%

Company	CEO Salary	CEO Bonus	CEO Other Compensation	Total Compensation
American Express (AXP)	$1,000,000	$6,000,000	$1,771,180	$ 8,771,180
Citigroup (C)	1,000,000	8,415,000	641,344	10,056,344
Exxon-Mobil (XOM)	3,600,000	3,920,500	395,382	7,915,882
General Electric (GE)	3,000,000	5,300,000	234,829	8,534,829
Home Depot (HD)	2,000,000	5,750,000	6,869,842	14,619,842
Honeywell (HON)	1,500,000	2,400,000	5,271,066	9,171,066
IBM (IBM)	1,660,000	5,175,000	316,206	7,151,206
J.P. Morgan (JPM)	1,000,000	7,500,000	418,515	8,918,515
Procter & Gamble (PG)	1,700,000	3,500,000	523,100	5,723,100
SBC Comm. (SBC)	2,124,000	6,213,000	2,347,897	10,684,897
United Technology (UTX)	1,200,000	3,500,000	389,960	5,089,960
Walt Disney (DIS)	1,000,000	7,250,000	62,373	8,312,373

Company	# of Options Granted	Other Stock Compensation
American Express (AXP)	799,233	17,213 Restricted Stock Award ($3.0 million)
Citigroup (C)	562,003	Restricted Stock Award ($6.78 million), # shares not provided
Coca-Cola (KO)	450,000	140,000 Restricted Stock Award ($6.9 million)
Du Pont (DD)	245,800	64,000 Performance-Based Restricted Stock Units, No value given
Exxon-Mobil (XOM)	0	550,000 Restricted Stock Award ($28.0 million), 1,206,310 LT Incentive Plan ($2.2 million)
General Electric (GE)	0	250,000 Performance-Based Units ($8.6 million)
General Motors (GM)	400,000	81,071 LT Incentive Shares, no dollar value given)
Home Depot (HD)	600,000	400,000 Restricted Stock Award ($13.9 million)
Honeywell (HON)	600,000	0
IBM (IBM)	250,000	Performance Stock Units ($1.7 million)
J.P. Morgan (JPM)	600,481	0
Pfizer (PFE)	525,000	125,000 Restricted Stock Award ($4.3 million), 220,800 Performance Restricted Shares ($4.29 million)
Procter & Gamble (PG)	705,834	Restricted Stock Award ($9.9 million)
SBC Comm. (SBC)	400,000	LTIP Payouts ($3.5 million)
Verizon (VZ)	468,300	Restricted Stock Award ($6.3 million)
Wal-Mart (WMT)	339,001	Restricted Stock Award ($6.3 million)

EXHIBIT 14.11   2004 SALARY NUMBERS FOR SOME BETTER-PAID CEOS AND EQUITY GRANTS

for the year, to $6.5 billion. However, the stock price dropped slightly for the year and underperformed the Dow. Perhaps Lafley was worth it based on earnings performance. United Technology's CEO George David exercised 1.1 million options worth $83.6 million, not to mention over $5 million in cash compensation. United Technology's net income rose 18% for 2004, and the stock substantially outperformed the Dow. In contrast, GM had a miserable year, although CEO Richard Wagoner received cash compensation of $4.8 million plus 400,000 options and 81,000 incentive shares.

Related-Party Transactions and Insider Trading

Related-party transactions involve buying, selling, and other transactions from officers, directors, partners, employees, family members, and so on. Current accounting and auditing standards require the disclosure of these related-party transactions (but only if material) and no more. These are not illegal or necessarily a violation of any kind. However, they signal potential earnings management issues. Thus, the perspective is qualitative—with a focus on corporate governance.

Directors and managers buy and sell the stock of their company on a somewhat regular basis. This is an important component of insider trading and is partially based on the use of stock options. Insider trading becomes illegal when someone (besides corporate directors or employees, it can include investment bankers, analysts, friends, and relatives) uses insider (nonpublic) information for personal gain. However, it is difficult to prove. Of course, there was Sam Waksal of Imclone and the involvement of Martha Stewart.

Of particular concern for evaluating the corporate governance environment is the potential for these executive insiders to profit from insider information. Purchases and sales do not prove illegal acts but provide potential signals of executive reaction to new events with opportunistic behavior. SEC Form 4 and Form 144 information is available by company on several financial Web sites (and these are more convenient than going directly to the SEC Web page). Both Yahoo! Finance and CNN Money have both disclosures available by company. For example, IBM CEO Samuel Palmisano exercised almost 194,000 stock options and sold over 123,000 for $9.4 million on May 24, 2005.

Internal Control Report

Internal control regulations are a major part of Sarbanes-Oxley reforms, and firms are screaming about the cost; auditors, however, are rather pleased at the windfall. It is difficult to criticize internal control requirements, because the concept of adequate internal controls has been central to auditing and also required by federal law for decades. Most of the complaints so far have been related to the high costs, presumably compared to expected minimal benefits, and the overregulation of the auditors in the field. Most outsiders cannot believe that internal controls at major corporations are so substandard. The auditor's internal control report is expected to be "boilerplate," much as the auditor's opinion usually is. When auditors find weaknesses and errors, they notify company officials and expect them to fix the problems. When that happens, a clean opinion is expected. Outsiders are almost always unaware of any major problems encountered by the auditors. In the majority of cases the internal control report is part of the auditor's report. As expected, the auditors at 28 of the Dow 30 reported no material weaknesses in internal control. The shock is that material weaknesses were reported by two companies, AIG and GE—both firms that restated earnings for 2004 and before. GE's weakness related to accounting controls for derivative transactions, which also caused the earnings restatement. AIG's reported weaknesses were extensive, including "control environment, controls over evaluation of risk transfer, controls over balance sheet reconciliation, controls over accounting for certain derivative transactions, and controls over income tax accounting." This is an unexpected red flag and, along with other AIG issues, suggests severe earnings magic problems.

OTHER ISSUES

The list of other issues can be long, but only two examples are used. Restated earnings and evidence of regulatory investigations are major red flags and likely indicators of extreme earnings magic. The market responds to bad news by selling, with potentially large stock price drops. Investor dissatisfaction should be investigated.

Restating Earnings and Regulatory Investigations

One of the most blatant signals of past earnings magic is an earnings restatement for earlier accounting periods. This requires an 8-K filing with the SEC, and, almost always, companies will announce an upcoming restatement. Until the last decade or so, this was a rare event. Unfortunately, it has become a relatively common occurrence. The Government Accountability Office conducted a major study of restatements in 2002 and discovered some 919 restatements from 1997 to the middle of 2002. This included 72 S&P 500 companies, indicating that restatements are a problem for both big and small firms. Most of these restatements involved revenue recognition or expense-related issues. Despite the increased regulations and audit oversight, this issue has not gone away. Both AIG and GE restated previous years' financial statements in 2005.

AIG had settled litigation with the SEC and Justice Department at the end of 2004, only to be hit with new investigations by the SEC and New York Attorney General in February 2005 on reinsurance transactions and nontraditional insurance products. AIG did not manage to issue its 2004 10-K until May 31, 2005; it included restatements for each year since 2000. The results included lowered net income for 2004 by $1.3 billion and $3.9 billion for the previous five years. Equity was reduced by $2.3 billion. For example, the reserve for asbestos and environmental exposure was increased by $850, offset by a comparable expense. Internal control weaknesses also were noted, indicating that AIG's troubles are not over.

GE's problems were much less severe than those of AIG. GE restated earnings for 2001 to 2004, reissuing its 2004 10-K on May 5, 2005. The problems related to accounting for derivative instruments based on internal audit findings. The result was a net increase in earnings of $0.6 billion, primarily from interest rate and asset swaps.

On November 9, 2005, General Motors filed an 8-K stating that the company would restate earnings from 2000–2005 to correct supplier credits recorded as income. GM estimated 2001 earnings were overstated by $300–$400 million. On the news, GM stock dropped another 5%.

Stock Prices: What Does the Market Tell Us?

The market is efficient; or maybe it is nuts much of the time. Academics stress market efficiency. Investors often claim the ability to beat the market, in part because it is obviously not efficient. It turns out that academics find real threats to efficiency, but still say that consistently beating the market is unlikely. Former hedge fund manager and financial media star Jim Cramer (2002) claims to "trade on the buzz"—the antithesis of market efficiency. In summary, there is no consensus on market behavior.

Having said that, there can be real information in stock prices. Stocks do reflect investor sentiment—rational or irrational. A large price change after an earnings announcement or some other event suggests market euphoria or dread. Earnings surprise—the difference between the consensus earnings per share (EPS) forecast and actual EPS—is the most common information signal. A stock can tumble even with a small negative surprise. When a company announces an acquisition, the stock price after the announcement tells the market reaction: A decline signals dissatisfaction. An early step to analyze the reaction to a news story is to analyze a stock chart, comparing the companies directly affected to competitors and market averages. Consider AIG, which announced SEC and New York Attorney General investigations in late February 2005 and restated earnings at the end of May 2005. A stock

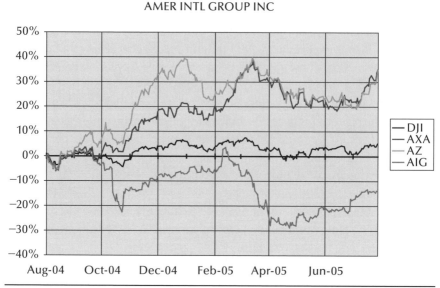

EXHIBIT 14.12   STOCK CHART FOR AIG

chart is shown in Exhibit 14.12 for the last year, along with competitors AZ (Allianz Aktiengesellschaft), AXA SA, and the Dow average.

The stock price drop at the end of February is obvious, with continuing negative reactions over the next couple of months (along with continued bad

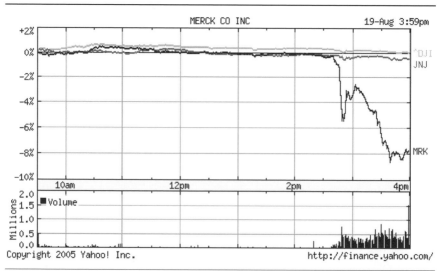

EXHIBIT 14.13   STOCK CHART FOR MERCK CO.

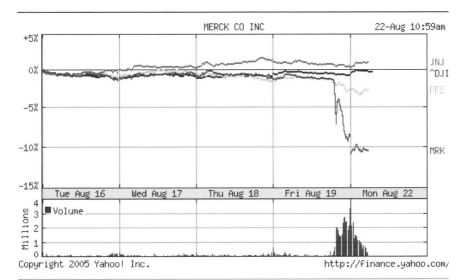

Reproduced with permission of Yahoo! Inc. © 2005 by Yahoo! Inc. Yahoo! and the Yahoo! logo are trademarks of Yahoo! Inc.

EXHIBIT 14.14   CHANGE IN MERCK'S STOCK CHART

news). During the same period, the Dow and competitors were flat or up slightly. Interestingly, AIG's stock price went up with the restatement because the results were actually better than expected (basically, a perverse form of "good news").

What about Merck and the recalled drug Vioxx? Merck was found guilty in the first case on August 19, 2005, and the jury awarded the victim's widow about $250 million. What was the market reaction? Bad—you bet! The stock dropped 8% in the last couple of hours of trading. When the market opened on Monday, the stock was down a bit more (see Exhibit 14.13).

In addition, Vioxx is a Cox-2 painkiller, and the court case should impact on other pharmaceutical firms with similar drugs, including Pfizer. That is exactly what happened: Merck was down about 10%, Pfizer down about 3%, Johnson & Johnson (without a similar drug) up a bit (see Exhibit 14.14).

Section 3

PUTTING IT ALL TOGETHER

The rule is *caveat emptor.* Financial fiascos have been a constant in the history of business. Despite the many layers of oversight and regulation, earnings magic and the lack of transparency continues. Severe manipulation becomes known only after the culprits are caught. In the meantime, analysts have to rely on diligent analysis and signals of likely magic. Major issues have been reviewed. Now it is time to put it all together. What process is most likely to reveal relative transparency, approximate financial reality, and discover earnings magic signals?

This is the payoff: a comprehensive analysis to determine if real transparency exists, which means that financial reality and the level of earnings magic can be estimated. Earnings magic correlates to nontransparency, which makes discovering financial reality somewhere between difficult and impossible. There is no way to guarantee transparency, only the relative confidence associated with signals of earnings quality.

Chapter	Discussion
15. Finding Signals of Financial Excellence and Earnings Magic	Start with basic financial analysis, including stock price and other market information—basic performance and market response. Then determine if this is financial reality, based on the Big 8 and the rest of the Dirty 30.
16. A Checklist for Evaluating Financial Excellence	A checklist is used to evaluate relative earnings quality, based on a scoring sheet to convert qualitative and quantitative analysis to specific scores.
17. An Investment Strategy	How would an earnings magic evaluation fit into an investment strategy? A simple game plan is presented, using selection criteria to pick which firms to evaluate and how to proceed.
18. Searching for Help: Useful Internet Sites	Most of the information is available in the annual reports and proxy statements, but there is lots of help available from the Internet and other sources.

EXHIBIT S3.1   CHAPTER DISCUSSIONS

221

15

FINDING SIGNALS OF FINANCIAL EXCELLENCE AND EARNINGS MAGIC

*By the fall of 1995, America Online's share already had taken
wing—up 2,000 percent since the company's initial public offering.
. . . AOL was trying to paper over its cash deficit by issuing more
and more stock. In other words, AOL was gaming its books.*
—Maggie Mahar

*History has shown that Wall Street is more apt to cross an
ethical line when seven-figure bonuses abound.*
—Roger Lowenstein

A basic market and financial analysis represents the first cut to earnings performance, balance sheet quality, and the market perception of quality and potential. How close is this picture to financial reality? Enron and WorldCom seemed pretty impressive given their financials; it just was not real. Both exhibited a lack of transparency and signals of earnings magic. Most companies are expected to be relatively transparent and earnings magic-free. But which ones? A comprehensive follow-up is needed to figure that out. Basically, that is using the Big 8 and the rest of the Dirty 30 to test for earnings quality and relative transparency and to look for signals of possible earnings magic.

Step one is a fundamental financial analysis. Doing this establishes the baseline of relative performance and financial position. Results such as erratic earnings or high leverage suggest earnings magic is more likely. A market analysis provides a perspective on investor sentiments on the overall corporate performance. For example, a high price/earnings ratio usually suggests relative confidence in the earnings quality and future prospects for growth.

Step two is the Dirty 30 analysis to determine the relative confidence in the financial reporting of the company. Does disclosure suggest high transparency and lack of signals of earnings magic? Low transparency and signals of earnings magic increase the need to reevaluate financial numbers and to recalculate and reinterpret ratios—and take a dim view of the company. For example, stock options are a major incentive for executives to meet earnings targets—by operating brilliance or earnings magic. Options dilute equity and are a real compensation expense (whether recorded or not). When significant (and not expensed), earnings can be reevaluated to include this expense. An arbitrary 10% rule for significance is used throughout for convenience.

Step three is recasting earnings and balance sheet information to come closer to financial reality. Doing this can include recalculating financial ratios and reinterpreting the overall results. For example, earnings less stock option expense can be used to recalculate performance measures, including return on sales and return on equity.

Step four is rating the corporations for relative transparency (earnings quality). More on this in the next chapter, which uses a scale of A to F to compare relative quality.

A FUNDAMENTAL FINANCIAL ANALYSIS

Financial Analysis Using Financial Statements

Chapter 4 introduced financial reporting, qualitative analysis, and the number crunching of quantitative analysis. The quantitative analysis converts financial statement data to percentages for comparisons across companies, over time, and various rules of thumb about what represents good or bad performance. Profitability can be measured by great ratios (e.g., return on sales and return on equity greater than competitors and market averages) that improve year after year. Strong balance sheets can be measured by relative liquidity and leverage.

The four high-tech firms of the Dow 30 were used as examples. There were substantial differences in the ratios, with Microsoft and Intel showing good performance and strong balance sheets for 2004. Both IBM and Hewlett-Packard were more problematic. Across the Dow 30 (see Appendix 5.1), the average firm had a current ratio of 1.2, long-term debt to equity of 49%, and return on equity (ROE) of 9.8%. ROE averaged 20.0% and ranged from 1.9% for GM to 38.5% for Procter & Gamble, with six firms having an ROE above 30%. Profitability ratios are relatively easy to evaluate: The bigger the better. However, multiple ratios provide more information, often resulting in mixed signals. Microsoft had a superb return on sales of 13.3%, but an average ROE at 19.1% because of low leverage (compared to P&G's 11.5 return on sales and 30% ROE).

Balance sheet ratios are harder to interpret. What is the optimum amount of liquidity or leverage? Increasing debt will increase ROE, but also increases credit risk. Higher liquidity improves the ability to pay bills and investment flexibility, but perhaps the cash can be used for better purposes. There are differences of opinion on appropriate actions. I believe in adequate liquidity and view negative working capital (current liabilities are greater than current assets) as a red flag. Other analysts favor high levels of accounts payable and low levels of current assets. Long-term debt to equity above 1 may be a concern for manufacturing and retail firms, but leverage ratios for banks and financial firms are much higher. A "strong balance sheet" is in the eyes of the analysts. Five Dow 30 firms had negative working capital; another five had current ratios greater than 2. Long-term debt to equity averaged 53%; 4 manufacturing firms had ratios above 1. Caterpillar, GE, and GM have large financing operations to explain high leverage, but GM's 11.4 ratio suggests very high credit risk.

A more thorough quantitative financial analysis is encouraged. It should incorporate additional ratios and analysis categories (including common-size and the Du Pont Model), comparisons to close competitors and industry averages, and include time series (most recent quarters and for the last three-plus years). For details, see Giroux (2003), especially Chapters 1, 4, and 5.

Market Comparisons

The appendix to Chapter 5 summarized a quick market comparison of the Dow 30. Despite substantial revenue and assets, GM had the lowest market cap at $18 billion, dinky compared to GE's $391 billion and Exxon-Mobil's $362 billion. GM was the only Dow company with a price-to-book less than 1. Investor votes were that GM was actually worth less than its book value. All the Dow firms paid dividends and had an average dividend yield of 2.7%, slightly overstated because of Microsoft's one-shot special dividend.

Particularly important market data are price/earnings ratio (P/E), five-year earnings forecast, and the price earnings to growth ratio (PEG), presented in Exhibit 15.1 based on July 13, 2005 stock prices.

The price/earnings ratio can be interpreted as the relative "premium" paid for current earnings. In this case, P/Es are based on the forecast EPS for the next fiscal year (2006). The average P/E was 15 (equivalent to EPS of about 7% of share price). Higher P/Es are normally associated with greater future earnings growth potential. P/Es ranged from 9.9 for Citigroup to 20 for Boeing. GM had a P/E of 22.3 because of a poor EPS and is not representative of a growth opportunity.

Company	P/E	5-Year Forecast	PEG
3M (MMM)	15.9	12	1.5
Alcoa (AA)	12.3	14	1.1
Altria (MO)	11.8	8.5	1.5
American Express (AXP)	15.2	13	1.3
American International Group (AIG)	11	13	1
Boeing (BA)	20	12	2.1
Caterpillar (CAT)	10.8	12	1
Citigroup (C)	9.9	11	1
Coca-Cola (KO)	18.8	8	2.5
Du Pont (DD)	14	10	1.6
Exxon-Mobil (XOM)	13	7.3	1.7
General Electric (GE)	17.2	10.5	1.8
General Motors (GM)	22.3	5	4.5
Hewlett-Packard (HPQ)	14.5	10	1.6
Home Depot (HD)	14.1	14	1
Honeywell (HON)	14.9	12	1.5
IBM (IBM)	15.1	10	1.7
Intel (INTC)	17.8	15	1.3
J.P. Morgan (JPM)	10.3	10	1.2
Johnson & Johnson (JNJ)	17.1	10	1.9
McDonald's (MCD)	13.8	8	1.9
Merck (MRK)	13.1	2.6	4.9
Microsoft (MSFT)	18.1	10	1.9
Pfizer (PFE)	12.5	8	1.7
Procter & Gamble (PG)	18.6	11	1.8
SBC Comm. (SBC)	14.9	6	2.7
United Technology (UTX)	15	12	1.4
Verizon (VZ)	12.8	4	3.3
Wal-Mart (WMT)	16.6	14	1.2
Walt Disney (DIS)	17.1	11.5	1.6
Average	15.0	10.1	1.8

EXHIBIT 15.1 P/E, 5-YEAR FORECAST, AND PEG BASED ON JULY 13, 2005 STOCK PRICES

The Dow 30 firms are predicted to have earnings growth that will average 10% annually for the next five years. Alcoa, Home Depot, and Wal-Mart top the list at 14%; Merck is expected to have only a 2.6% annual growth rate. Normally, growth stocks will have double-digit earnings growth, while value stocks will have single-digit (or less) earnings growth. Consequently, the results are unexpected. Historically, pharmaceuticals have been high-growth stocks. Merck's expected growth of 2.6% is unusual, but Merck has problems (especially the recall of Vioxx) and competitors Johnson & Johnson and Pfizer are doing only slightly better.

PEG is measured as P/E divided by the five-year earnings growth rate. Assuming that the primary reason for the "price premium" as measured by P/E is earnings growth, then PEG captures this. The average PEG of 1.8 means that investors are willing to pay 1.8 times the expected earnings growth rate. PEG varies from 1 for AIG, Boeing, and Citigroup to 4.9 for Merck. The high PEGs for both Merck and GM are because of low current earnings and suggest nothing relevant about growth potential. For more typical cases, PEG suggests information on the potential quality associated with reported earnings. GE has a PEG of 1.8, average for the group. This can be interpreted to mean that GE's earnings quality has been considered "average" by the market; the relative quality of GE's earnings is above AIG (PEG of 1) but below Coca-Cola at 2.5. Whether this perspective is correct will take considerably more analysis, but it is a reasonable starting point.

DETECTING EARNINGS MAGIC AND THE SEARCH FOR TRANSPARENCY—A SUMMARY

Financial and market analysis can be brief or thorough and establishes the base financial statement reality for each firm investigated. The key question: Does this analysis result in financial reality and transparency, free of earnings magic? The higher the earnings quality of the financial statements, the closer the statements are to financial reality. Thanks to generally accepted accounting principles (GAAP), not to mention corporate hanky panky, the answer is most likely no—as extensively demonstrated in Section 2. However, the analysis of notes and other disclosures will provide three benefits: (1) the information to restate financial statement numbers with more economically realistic numbers (e.g., options, pension, and operating leases); (2) the review of the Dirty 30 will turn up transparency concerns and signals of earnings magic; and (3) the clarity and thoroughness of disclosures and other sources will indicate the relative transparency present. Basic concerns by category are summarized in Exhibit 15.2 for the Big 8.

Stock Options

The existence of options signals that executives have increased incentives for meeting earnings targets, especially quarterly consensus analysts' EPS forecasts. In terms of incentives, it is preferred if executives are given restricted

Issue	Concerns
Stock Options	Signal of executive incentives to meet earnings targets, increasing the potential for earnings magic. Options dilute equity and, if not expensed, are a real compensation cost that should be recognized.
Pensions and OPEB	Defined benefit pension plans and other postemployment benefits can represent big obligations and major expenses. Even worse, substantial obligations can be off–balance sheet, and pension/OPEB expenses can be misstated.
Revenues	Revenue recognition has the largest potential for earnings magic, since there are so many ways to manipulate. It is difficult to detect earnings magic signals, but it is worth attempting.
Earnings, Expenses, and Expectations	There are several categories of earnings, such as EBIT, income from continuing operations, and net income. Expense categories and earnings should line up reasonably well (especially over time and when compared to competitors); if not, search for possible earnings magic.
Strange Special Items	Special items are beyond normal operations, generally suspect, and include both nonrecurring and unusual items that are treated as part of continuing operations. All need to be investigated for reasonableness. Repeat offenders are more likely manipulating.
Treasury Stock	Companies buy back their own shares to fund options likely to be exercised and for other purposes. Treasury stock is antidilutive, uses cash, and reduces equity. It also can be used to prop up stock price.
Off–Balance Sheet	Operating leases and special-purpose entities are used specifically to keep liabilities unrecorded, i.e., off–balance sheet. When these are big amounts, manipulation is suspected.
Acquisitions	Big business gets even bigger through acquisitions. Many manipulative techniques are possible, including the use of goodwill. Only limited information on acquisitions is presented, but signals of potential manipulation exist. Habitual acquirers and big acquisitions are particularly suspect.

EXHIBIT 15.2   SOME BASIC CONCERNS FOR THE BIG 8 BY CATEGORY

stock or other stock-related incentives. When stock options represent a large percentage of overall compensation and alternative equity-based compensation is not used, the warning is that quarterly earnings are more likely to be manipulated.

The major problem is that stock options are not expensed (which will be corrected beginning in 2006), increasing the rationale to use them. Check for the dilution effect as measured by options outstanding divided by share outstanding. A ratio greater than 10% is one signal of substantial potential dilution. Note disclosure requires that compensation expense must be calculated and presented in the notes as the difference between net income and net income pro forma. If the difference is greater than 10%, recalculate all the performance ratios that include net income.

Pensions and OPEB

Relatively newer companies, such as Microsoft and Home Depot, have neither defined benefit pension plans nor other postemployment benefits (or OPEB is immaterial)—therefore, a nonissue for these firms. Most of the Dow 30 have big pension and OPEB expenses, as well as pension and OPEB obligations. These are seldom presented as line items on the income statement and balance sheet, but substantial note disclosures exist. The primary issue is financial reality, not earnings magic (earnings magic may exist here, but it is less important). Disclosures indicate the amounts shown on the income statement as expenses and the net amount shown on the balance sheet. A net asset position is overfunded and a net liability is underfunded.

Pension and OPEB expenses greater than 10% of net income can be concerns. More critical is the funding level, especially economic reality. Most of the Dow 30 report a net asset position (overfunded) for pension but a net liability position (underfunded) for OPEB (because of tax laws that limit the deductibility of invested assets for OPEB). But this is not economic reality because of GAAP "smoothing requirements." Financial reality is funded status for both pension and OPEB. Most of the Dow 30 pension and OPEB plans were underfunded based on funded status. The difference between the net asset or liability position and funded status is off–balance sheet. Underfunded pension plans and OPEB plans underfunded by more than 10% of total assets could be considered significant concerns. A transparency issue also exists, because disclosure and terminology can be particularly confusing for some companies.

Revenues

The driver of profitability is sales, with the open question of when and how much to recognize. Manipulation can be relatively easy, especially whether to recognize revenue this quarter or next quarter. Short of outright fraud, the issue is timing, which means it is almost impossible to detect manipulation from annual reports and other public documents. Instead, look for unusual changes in revenues from period to period, especially compared to receivables and inventory levels. Management Discussion and Analysis (MD&A) and notes may suggest possible earnings magic. If revenues are unusually brisk but receivables are rising even faster, it is likely that credit terms are being relaxed. This is a bad strategy because of increased bad debts. Magic is more likely if revenues are rising, receivables are rising much faster, and the allowance for doubtful accounts is actually falling. It is much more likely that revenue manipulation will be discovered externally: restated financial statements, an SEC investigation, or business media stories that suggest fraud.

Earnings, Expenses, and Expectations

The bottom line is that earnings are everything in business. Earnings and the various expense categories should be relatively stable over time. If earnings rise by 10%, revenue and cost of sales also should rise about the same. It is likely that expenses and earnings results will be similar to direct competitors. Pharmaceuticals have low cost of sales, but high selling, general and administrative and research and development costs, for example. Changing patterns and unusual amounts should be investigated for magic signals.

Strange Special Items

Nonrecurring items and other strange stuff should not exist and, therefore, should be treated skeptically. As demonstrated by the Dow 30, they can be fairly common. Nonrecurring items are listed on the income statement as separate line items and usually disclosed with some detail in the notes. Special items also get note coverage. They must be evaluated individually for reasonableness and to what extent they represent earnings magic. Poor coverage in the notes suggests a lack of transparency. Repeat offenders should be viewed with particular skepticism. Some items, such as gains on discontinued operations that are treated as "normal operations," especially when the company is otherwise having a poor year, just scream manipulation.

Treasury Stock

Why would a company even buy back its own shares? Companies give good rationales, such as to fund stock options and other stock incentive programs or because it is the best available use of cash. Some analysts find buybacks "good news": The company believes in itself. I do not. Beyond the bad stuff that it does to the balance sheet (reducing cash and equity) is the likelihood that the company is propping up share price. The antidilutive effect can also increase EPS when net income is not rising. Treasury stock rising above 10% of equity suggests that bad stuff is particularly likely. Are executives manipulating stock price when they want to exercise and sell options? If the companies are increasing outstanding debt at the same time, the signal is manipulation. Another problem is companies that do not record treasury stock on the balance sheet (but must record treasury stock in the cash flow statement and statement of stockholders' equity). This may be a big item, but it is impossible to tell how much stock they actually bought back—a real lack of transparency.

Off–Balance Sheet

Operating leases should reasonably be used for relatively minor equipment. Operating leases are very common, including among the majority of the Dow 30. The key characteristic is that the obligation is off–balance sheet, reasonable for minor equipment but not for major fixed asset items. To determine the significance of operating leases, go to the lease note. Add the obligations together. (They are stated by year plus the current year rent expense.) The relative magnitude can be estimated by the ratio operating leases to total assets. A ratio above 10% is one measure of concern. At that level, liabilities should be reestimated to include operating leases. The leases should be discounted; for example, using the same discount rate as capital leases. Then recalculate the leverage ratios.

Special-purpose and other strange entities can be important—Enron was the SPE manipulation champ—but likely are not disclosed adequately. There should be one or more notes plus a discussion in MD&A that focus on variable interest entities and qualified SPEs. Large financial institutions are big users and usually have considerable disclosure. The problem is the number can be huge, and it is somewhere between difficult and impossible to determine the outstanding risks involved in these entities. Nonfinancial firms typically have little disclosure on SPEs, and what is disclosed can be muddled. That is a lack of transparency, which can camouflage the impact on financial reality.

Acquisitions

Acquisitions make big companies bigger, almost always guaranteeing increased revenues and earnings. Performance and leverage ratios may not improve. These mergers may be brilliant decisions or complete disasters. The merger of AOL and Time Warner was sold as a creative combination of old economy and new economy media giants; then the Internet bubble collapsed and AOL-Time Warner was viewed as the major merger blunder of the twenty-first century. Conglomerates seem to be in a perpetual buying mode, with mixed success. Tyco is viewed as a major financial fiasco, while GE is a long-term success. How do you tell which is which? This is mainly a qualitative analysis, based on business strategy and corporate discipline. GE gets high marks here, while Tyco seemed to be an earnings magic specialist. The starting point for analysis is the goodwill amount on the balance sheet, plus additional disclosures on intangibles. Goodwill divided by total assets indicates the relative accumulated "goodwill premium." Goodwill is not a real asset. The bigger the amount, the weaker the balance sheet. Limited disclosure also is presented on current mergers, with the most useful information the relative allocation among physical and financial net assets, goodwill, and other intangibles. Because goodwill is not expensed (but subject to possible impairment), high goodwill percentages suggest acquisition magic.

The Rest of the Dirty 30

The rest of the Dirty 30 include:

1. A more detailed ratio analysis, such as liquidity, leverage, inventory, receivables, and taxes
2. Complex accounting issues including derivatives, the equity method, and segment reporting
3. Corporate governance and auditing issues, such as executive compensation and auditor fees

Additional issues include restated earnings and stock prices. The detailed ratio areas are primarily quantitative, looking for unusual amounts that may signal earnings magic. High leverage and changing allowance for doubtful accounts are examples. Complex accounting issues usually affect certain industries and companies. The equity method is not that common but is significant for Coca-Cola. Segment reporting is especially important for conglomerates. Corporate governance and auditing areas are useful primarily as oversight signal. An independent board of directors is more likely to be skeptical of senior executives and provide more thorough oversight. Executive compensation suggests the relative incentives of the CEO and other executives. Restated earnings are usually a red flag of earnings magic—caught with their collective executive hands in the cookie jar. Reviewing stock prices is useful for evaluating specific events, such as acquisitions, and the overall market response to the company.

Quantitative versus Qualitative and Industry Analysis

Most of the Big 8 items can be analyzed quantitatively with relative magnitude the indicator of the level of financial transparency and possible earnings magic. Most of the rest of the Dirty 30 requires a mix of quantitative and qualitative analysis, in other words, judgment based on numbers and disclosures. The quantitative part is easier, although issues such as contingencies and risk management are equally important.

Industry analysis is a key factor. The pharmaceuticals (Pfizer, Johnson & Johnson, and Merck in the Dow) have unusual expense category relationships and huge contingencies. Financial institutions have high leverage, lots of SPEs, and extreme derivatives. High-tech companies tend to have lots of stock options, and retailers, lots of operating leases and high inventories. Consequently, what appears to be serious earnings magic may be an industry standard.

16

A CHECKLIST FOR EVALUATING FINANCIAL EXCELLENCE

*Certainly capitalism intends to reward ambition
and hard work, but it is not set up to punish dishonesty
or penalize a lack of integrity.*

—Maggie Mahar

*Starting with the unfolding of the Enron story in October 2001,
it became apparent that the boom years had been
accompanied by a serious erosion in business principles.*

—William Donaldson, Former SEC Chairman

Companies can be rated on an arbitrary scale, such as from A to F—but with no grade inflation (see Exhibit 16.1). If A represents complete transparency and financial reality, few if any companies would meet this hurdle. From an analyst's perspective, A would be expected. It is just that the analyst is disappointed most of the time and for a variety of reasons. Unfortunately, quite a few companies would be graded F—these are the corporate scandals that make the financial headlines. Most companies are in the B to D range, with too many Cs and Ds. These are companies that are far from transparent and financial reality and signal that manipulation and potential scandal are possible.

A	Transparent company—thorough disclosure, near financial reality, no evidence of earnings magic, and no history of past abuse
B	Good disclosure and high financial reality, with limited evidence of potential problems and little or no history of past abuse (or evidence that the company has changed its ways)
C	Average company—adequate disclosures and level of financial reality, potential manipulation, but consistent with industry practices

(continues)

EXHIBIT 16.1 ARBITRARY RATING SCALE FOR COMPANIES

D	Indicators of inadequate disclosure, not close to financial reality, signals of poor transparency, potential manipulation problems, or evidence of past abuse
F	Substantial evidence of serious issues, history of past abuse; company with serious problems, probably made worse by financial mismanagement and misleading disclosures

EXHIBIT 16.1   ARBITRARY RATING SCALE FOR COMPANIES (CONTINUED)

A SUGGESTED GRADING SYSTEM

The grading scale can be used by analysis category to see the relative strengths and weaknesses of each company and make analysis by industry somewhat easier. The basic categories are shown in Exhibit 16.2.

The key checklist issues by category are shown in Exhibit 16.3.

Category	Discussion
Overview: Financial and Market Analysis	Number crunching for basic ratios and related analysis. This is the starting point and assumes that the financial statement information is economic reality. Not likely, but it is the place to start to understand the corporate fundamentals and the market's reaction.
Big 8	These are the biggies of earnings magic and financial reality. From stock options to acquisitions, these are the items most likely to distort financial reality and signal possible manipulation.
Other Dirty 30 Items	Categories include more detailed ratios and financial analysis by category, complex accounting issues, and corporate governance.
Wild Card	Anything else, which includes companies that restated financials, are being investigated by the SEC, and business media analysis. Recent stock price trends should be reviewed to determine investor sentiment.

EXHIBIT 16.2   BASIC CATEGORIES FOR ANALYSIS

Financial and Market Analysis:

Analysis	Discussion	Concerns
Financial Overview	Review financial statements and general annual report disclosures; use common-size analysis for initial standardization of income statement and balance sheet.	Any item that appears unusual; unexpected common-size ratios, based on comparisons over time and to competitors.
Standard Ratios by Category	Basic ratios for liquidity, leverage, activity, and performance; compare over time (e.g., last three years) and to major competitors.	Various, including negative working capital, high leverage, and low performance ratios.

(continues)

EXHIBIT 16.3   KEY CHECKLIST ISSUES BY CATEGORY

Analysis	Discussion	Concerns
Stock Charts and Standard Market Ratios	Stock charts for the last year and 5 years, including comparisons to competitors and market averages (e.g., DJIA). Market ratios of interest include market-to-book, P/E, PEG, and dividend yield; plus quarterly and 5-year consensus forecasts.	Large unexpected drops in stock price relative to competitors and market averages; market-to-book below 1; extremely high or low PEGs; dividend payouts greater than net income.
Advanced Ratios	Vary by industry and other factors; Altman's Z-score is useful for evaluating credit risk; separate ratios for financial institutions on loan portfolios, etc.; detailed ratio analysis when warranted.	Various, including failing Altman's Z- score; most concerns are industry related.

Big 8:

Analysis	Discussion	Concerns
Stock Options	Options divided by total shares; difference between net income and net income-pro forma: if greater than 10%, recalculate performance ratios.	Options greater than 10% of total shares outstanding; options expense greater than 10% of net income.
Pensions and OPEB	Relative reported funding level; more critical is funding level based on funded status; calculate pension and OPEB expense as a percent of net income.	Underfunded pension and OPEB plans; underfunded plans based on funded status (note: the difference between reported amount and funded status is off–balance sheet). Pension and OPEB expenses greater than 10% of net income.
Revenues	Focus on revenue changes over time and compared to major competitors; check revenue changes to impact on receivables and bad debts reserve.	Large drops in revenues; large gains especially if receivables are rising and changes if reserve for doubtful accounts are noted.
Earnings and Expenses	Compare alternative bottom-line numbers for reasonableness, including over time and to competitors; calculate expense categories as a percent of revenues and compare to competitors.	Declining or erratic changes in earnings; unusual percentages in earnings categories; other indicators of likely aggressive expense recognition.
Strange Special Items	Evaluate all nonrecurring items (including previous years); check for reasonableness and likely earnings magic. Evaluate all special items, including restructuring costs and impairment evaluations.	All special items are problematic; a particular concern if they are common and a large percentage of earnings; evidence of earnings magic, e.g., a gain from discontinued operations in an otherwise low-performance year.

(continues)

EXHIBIT 16.3   KEY CHECKLIST ISSUES BY CATEGORY (CONTINUED)

Analysis	Discussion	Concerns
Treasury Stock and Dividends	Treasury stock divided by total stockholders' equity; dividend yield and dividend payout; evaluate relationships among treasury stock, dividends, and stock options.	Treasury stock greater than 10% of equity; high leverage caused, in part, by high treasury stock levels; dividend payout ratios greater than 1; unusual patterns across items.
Off–Balance Sheet	Operating leases divided by total assets; evaluate disclosure of SPEs.	Operating leases greater than 10% of total assets: restate leverage ratios by including discounted operating leases as part of liabilities; poor reporting of SPEs or poor fit to business strategy.
Acquisitions	Goodwill divided by total assets; calculate allocation percentages for current-year acquisition, especially goodwill as a percent of total acquisition cost.	Goodwill greater than 10% of total assets; goodwill a large percentage of acquisition price on recent acquisitions.

Other Dirty 30 Categories:

Issue	Discussion	Concerns
Detailed Financial Analysis	Analysis of liquidity, credit risk, and other quantitative techniques, including receivables and inventory, SG&A, R&D, cash flows, and taxes.	Negative working capital, high leverage, unusual receivables and inventory patterns, large SG&A, negative operating cash flows, or unusual effective tax rates.
Complex Accounting Issues	A whole host of issues usually involving qualitative characteristics, including derivatives, contingencies, and segment reporting.	Accountings issues that are not consistent with business strategy, such as unexpected segments; high-risk items such as the misuse of derivatives; excessive contingencies.
Corporate Governance	Policy and oversight provided by the board of directors, including board independence, role and compensation of CEO, and other factors such as related party transactions and insider trading.	Too many insiders on the board; CEO also chairman and exerting too much influence; excessive compensation for CEO, overuse of stock options, shady related party transactions, and unexpected insider trading.
Auditing	Auditor should be Big 4; opinion clean and issued relatively soon after the end of the fiscal year; low nonaudit fees expected as a percent of total fees; clean internal control report.	Auditor report date close to the 10-K required report date; high nonaudit fees; qualified opinion or internal control exceptions.

(continues)

Exhibit 16.3   Key Checklist Issues by Category (continued)

Wild Card:

Analysis	Discussion	Concerns
Restated Earnings, Regulatory Investigations	Review financial report when earnings are restated for earlier periods; bad-news items usually reported in the business media.	Usually an indicator of earnings magic in action, a red flag.
Stock Prices	Big changes in stock price indicate an investor reaction to some information, which should be investigated.	Big stock price drop, which may relate to a specific known event (company announced restated earnings) or unknown reasons.
Joker	Could be anything, from a corporate announcement to a *Wall Street Journal* article.	Any evidence of bad news.

EXHIBIT 16.3   KEY CHECKLIST ISSUES BY CATEGORY (CONTINUED)

GRADING CHECKLIST

Now these analytical categories are turned into grading checklists (see Exhibit 16.4).

Financial and Market Analysis:

Analysis	Grade	Discussion
Financial Overview		
Standard Ratios by Category		

Big 8:

Analysis	Grade	Discussion
Stock Options		
Pensions and OPEB		
Revenues		
Earnings and Expenses		
Strange Special Items		
Treasury Stock and Dividends		
Off–Balance Sheet		

(continues)

EXHIBIT 16.4   GRADING CHECKLIST

Analysis	Grade	Discussion
Acquisitions		

Other Dirty 30 Categories:

Issue	Grade	Discussion
Detailed Financial Analysis — Quantitative		
Complex Accounting Issues — Qualitative		
Corporate Governance		
Auditing		

Wild Card:

Analysis	Grade	Discussion
Restated Earnings, Regulatory Investigations		
Stock Prices		
Joker		

EXHIBIT 16.4 GRADING CHECKLIST (CONTINUED)

PUTTING THE CHECKLIST TO WORK

The checklist is completed for two disappointing firms from the Dow: AIG and General Motors (see Exhibit 16.5). Note that the focus is on problems; little discussion is presented when the results are okay.

American International Group (AIG)
Financial and Market Analysis:

Analysis	Grade	Discussion
Financial Overview	F	Insurance giant AIG had been run by CEO and Chairman Hank Greenberg for decades. But a 2005 accounting scandal forced him and several other executives out. This is the most blatant earnings magic case of the Dow 30. There are few problems when looking solely at the financial statements.
Standard Ratios by Category	B	Normal range.

(continues)

EXHIBIT 16.5 AIG AND GENERAL MOTORS CHECKLISTS

Big 8:

Analysis	Grade	Discussion
Stock Options	B	Moderate dilution (2% of shares outstanding) and compensation expense (less than 1% of net income).
Pensions and OPEB	C	Underfunded pension (balance sheet and funded status, $1.3 billion); underfunded OPEB (balance and funded status, $278 million).
Revenues	C	Rising revenues (20.5%) but declining return on sales.
Earnings and Expenses	C	High SG&A (85% of revenues).
Strange Special Items	C	Accounting change in 2004.
Treasury Stock and Dividends	B	Low treasury stock ($2.2 billion); moderate dividends.
Off–Balance Sheet	C	Moderate operating leases; substantial Qualified Special Purpose Entities and Variable Interest Entities, poor reporting of SPEs.
Acquisitions	B	Low goodwill.

Other Dirty 30 Categories:

Issue	Grade	Discussion
Detailed Financial Analysis—Quantitative	B	Adequate to good; receivables decreased over 50%, despite increase in revenues.
Complex Accounting Issues—Qualitative	B	Adequate to good; substantial contingencies.
Corporate Governance	F	**Accounting scandal;** CEO and many senior executives terminated; evidence of ineffective board.
Auditing	F	**147 days to opinion; substantial internal control weaknesses** (risk transfer, balance sheet reconciliation, derivative accounting, income tax accounting, and others).

Wild Card:

Analysis	Grade	Discussion
Restated Earnings, Regulatory Investigations	F	**Earnings restatement in 2005 for fiscal years 2000–2004.**
Stock Prices	D	Substantial drop in stock price after announcement of New York State Attorney General and SEC investigations in February 2005 (from over 70 to about 50).
Joker	D	Investigations continuing; new CEO and other executives; **10-K filed two months late.**

Summary:

Category	Grade	Discussion
Financial Overview	C	Financial statements normal, except for impact of accounting scandal.

(continues)

EXHIBIT 16.5   AIG AND GENERAL MOTORS CHECKLISTS (CONTINUED)

Summary: (Continued)

Category	Grade	Discussion
Big 8	C	Adequate on most dimensions.
Other Dirty 30	D	**Late audit report; internal control weaknesses.**
Wild Card	D	**Continuing investigation of insurance practices.**
Overall	F	**Accounting scandal dominates analysis;** investigations and earnings restatements: **substantial earnings magic!**

General Motors
Financial and Market Analysis:

Analysis	Grade	Discussion
Financial Overview	D	Poor performance, high compensation and related costs; large losses in 2005.
Standard Ratios by Category	D	Poor liquidity, high leverage, and poor performance (note $89 million loss on automotive operations, overall return on sales of 1.4%).
Stock Charts and Standard Market Ratios	F	Market-to-book below 1. Large stock price drop: over 50% for the last 2 years.
Advanced Ratios	D	Poor ratios on most dimensions, failing Altman's Z-score; evidence of using cookie-jar reserves for doubtful accounts.

Big 8:

Analysis	Grade	Discussion
Stock Options	C	Stock option dilution (18.9% of shares outstanding), but small options expense (less than 1% of net income).
Pensions and OPEB	F	**Pension underfunded: $7.5 billion funded status ($42.3 billion off–balance sheet); pension expense 87.6% of net income; OPEB underfunding of $7.6 billion, funded status; OPEB expense 162.3% of net income.**
Revenues	C	Revenues recorded when products are shipped; various incentive awards at time of vehicle sales—somewhat aggressive.
Earnings and Expenses	F	High cost of sales (82.7% of revenues), tax "income" (income increasing); substantial net losses in 2005.
Strange Special Items	C	Discontinued operations (2002–2003); disposal activities to close plants and relocate employees; asset impairment.
Treasury Stock and Dividends	D	Treasury stock not listed on balance sheet, but **treasury stock purchases equal to 84% of net income last six years;** dividend payout 230% of net income.
Off–Balance Sheet	C	Low operating leases; substantial SPEs in several financial categories.
Acquisitions	B	Low goodwill; no significant recent acquisitions.

(continues)

EXHIBIT 16.5   AIG AND GENERAL MOTORS CHECKLISTS (CONTINUED)

Other Dirty 30 Categories:

Issue	Grade	Discussion
Detailed Financial Analysis — Quantitative	D	Negative working capital; high leverage; receivables increased 13%, while revenues declined; negative other comprehensive income resulting in loss based on comprehensive income; failing Altman's Z-score; **BB bond rating** (below investment grade).
Complex Accounting Issues — Qualitative	C	Adequate on most dimensions. Equity method for foreign operations; poor performance for automotive segment, especially GM-Europe; substantial contingencies.
Corporate Governance	C	Chairman also CEO; 400,000 options + 81,000 Long-Term incentive shares to CEO.
Auditing	C	73 days to audit report date.

Wild Card:

Analysis	Grade	Discussion
Restated Earnings, Regulatory Investigations	F	8-K issued in November 2005 indicating that earnings would be restated for 2000–2005 due to misstated revenues.
Stock Prices	F	Market-to-book below 1; GM underperforming the Dow: stock price down over 50% in the last 2 years.
Joker	F	$3.8 billion in net losses for first three quarters of 2005.

Summary:

Category	Grade	Discussion
Financial and Market Analysis	D	Poor performance, negative market reaction; evidence of cookie-jar reserves.
Big 8	D	Pension & OPEB performance problematic; treasury stock purchases.
Other Dirty 30	D	Junk (BB) bond rating.
Wild Card	F	Restating earnings; poor performance for 2005.
Overall	F	Earnings restatements, poor performance, and high leverage including large losses in 2005; major problems with employee compensation, especially pension and OPEB costs.

EXHIBIT 16.5   AIG AND GENERAL MOTORS CHECKLISTS (CONTINUED)

GRADING THE DOW 30

Based on the checklist shown in Exhibit 16.5, the reporting excellence results are summarized in Exhibit 16.6 for the 2004 fiscal year. (Discussion focuses on concerns.)

Company	Grade	Discussion
3M (MMM)	C	Stock option dilution (10.1% of shares), pension and OPEB underfunding, pension expense (10.9% of NI), treasury stock (53.0% of equity), goodwill (12.8% of TA).
Alcoa (AA)	C	Pension underfunding, pension expense (15.4% of NI), OPEB underfunding (FS 11.2% of TA), OPEB expense (21.3% of NI), treasury stock (14.5% of TA), goodwill (19.5% of TA), discontinued operations (2002–2004), special items (asset retirement, restructuring), large decrease in bad debt reserve.
Altria (MO)	D	Pension and OPEB underfunding, **treasury stock (80.9% of equity), goodwill (27.6% of TA), BBB bond rating,** negative working capital, **substantial contingencies.**
American Express (AXP)	C	Stock option dilution (10.6% of shares), pension and OPEB underfunding, SG&A (46.1% of revenue), treasury stock not listed but **treasury stock purchases equal to 59% of net income for the last six years,** option grant to CEO of 800,000 options, substantial SPEs and derivatives.
American International Group (AIG)	F	Pension and OPEB underfunding, poor disclosure on SPEs, substantial contingencies, **earnings restatement, accounting investigations by regulators, 147 days to issue audit report, substantial internal control weaknesses.**
Boeing (BA)	C	Pension underfunding, pension expense (24.1% of NI), OPEB underfunded (14.9% of TA, FS; OPEB expense 39.2% of NI), treasury stock (16.3% of TA), negative working capital, substantial contingencies, failing Altman's.
Caterpillar (CAT)	C	Stock option dilution (12.0% of shares), pension underfunding (13.5% of TA), OPEB expense (17.5% of NI), treasury stock (43.9% of equity), large increase in inventory, negative CFO, nonaudit fees (62.4% of total fees).
Citigroup (C)	C	Pension underfunding, negative CFO & FCF, SG&A (50.4% of revenue), CEO paid $10.1 million and exercised 1.8 million options ($12.3 million), substantial exposure to SPEs and derivatives, large decrease in bad debts reserve, history of past financial abuse, and regulatory investigations.
Coca-Cola (KO)	C	Pension and OPEB underfunding, **treasury stock (110.6% of equity),** substantial use of equity method for bottling, accounting change, special items (goodwill impairment, franchise impairment, "streamlining costs").
Du Pont (DD)	C	Pension underfunding (10.0% of TA, FS), **pension expense (56.0% of NI),** treasury stock (31.9% of equity), increase in receivables much larger than increase in revenues, substantial contingencies.

(continues)

EXHIBIT 16.6 SUMMARY OF REPORTING EXCELLENCE RESULTS

Company	Grade	Discussion
Exxon-Mobil (XOM)	B	Pension and OPEB underfunding, treasury stock (37.6% of equity), CEO exercised 1.8 million options ($43.7 million).
General Electric (GE)	C	Pension and OPEB underfunding, treasury stock (11.5% of equity), substantial exposure to SPEs and derivatives, large other comprehensive loss, restated earnings, internal control weaknesses.
General Motors (GM)	F	Earnings restatements announced in 2005; stock options (18.9% of shares), pension underfunding, **pension expense (87.6% of NI), OPEB underfunding (12.8% of TA, FS — $61.5 billion), OPEB expense (162.8% of NI), [negative equity if funded status is used], dividend payout 229.9% of NI,** treasury stock not listed but **treasury stock purchases equal to 84% of net income last six years,** substantial exposure to SPEs and derivatives, rising receivables despite declining revenues, evidence of cookie-jar reserves, substantial contingencies, failing Altman's, **non-investment grade bond rating (BB),** 73 days to audit report, large net losses in 2005.
Hewlett-Packard (HPQ)	C	Stock options (18.9% of shares; net income down 20.5%), pension underfunding, pension expense (17.2% of NI), OPEB underfunding, treasury stock not listed but **treasury stock purchases equal to 90.5% of net income last six years,** goodwill 20.1% of total assets; 2002 acquisition of Compaq.
Home Depot (HD)	B	Operating leases (22.1% of TA), CEO salary $14.6 million.
Honeywell (HON)	C	Pension underfunding, pension expense (30.1% of NI), OPEB underfunding, OPEB expense (17.1% of NI), goodwill (19.4% of TA).
IBM (IBM)	C	Stock options (15.3% of shares, 11.3% decrease in NI), pension underfunding, pension expense (12.7% of NI), OPEB underfunding, **treasury stock (104.5% of equity),** acquisition in 2004 ($24 billion, $14.5 billion charged to goodwill, 67.8%), discontinued operations (2002–2004), nonaudit fees (72.2% of total fees).
Intel (INTC)	B	Stock options (14.1% of shares, 16.9% decrease in NI), pension and OPEB underfunding, treasury stock not listed but **treasury stock purchases equal to 80% of net income last six years.**
J.P. Morgan (JPM)	C	Stock options (10.6% of shares), OPEB underfunding (FS), negative CFO and FCF, SG&A (49.8% of revenue), substantial exposure to SPEs and derivatives, regulatory problems; acquisitions of Chase Manhattan in 2001 and Bank One in 2004.
Johnson & Johnson (JNJ)	C	Pension and OPEB underfunding, treasury stock (18.9% of shares), goodwill (11.0% of TA), non-audit fees (61.1% of total fees), substantial contingencies.

(continues)

EXHIBIT 16.6   SUMMARY OF REPORTING EXCELLENCE RESULTS (CONTINUED)

Company	Grade	Discussion
McDonald's (MCD) (Continued)	C	Stock options (13.1% of shares), **treasury stock (67.4% of equity), operating leases (45.6% of TA)**, negative working capital, substantial contingencies.
Merck (MRK)	C	Stock options (11.6% of shares), pension and OPEB underfunding, **treasury stock (151.5% of equity), substantial contingencies including Vioxx,** CEO exercised options (1.1 million, $34.8 million).
Microsoft (MSFT)	B	Substantial nonaudit fees (61.1% of total fees), regulatory contingencies, treasury stock not disclosed, large decrease in bad debts reserve (31%).
Pfizer (PFE)	C	Pension underfunding (FS), treasury stock (52.7% of equity), goodwill (19.2% of TA), discontinued operations, accounting change, special items (merger-related costs, restructuring), substantial contingencies.
Procter & Gamble (PG)	C	Stock options (10.8% of shares), **goodwill (34.4% of TA),** negative working capital, large decrease in bad debts reserve, treasury stock not listed but **treasury stock purchases equal to 60% of net income last six years,** CEO granted 706,000 options, Gillette acquisition.
SBC Comm. (SBC)	C	OPEB underfunding (15.1% of TA, FS), OPEB expense (21.7% of NI), negative working capital, discontinued operations (2002–2004), accounting change, extraordinary item, restructuring, use of equity method for Cingular (60% ownership), CEO compensation ($10.7 million), AT&T Wireless acquisition, AT&T acquisition.
United Technology (UTX)	C	Pension and OPEB underfunding, **goodwill (25.3% of TA),** large decrease in bad debts reserve, CEO exercised options (1.1 million, $83.6 million).
Verizon (VZ)	C	OPEB underfunding (13.6% of TA, FS), OPEB expense (22.7% of NI), failing Altman's, negative working capital, discontinued operations, accounting changes (2002–2004), special charges, large increase in inventory, large decrease in bad debts reserve; established as a 2000 merger of Bell Atlantic and GTE.
Wal-Mart (WMT)	C	Pension underfunding, operating leases ($10.3 billion, 8.6% of TA), treasury stock not listed but **treasury stock purchases equal to 38% of net income last six years,** negative working capital, substantial contingencies.
Walt Disney (DIS)	C	Stock options (11.1% of TA, 10.9% decrease in NI), underfunded OPEB, BBB+ bond rating, negative working capital, SG&A (86.8% of revenue), 70 days to audit report.

CEO = chief executive officer, CFO = cash from operations, FCF = free cash flows, FS = funded status, NI = net income, OPEB = other post-employment benefits, SG&A = selling, general and administrative expenses, SPEs = special purpose entities, TA = total assets.

EXHIBIT 16.6 SUMMARY OF REPORTING EXCELLENCE RESULTS (CONTINUED)

The results are not a pretty sight. There is not an A in sight and only four Bs. The two Fs (AIG and GM) and a D (Altria) indicate firms with big earnings quality issues. All the firms have transparency issues, and many are substantial. AIG represents a current accounting scandal. General Motors has significant earnings quality issues. GM's biggest problems center on employee compensation issues, especially pension and other postemployment benefits (OPEB). With high-cost labor and problems selling cars, GMs junk bond rating is well deserved. But that's not all. GM indicated a restatement of earnings from 2000–2005 to correct overstated revenues. Additional concerns center on cookie-jar reserves and other issues. Altria has big contingency concerns. In addition to the massive U.S. lawsuits, the company is being sued around the world—a new wrinkle to globalization.

Closing in on Financial Reality

Now what? Big problems exist with some of the Dow 30, a group expected to be among the biggest and best American corporations. Can financial reality be achieved? The short answer is no. However, we can move closer by recalculating selected financial statement information—a process called "normalization." Home Depot, for example, has substantial operating leases (22.1% of total assets). As demonstrated earlier, an estimated present value can be calculated based on the discount used for capital leases. This results in estimated operating lease obligations of $2.7 billion for Home Depot and increased total liabilities by 18.5%. New leverage ratios can be calculated using the adjusted liability total.

Similar adjustments can be made for several issues. Stock options expense is a note disclosure, and net income pro forma can be used as an alternative bottom line to recalculate performance ratios. Hewlett-Packard's net income pro forma at $2.8 billion was over 20% lower than reported net income. H-P's reported return on sales of 4.4% drops to 3.5% using pro forma net income. H-P's price/earnings ratio of 13.9 looks much less attractive at 16.7.

Pension and OPEB net obligations are reported based on various "smoothing" calculations. Economic reality means funded status, which is presented in the pension/OPEB notes. Funded status can be substituted to give a more accurate picture of relative financial position. An extreme case is General Motors, which has big pension/OPEB problems. The balance sheet differences for 2004 are shown in Exhibit 16.7.

GM reported a combined pension/OPEB net asset position of $31 billion, substantially overfunded. Unfortunately, funded status shows that GM

	Pension	OPEB	Total
Reported	$ 34,817	$−3,847	$ 30,970
Funded Status	−7,531	−7,598	−15,129
Difference	$−42,348	$−3,751	$−46,099

EXHIBIT 16.7   BALANCE SHEET DIFFERENCES FOR 2004

was really underfunded by over $15 billion. Fifteen billion dollars is not bad for a company with $449 billion in total assets. However, the difference of $46 billion represents what amounts to off–balance sheet obligations of over 10% of assets. That effectively increases the leverage of a highly leveraged company. Reported liabilities of $423 billion resulted in a debt ratio of 94.2% ($423/$449). Using funded status would more than wipe out equity of $25 billion.

Procter & Gamble has about a third of assets recorded as goodwill. This represents the total acquisition payment beyond restated net assets—perhaps money well spent or just an indicator of accumulated overpayment. In any case, it is an accounting plug figure rather than a "real asset." It could be deducted from total assets, and then leverage and other ratios could be recalculated. P&G is a highly leveraged firm (debt-to-equity of 2.3). Deducting goodwill ($19.6 billion) would wipe out equity. An alternative would be to use net tangible assets, which deducts all intangibles. Many companies do poorly under this perspective, including most pharmaceuticals. Pfizer, for example, has $23.8 billion in goodwill and $22.3 billion in other intangibles: total intangibles of $57.0 billion compared to total assets of $123.7 billion. Net tangible assets were $66.7 billion, or only 53.9% of total assets.

For most concerns, no adjustments are readily available. Companies that have massive amounts of treasury stock just have much less equity and fewer shares outstanding. This is great for earnings per share and return on equity but has no effect on return on sales (except for missing out on alternative uses of cash) and a negative effect on leverage. The use of the equity method for investments may be a great use of risk management (giant oil companies often use joint ventures on risky drilling ventures) or a major earnings magic tool—equity method investments are effectively off–balance sheet, and spinning off subsidiaries may be timed to strategically result in gains or losses in a specific period.

Then there are issues that are hard to analyze in detail. Companies such as Altria or Merck with massive contingencies have sizable uncertainty, with no obvious way to effectively evaluate long-term outcomes effectively. The use of derivatives is all about risk management for most firms. However, to what extent firms are effectively hedging versus poor hedging or outright speculation is difficult to determine. Reporting is limited on these issues (e.g., companies are supposed to report non-hedging derivatives), but most specific risks are not often evaluated. The impact of previous acquisitions also is hard to determine. Companies may provide disclosures, especially on restructuring associated with specific acquisition or segment reporting if the acquisition becomes a specific separate reporting segment. However, there are no specific generally accepted accounting principles (GAAP) requirements beyond the acquisition year.

In addition, there are differences of opinion on what is "bad news." Thus, negative working capital and treasury stock are "bad news" signals in the current analysis. However, some analysts favor both of these items. There are trade-offs in various items, such as leverage. Accumulating debt may be important for acquisitions or to fund new operating investments. Since added debt increases credit risk, how much is too much?

In summary, there are substantial disclosures to evaluate financial statements and numerous tools and techniques to effectively evaluate earnings magic and relative transparency. Given the recent history of corporate scandal, the tools are useful and possibly essential. However, no analysis is foolproof.

17

AN INVESTMENT STRATEGY

*In 1982, stocks were dirt cheap—but this is only another
way of saying that no one wanted to buy them. The Dow
was now trading at seven times earnings.*

—Maggie Mahar

Bears are people who do their arithmetic.

—Peter Bernstein

How does the evaluation of earnings magic and transparency fit into an investment decision? The additional information on financial reality should be an
important component. One possibility is to focus on companies that get A
(good luck) or B ratings. Doing this substantially cuts down on the investment
set and is probably a good idea, everything else being equal. Of course, everything is not equal. At some price, D and F companies become attractive.

Investors have short- and long-term goals, and should invest around
these specific goals. How much risk an investor is willing to assume is a key
factor for evaluating investment decisions. In a well-diversified portfolio,
assuming greater risk should result in a higher return over the long run. Avoiding the Enrons and WorldComs also helps. Fundamental factors related to
investment goals and basic financial analysis are reviewed in this chapter.

Let us assume a long-term investment horizon, a focus on large-
capitalization stocks, and a relatively conservative approach to picking
stocks. A well-diversified portfolio is a standard feature, and the investment
mix will include cash equivalents, bonds, and stocks. But the focus is on
stock picking for a diversified portfolio. The strategy is to concentrate on
evaluating many stocks with appealing characteristics and conduct two levels of analysis. First is an initial screening based on specific investment criteria; next is the earnings magic/transparency analysis.

Experts usually describe three investment strategies. First are growth
stocks, with longer-term investors focusing on high earnings growth expected

throughout the foreseeable future. Growth stocks are expected to have double-digit earnings growth prospects and usually expected to outpace competitors. Second are income stocks that have high dividend yields. An investor needing a cash return (e.g., at or near retirement) may consider mainly high-dividend-yielding companies. They pay cash and usually have limited earnings growth opportunities. The recent tax law changes make high-yield companies even more attractive. Third are value stocks that are "undervalued" based on some criteria, possibly because of a recent stock price drop. These may be "cyclically out of favor," badly in need of restructuring or changing business strategy, suffering a short-term earnings blip, and, it is hoped, not on the road to bankruptcy.

Starting with a preliminary list of potential buys (limited to the Dow 30 for this example), a quick financial and market analysis is made to determine important financial characteristics: how much cash and liquidity, how much debt, basic profitability and efficiency characteristics, and recent market response to the firms. Ratios and other analytical techniques can be calculated quickly, or various Internet sites can be used where these have already been calculated. Yahoo! Finance, for example, presents many key ratios as well as abbreviated financial statements.

Particularly important are current stock prices and relative valuations. The point is to determine which stocks appear to be overpriced and which seem to be bargains. There are several techniques to attempt these valuations, but all have limitations. Price earnings to growth ratio (PEG) and market-to-book (market capitalization divided by stockholders' equity) should roughly signal whether the stock is reasonably priced.

The information so far assumes that the stated numbers on the financial statements represent economic reality; that is, they are 100% correct and need no further adjustments. That is where earnings magic analysis comes in: Determine if reasonable transparency really exists, if there are signals of substantial earnings magic, and recalibrate financial statement information to approximate financial reality if necessary.

ANALYZING THE DOW 30

The Dow 30 are huge, mature firms with long histories of success. All pay dividends and many tend to be attractive as income stocks. Sheer size makes huge earnings growth unlikely, although the majority have projected five-year earnings growth of at least 10%. Thus, there are some growth stock candidates. Almost by definition, they are seldom out of favor. Stocks are usually dumped from the Dow if they stay out of favor for very long, but note that GM's stock price has been declining for the last five years.

Arbitrary criteria can be used initially to classify firms into potential investments for any of three "portfolios:" growth, income, or value. For this exercise, assume that: (1) potential growth investment stocks must have five-year earnings growth forecasts of at least 12% annually (preferably with a five-year earnings history of at least double-digit growth); (2) potential income stocks must have dividend yields of at least 3%; and (3) potential value stocks must have a price-to-book of less than two and a PEG of 1.2 or less. Appendix 17.1 sorts the Dow 30 first by five-year earnings forecasts, and Appendix 17.2 sorts them by dividend yield.

Growth Investments

Typical growth companies might include high-tech companies like eBay (price/earnings ratio [P/E] of 60.3 and five-year earnings forecast of 27.9%) and Google (P/E of 44.4 and five-year earnings forecast of 30.0%). By comparison, the fastest growing of the Dow 30 are stodgy. Intel leads the list with a five-year earnings growth of 15% and a P/E of 17.8. Still, some big names can add some stability. Home Depot looks attractive with a 14% forecast and a five-year earnings growth history of 17.9%. Eleven of the Dow have earnings growth forecasts of at least 12%, but only six also have a recent history of double-digit earnings growth (last five years). Eliminate AIG for obvious earnings magic and the list is five. Summary market information for these five, compared to the two high flyers, is shown in Exhibit 17.1.

The Dow Five are no match to the two high flyers for earnings expectations and related market information. eBay and Google pay no dividends, have high P/Es and price-to-book, but also higher PEGs (the high P/Es are

Company	5-Year Earnings Forecast	P/E	PEG	Price-to-Book	Yield
Google	30.0%	44.4	1.5	23.5	0
eBay	27.9	60.3	2.2	7.3	0
Home Depot	14	14.1	1	3.7	0.9%
Wal-Mart	14	16.6	1.2	4.2	1.2
American Express	13	15.2	1.2	4.1	0.9
3M	12	15.9	1.3	5.8	2.0
Caterpillar	12	10.8	1.1	4.2	1.8

EXHIBIT 17.1   FIVE-YEAR SUMMARY MARKET INFORMATION COMPARED TO TWO HIGH FLYERS

Company	Grade	Concerns
3M (MMM)	C	Stock option dilution (10.1% of shares), pension and OPEB underfunding, pension expense (10.9% of NI), treasury stock (53.0% of equity), goodwill (12.8% of TA).
American Express (AXP)	C	Stock option dilution (10.6% of shares), pension and OPEB underfunding, SGA (46.1% of revenue), treasury stock not listed but **treasury stock purchases equal to 59% of net income last six years,** option grant to CEO (800,000), substantial SPEs and derivatives.
Caterpillar (CAT)	C	Stock option dilution (12.0% of shares), pension underfunding (13.5% of TA), OPEB expense (17.5% of NI), treasury stock (43.9% of equity), large increase in inventory, negative CFO, nonaudit fees (62.4% of total fees).
Home Depot (HD)	B	Operating leases (22.1% of TA), CEO salary $14.6 million.
Wal-Mart (WMT)	C	Pension underfunding, operating leases ($10.3 billion, 8.6% of TA), treasury stock not listed but **treasury stock equal to 38% of net income last six years,** negative working capital, substantial contingencies.

EXHIBIT 17.2 SCORES FOR DOW FIVE

partially compensated by the high earnings growth rates). The Dow Five P/Es are similar to the rest of the Dow 30 but have lower price-to-book and lower dividend yields. Assuming the earnings forecasts are accurate, all five seem likely investment candidates. But how do they do on the earnings magic scale? The scores from the last chapter are outlined in Exhibit 17.2.

The good news is that all five are relatively clean companies; no major issues exist with any of them. Home Depot is rated B, a reasonable indicator of relative transparency. The major item is operating leases, which suggests that liabilities should be restated to approximate the impact of the leases. The use of operating leases is a common industry practice. The four remaining companies had more serious issues, but none is serious enough to reject them as a possible investment.

Income Investments

Income investments are expected to have relatively large dividend yields and stable characteristics that suggest continuing dividend payments. The Dow 30 have an average yield of 2.7% and, therefore, are likely to provide several investment candidates. Six firms (excluding Microsoft because of the special dividend and GM as an earnings magic disaster) have dividend yields of at least 3%. Summary market information for these six is shown in Exhibit 17.3.

Company	5-Year Earnings Forecast	P/E	PEG	Price-to-Book	Yield
SBC Comm.	6%	14.9	2.7	1.9	5.4%
Merck	2.6	13.1	4.9	4	4.6
Verizon	4	12.8	3.3	2.6	4.4
J.P. Morgan	10	10.3	1.2	1.2	3.8
Citigroup	11	9.9	1	2.3	3.5
Du Pont	10	14	1.6	4	3.0

EXHIBIT 17.3 SUMMARY MARKET INFORMATION

It is not unusual to have income stocks that have poor market characteristics, and these companies are no exception. Despite the hefty dividends, the remaining market factors are mediocre at best—the high-yield firms are called "Dogs of the Dow" for a reason. J.P. Morgan, Citigroup, and Du Pont have the lower yields in the group, but also have double-digit earnings forecasts and reasonable P/Es and PEGs.

What about the earnings magic characteristics? Let us review Exhibit 17.4.

Company	Grade	Concerns
Citigroup (C)	C	Pension underfunding, negative CFO, SGA (50.4% of revenue), CEO paid $10.1 million and exercised 1.8 million options ($12.3 million), substantial exposure to SPEs and derivatives, large decrease in bad debts reserve, history of past financial abuse and regulatory investigations.
Du Pont (DD)	C	Pension underfunding (10.0% of TA, FS), **pension expense (56.0% of NI)**, treasury stock (31.9% of TA), increase in receivables much larger than increase in revenues, substantial contingencies.
J.P. Morgan (JPM)	C	Stock options (10.6% of shares), OPEB underfunding (FS), negative CFO, SG&A (49.8% of revenue), substantial exposure to SPEs NS derivatives, regulatory problems, acquisitions of Chase Manhattan in 2001 and Bank One in 2004.
Merck (MRK)	C	Stock options (11.6% of shares), pension and OPEB underfunding, **treasury stock (151.5% of equity), substantial contingencies including Vioxx,** CEO exercised options (1.1 million, $34.8 million).
SBC Communications (SBC)	C	OPEB underfunding (15.1% of TA, FS), OPEB expense (21.7% of NI), negative working capital, discontinued operations (2002–2004), accounting change, extraordinary item, restructuring, use of equity method for Cingular (60% ownership), CEO compensation ($10.7

(continues)

EXHIBIT 17.4 COMPANY CONCERNS

SBC Communications (SBC) (Continued)		million), AT&T Wireless acquisition, AT&T acquisition pending.
Verizon (VZ)	C	OPEB underfunding (13.6% of TA, FS), OPEB expense (22.7% of NI), failing Altman's, negative working capital, discontinued operations, accounting changes (2002–2004), special charges, large increase in inventory, large decrease in bad debts expense; established as a 2000 merger of Bell Atlantic and GTE.

EXHIBIT 17.4   COMPANY CONCERNS (CONTINUED)

The firms have C ratings, but these include some sizable problems. Merck has a few questionable areas, with contingencies—especially the Vioxx recall—a big unknown. The others are at least worth taking a look at. It may be worth considering firms with lower dividend yields. There are 9 other Dow 30 companies that have a yield of at least 2%. In that group, Exxon-Mobil is rated B and has a yield of 2%. Utilities have been traditional high-yield stocks, and even with deregulation many utilities have reasonable dividend yields. For example, Duke Energy has a yield of 3.7%.

Value Investments

Value investing is hard to define, since the idea is finding undervalued stock—whatever that means. A typical stimulus is a specific big event (notification of a Securities and Exchange Commission investigation or a particularly bad earnings forecast) that results in a big stock price decline. However, a company could be considered out of favor for any number of reasons, and an analyst could be adamant about an eminent turn-around.

Two signs of possible out-of-favor stock are low price-to-book ratios and low PEGs. For this example, assume that a price-to-book below 2 and a PEG of 1.2 or less are possible value investments. Based on these criteria, only three Dow 30 companies are considered: Alcoa, AIG, and, unexpectedly, J.P. Morgan. Several companies have one but not both characteristics, as shown in Exhibit 17.5.

These are three diverse companies and make this list for different reasons. AIG is a real corporate scandal, with an earnings magic F. The investigations and follow-up events dropped the company to potential bargain range. Alcoa is a commodity play, with investors skeptical that stellar earnings will continue. J.P. Morgan is a bank susceptible to interest rate changes and has suffered some regulatory problems. Both Alcoa and J.P. Morgan have earnings magic Cs.

Company	5-Year Earnings Forecast	P/E	PEG	Price-to-Book	Yield
Alcoa	14%	12.3	1.1	1.8	2.2%
AIG	13	11	1	1.8	0.7
J.P. Morgan	10	10.3	1.2	1.2	3.8

EXHIBIT 17.5   SIGNS OF POSSIBLE OUT-OF-FAVOR STOCK

Stock charts are useful to evaluate recent stock drops and general investor disenchantment with a stock. The scandal at AIG started in February 2005, and the impact on stock price is obvious, as shown in Exhibit 17.6.

It has recovered a bit since the end of April. AIG's 2004 10-K with restatements since 2000 was not as bad as anticipated. However, the investigation continues, and the scandal is not necessarily over.

A five-year stock chart for Alcoa is shown in Exhibit 17.7.

Alcoa is somewhat more volatile than the Dow. It is down about 15% relative to the Dow over the last five years, with a drop since the beginning of 2004.

J.P. Morgan's one-year stock chart, shown in Exhibit 17.8, is compared to competitor Citigroup and the Dow.

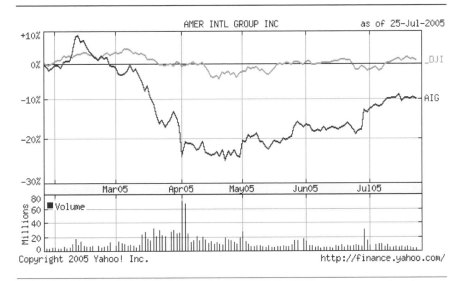

EXHIBIT 17.6   STOCK CHART FOR AIG

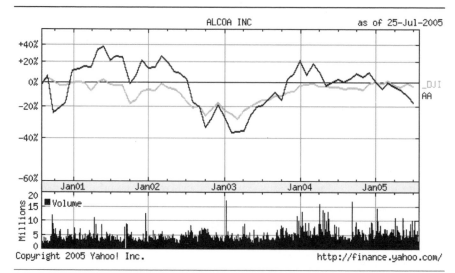

EXHIBIT 17.7   FIVE-YEAR STOCK CHART FOR ALCOA

Morgan has underperformed both Citi and the Dow year-to-date, especially the first quarter or so. Generally, all three potential value investments have shown recent stock price drops and can be viewed as out of favor.

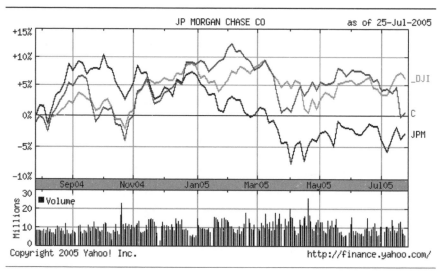

EXHIBIT 17.8   J.P. MORGAN'S ONE-YEAR STOCK CHART COMPARED TO CITIGROUP AND THE DOW

Company	Grade	Concerns
American International Group (AIG)	F	Pension and OPEB underfunding, poor disclosure on SPEs, earnings restatement, accounting investigations by regulators, 147 days to issue audit report, substantial internal control weaknesses.
Alcoa (AA)	C	Pension underfunding (pension expense 15.4% of NI), OPEB underfunding (FS 11.2% of TA), OPEB expense (21.3% of NI), treasury stock (14.5% of TA), goodwill (19.5% of TA), discontinued operations (2002–2004), special items (asset retirement, restructuring).
J.P. Morgan (JPM)	C	Stock options (10.6% of shares), OPEB underfunding (FS), negative CFO, SG&A (49.8% of revenue), substantial exposure to SPEs and derivatives, regulatory problems, acquisitions of Chase Manhattan in 2001 and Bank One in 2004.

CFO = cash from operations, FS = funded status, NI = net income, OPEB = other post employment benefits, SG&A = selling, general and administrative, SPEs = special purpose entities, TA = total assets.

Exhibit 17.9   Summary Earnings Magic Grades

The summary earnings magic grades are shown in Exhibit 17.9. With an F rating based on the revised 2004 10-K, there is no indication of transparency for AIG. As an investment: not a chance. Alcoa and J.P. Morgan are possibilities, but it is hard to get enthusiastic about them.

Are You Ready to Invest?

The purpose of this chapter is to illustrate how earnings magic can be integrated into an investment choice analysis. The investment scheme is relatively simple and categories are arbitrary. There are a host of Internet sites and investment books designed to assist in making reasonable investment choices. This quick analysis was not designed to replace any of these investment approaches, only to show the importance of evaluating earnings magic and relative transparency as part of the analysis.

APPENDIX 17.1

MARKET INDICATORS FOR THE DOW 30 (GROWTH ANALYSIS)

Company	5-Year Forecast*	5-Year History*	Price/Earnings Ratio	Price/Earnings to Growth Ratio
Intel (INTC)	15%	−2.1%	17.8	1.3
Alcoa (AA)	14	−5.8	12.3	1.1
Home Depot (HD)	14	17.9	14.1	1
Wal-Mart (WMT)	14	13.6	16.6	1.2
American Express (AXP)	13	14.2	15.2	1.3
American International Group (AIG)	13	14.7	11	1
3M (MMM)	12	12.6	15.9	1.5
Boeing (BA)	12	−17.3	20	2.1
Caterpillar (CAT)	12	14.5	10.8	1
Honeywell (HON)	12	−13.1	14.9	1.5
United Technology (UTX)	12	9.9	15	1.4
Walt Disney (DIS)	11.5	4	17.1	1.6
Citigroup (C)	11	10.5	9.9	1
Procter & Gamble (PG)	11	NA	18.6	1.8
General Electric (GE)	10.5%	5.3	17.2	1.8
Du Pont (DD)	10	0.5	14	1.6
Hewlett-Packard (HPQ)	10	−1.6	14.5	1.6
IBM (IBM)	10	0.2	15.1	1.7
J.P. Morgan (JPM)	10	5.9	10.3	1.2
Johnson & Johnson (JNJ)	10	15.1	17.1	1.9
Microsoft (MSFT)	10	NA	18.1	1.9
Altria (MO)	8.5	6.2	11.8	1.5
Coca-Cola (KO)	8	8.9	18.8	2.5
McDonald's (MCD)	8	5.9	13.8	1.9
Pfizer (PFE)	8	16.9	12.5	1.7

(continues)

Company	5-Year Forecast*	5-Year History*	Price/Earnings Ratio	Price/Earnings to Growth Ratio
Exxon-Mobil (XOM)	7.3	11.2	13	1.7
SBC Comm. (SBC)	6	−12.3	14.9	2.7
General Motors (GM)	5	−0.3	22.3	4.5
Verizon (VZ)	4	−4.3	12.8	3.3
Merck (MRK)	2.6	−2.7	13.1	4.9
Average	10.1%	4.6%	15	1.8

*Annual percentage growth rate.

APPENDIX 17.2

MARKET INDICATORS FOR THE DOW 30 (INCOME AND VALUE ANALYSIS)

Company	Yield	Market Cap*	Price-to-Book
Microsoft (MSFT)	12.9%**	$281.7	5.9
General Motors (GM)	6.4	18	0.7
SBC Comm. (SBC)	5.4	78.2	1.9
Merck (MRK)	4.6	71.5	4
Verizon (VZ)	4.4	98.1	2.6
J.P. Morgan (JPM)	3.8	126	1.2
Citigroup (C)	3.5	246	2.3
Du Pont (DD)	3	46.7	4
Altria (MO)	2.9	139.9	4.3
Pfizer (PFE)	2.5	210.8	3.2
Coca-Cola (KO)	2.3	108.2	6.6
General Electric (GE)	2.3	391.2	3.5
Alcoa (AA)	2.2	24	1.8
Honeywell (HON)	2.2	31.3	2.7
Exxon-Mobil (XOM)	2	361.6	3.5
3M (MMM)	2	59.2	5.8
Procter & Gamble (PG)	1.9	139.1	8.1
Caterpillar (CAT)	1.8	32.2	4.2
Johnson & Johnson (JNJ)	1.8	200.5	6
McDonald's (MCD)	1.8	39.6	2.7
United Technology (UTX)	1.5	55.2	3.6
Hewlett-Packard (HPQ)	1.4	65.9	1.8
Wal-Mart (WMT)	1.2	200.1	4.2
IBM (IBM)	1	124.4	4.2
American Express (AXP)	0.9	66.3	4.1
Boeing (BA)	0.9	52.1	4.5
Home Depot (HD)	0.9	86.3	3.7
Intel (INTC)	0.9	169.1	4.5

(continues)

Company	Yield	Market Cap*	Price-to-Book
Walt Disney (DIS)	0.9	56.9	2.2
American International Group (AIG)	0.7	146.9	1.8
Average	2.7%	$124.2	3.7

* In billions.
** Includes a special dividend of $3 a share (the current yield is 1.2%).

18

SEARCHING FOR HELP: USEFUL INTERNET SITES

"Dr. Livingstone, I presume."
—Henry Stanley

The compensation for greater risk is only apparently a greater return: It has to be multiplied by a probability coefficient, whereby its real value is again reduced.
—Joseph Schumpeter

There is nothing like the information magic of the Internet. There are literally thousands of sites that can be used to assist in financial analysis, financial planning, detailed information on virtually any company, and general knowledge. Because I used Internet sites extensively for this book, here are some of my favorites. This is by no means a complete list.

GENERAL FINANCIAL INFORMATION

Yahoo! Finance is my favorite site. It has financial news, but more important is the detailed financial analysis on individual companies that can be accessed by ticker symbol. The information is easy to use and the format is convenient. Many other sites are somewhat similar and also provide some unique information (see Exhibit 18.1), listed in order of relative usefulness.

Internet Site	Web Address	Description
Yahoo! Finance	finance.yahoo.com	Financial news, plus detailed information on individual companies including summary financial statements.

(continues)

EXHIBIT 18.1 INTERNET SITES AND DESCRIPTIONS

Internet Site	Web Address	Description
Motley Fool (Continued)	www.fool.com	Useful for "fool school," basic information on investing and financial planning.
CNNMoney	Money.cnn.com	Useful for financial news and articles from *Money Magazine*.
Fortune	www.fortune.com/fortune	Financial news, with substantial information on *Fortune* 500 (and other *Fortune* lists) plus articles from *Fortune* magazine.
Business Week	www.businessweek.com	Detailed financial news, with articles from *Business Week*.
Wall Street Journal	Online.wsj.com/public/us	Financial news, access to *Wall Street Journal*, but subscription required for most information.
Hoovers	www.hoovers.com/free/	Information on specific companies, but subscription required for most information.
Market Watch	www.marketwatch.com	Extensive financial news and investor tools.
Financial Times	News.ft.com/home/us	Financial news with a European flavor.
Reuters	www.reuters.com	Financial news with an international focus.

EXHIBIT 18.1 INTERNET SITES AND DESCRIPTIONS (CONTINUED)

SPECIALIZED BUSINESS TOOLS

Exhibit 18.2 provides a few sites with a specialized focus.

Raw Data Sources

Internet Site	Web Address	Description
Black-Scholes	www.optionanimator.com	Basic options discussion.
Federal Reserve	www.federalreserve.gov	Extensive discussion on the role of the Fed, banking, monetary policy, and other economic factors.
Lexis/Nexis	Web.lexis-nexis.com/universe	Detailed business tools, especially useful for downloading SEC reports (subscription service usually associated with libraries).
State-of-the-Nation	www.stat-usa.gov/econtest.nsf	Extensive list of current economic indicators.

(continues)

EXHIBIT 18.2 INTERNET SITES WITH A SPECIALIZED FOCUS (CONTINUED)

Raw Data Sources (Continued)

Internet Site	Web Address	Description
wrds	Wrds.wharton.upenn.edu	Vast financial and stock price database, used primarily for academic research (expensive subscription service).
Zacks	www.zacks.com	Financial tools, especially useful for analysts' earnings forecasts.

Regulatory-Accounting

Internet Site	Web Address	Description
SEC	www.sec.gov	Extensive listings, including role of the SEC and all pronouncements and actions.
FASB	www.fasb.org	Extensive site on FASB, including procedures, all pronouncements, and current projects.
Deloitte & Touche	www.deloitte.com	Big Four, good discussion of firm history.
Ernst & Young	www.ey.com	Big Four, discussion of some issues such as Sarbanes-Oxley.
KPMG	www.us.kpmg.com	Big Four.
PricewaterhouseCoopers	www.pwcglobal.com	Big Four.
New York Stock Exchange	www.nyse.com	Discussion of NYSE history and regulations, plus listed company directory.
Nasdaq	www.nasdaq.com	Includes listed companies.

EXHIBIT 18.2   INTERNET SITES WITH A SPECIALIZED FOCUS (CONTINUED)

DOW 30

Virtually all companies have Web sites, some extensive. Exhibit 18.3 lists the Dow 30. Company Web sites can be a source for important financial information (including annual reports and proxy statements). The Web site of any company considered for investing should be reviewed for information disclosure (a transparency indicator) and usefulness to investors and customers. As a group, the Web sites were quite diverse but generally disappointing. The 2004 annual report could be downloaded but was not always easily found. Fewer than half had a company history page.

Internet Site	Web Address	Description
3M (MMM)	www.3m.com	Adequate.
Alcoa (AA)	www.alcoa.com	Adequate.
Altria (MO)	www.altria.com	History timeline, adequate financial information.
American Express (AXP)	www.americanexpress.com	Focus on services, adequate investor relations.
American International Group (AIG)	www.aig.com	Adequate.
Boeing (BA)	www.boeing.com	Adequate.
Caterpillar (CAT)	www.cat.com	History timeline, better than most.
Citigroup (C)	www.citigroup.com	Focus on services, includes history timeline.
Coca-Cola (KO)	www.cocacola.com	Adequate.
Du Pont (DD)	www.dupont.com	Extensive site, including substantial information useful to investors.
Exxon-Mobil (XOM)	www.exxonmobil.com	Adequate.
General Electric (GE)	www.ge.com	Adequate.
General Motors (GM)	www.gm.com	Focus on selling cars; investor information adequate.
Hewlett-Packard (HPQ)	www.hp.com	Adequate.
Home Depot (HD)	www.homedepot.com	Good layout; financial information adequate.
Honeywell (HON)	www.honeywell.com	History page, financial information adequate.
IBM (IBM)	www.ibm.com	Okay for selling goods and services, plus adequate investor information.
Intel (INTC)	www.intel.com	Above-average content.
J.P. Morgan (JPM)	www.jpmorganchase.com	History page, adequate financial information.
Johnson & Johnson (JNJ)	www.jnj.com	Extensive investor relations information.
McDonald's (MCD)	www.mcdonalds.com	Adequate information but goofy format.
Merck (MRK)	www.merck.com	Adequate.
Microsoft (MSFT)	www.microsoft.com	Above-average disclosure.

(continues)

EXHIBIT 18.3 DOW 30 WEB SITES

Internet Site	Web Address	Description
Pfizer (PFE)	www.pfizer.com	Good on products, history page, adequate financial information.
Procter & Gamble (PG)	www.pg.com	Adequate.
SBC Communications (SBC)	www.sbc.com	Adequate.
United Technology (UTX)	www.utc.com	Above-average investor relations.
Verizon (VZ)	www.verizon.com	Adequate.
Wal-Mart (WMT)	www.walmartstores.com	Adequate.
Walt Disney (DIS)	www.disney.go.com	Fabulous visualization—not unexpected; adequate financial information.

EXHIBIT 18.3   DOW 30 WEB SITES (CONTINUED)

MUTUAL FUND COMPANIES

Mutual fund companies want to sell their funds but also have useful information on investing and financial planning. Exhibit 18.4 lists a few of the bigger ones.

Internet Site	Web Address	Description
Fidelity Investments	www.fidelity.com	Most extensive list of funds, substantial investment advice.
Merrill Lynch	www.ml.com	Investment planning tools.
T. Rowe Price	www.troweprice.com	Investment planning tools.
Vanguard	www.vanguard.com	Big listing of index funds plus financial planning tools.

EXHIBIT 18.4   MUTUAL FUND COMPANY WEB SITES

EPILOGUE

Earnings Magic focuses on current events and new issues, which continue to surface. Here is an update from early 2006.

Will General Motors continue to be a Dow 30 member? Its F grade is well-deserved based on earnings magic issues, but this venerable company is still the largest auto company in the world; historically, the GM management style of Alfred Sloan became a model for big industry in mid-20th-century America. Of course, that doesn't save the company from bankruptcy. GM's stock price is still dropping as bad news continues, including an earnings restatement announced in late 2005. GM's performance is a major reason for the poor stock performance of the Dow 30 in 2005.

SBC completed its acquisition of AT&T and now goes by the AT&T name (stock symbol T). The headquarters is still in San Antonio, Texas, and the Web site is still www.sbc.com. The stock price is up a bit since the acquisition; apparently, investors are adjusting to the new name.

AIG was the big Dow 30 scandal of 2005. It looks like AIG's earnings magic problem will continue in 2006. According to the *Wall Street Journal,* AIG is expected to pay about $1.5 billion to settle government (New York Attorney General, New York State Insurance Department, Securities & Exchange Commission, among others) fraud investigations over its improper accounting—one of the largest penalties ever. Better corporate governance by AIG is also part of the settlement.

Stock options are now being expensed for fiscal year 2006, a big change in earnings magic incentives—that is, no more "free compensation." Ironically, this means that earnings magic will increase and the analysis will be a bit more difficult. The Dow 30 and many other companies piled up huge options commitments, which, in financial reality terms, means big expenses to record. But earnings magic is not dead. First, many companies accelerated options vesting to 2005 to avoid options expense in 2006. Others will manipulate the options value formulas used to estimate the expense. The Black-Scholes Model of option pricing is based on stock price, the exercise price of the options, when the options expire, the so-called risk-free rate of return, and volatility (technically, the standard deviation of stock return). The options expense can be reduced by lowering the estimate for volatility and the risk-free rate, for example. Expect companies to do exactly that; the stock options note will then be used to estimate the amount of options magic.

The Financial Accounting Standards Board, Securities & Exchange Commission, Public Company Accounting Oversight Board, and other regulators have stayed active and continue to influence the New Accounting. The FASB has major projects on business combinations, financial instruments, revenue recognition, fair value, and so on. Some of these are joint projects with the International Accounting Standards Board to enhance international accounting standards convergence. The PCAOB has over 1,600 registered accounting firms and continues to inspect auditors and post the reports online—potentially useful for evaluating auditor quality. The new chairman of the SEC is Chris Cox, a former California Congressman. Somewhat surprising has been Cox's support for investor interests (he had a reputation of supporting business interests in Congress), including new rules on disclosing executive pay, stiff enforcement penalties on business, and a pledge not to undo Sarbanes-Oxley-related regulations.

One of the FASB projects is pensions and other postretirement obligations. A likely possibility is that future FASB pronouncements will eliminate the off-balance sheet items; that is, moving closer to recording funded status (financial reality) on the balance sheet. As demonstrated in Chapter 7, pensions and related obligations are a huge earnings magic issue and this won't go away. General Motors and Ford seem to be moving towards bankruptcy in part because of these massive liabilities. Other companies are eliminating or reducing future pensions, including IBM.

In summary, analyzing earnings magic and searching for financial reality will be a dynamic process in 2006 and beyond. These are a few of the major issues and companies involved. Expect new issues and new scandals to pop up.

REFERENCES

Altman, E., *Corporate Financial Distress* (New York: John Wiley & Sons, Inc., 1983).

Bauman, C., M. Mauman, and R. Halsey. "Do Firms Use the Deferred Tax Asset Valuation Allowance to Manage Earnings?" *Journal of the American Taxation Association* 23 Supplement (2001): 27–48.

Bentson, G., and A. Hartgraves. "Enron: What Happened and What We Can Learn From It," *Journal of Accounting and Public Policy* (Summer 2002): 105–127.

Berenson, A. *The Number: How the Drive for Quarterly Earnings Corrupted Wall Street and Corporate America* (New York: Random House, 2003).

Blankley, A., and E. Swanson. "A Longitudinal Study of SFAS 87 Pension Rate Assumptions," *Accounting Horizons* (December 1995): 1–21.

Botosan, C. "Disclosure Level and the Cost of Equity Capital," *The Accounting Review* 72 (1997): 323–349.

Buffett, W., *Letters to Berkshire Shareholders 1977–2004; www.berkshirehathaway.com/*.

Byrne, J., "Joe Berandion's Fall from Grace," *Business Week,* August 12, 2002, 50–56.

Charan, R., and J. Useem, "Why Companies Fail," www.fortune.com, 2002.

Committee of Sponsoring Organizations of the Treadway Commission (COSO). *Report of the National Commission on Fraudulent Financial Reporting* (New York: COSO, 1987).

COSO. *Fraudulent Financial Reporting: 1987–1997—An Analysis of U.S. Public Companies* (New York: COSO, 1999).

Cramer, J. *Confessions of a Street Addict* (New York: Simon & Schuster, 2002).

Dhaliwal, D., C. Gleason, and L. Mills. "Last-Chance Earnings Management: Using the Tax Expense to Meet Analysts' Forecasts," *Contemporary Accounting Research* (Summer 2004), pp. 431–459.

Dechow, P., and D. Skinner. "Earnings Management: Reconciling the Views of Accounting Practitioners, and Regulators," *Accounting Horizons* 14 (2000): 235–250.

Donaldson, W., "Speech by SEC Chairman: Remarks to the National Press Club," July 30, 2003, www.sec.gov.

Eichenwald, K. *Conspiracy of Fools* (New York: Broadway Books, 2005).

Erickson, M., M. Hanlon, and E. Maydew. "How Much Will Firms Pay for Earnings That Do Not Exist? Evidence of Taxes Paid for Allegedly Fraudulent Earnings," SSRN Working Paper, 2004.

Fields, T., T. Lys, and L. Vincent. "Empirical Research on Accounting Choice," *Journal of Accounting and Economics* 31 (2001), pp. 255–307.

Financial Accounting Standards Board, *FASB Response to SEC Study on the Adoption of a Principles-Based Accounting System* (Norwalk, CT, July 2004).

Foster, J. "Observations on the Current Crisis and Its Affect on the Development of Accounting Standards," Speech at Texas A&M: Profession at a Crossroads Series, November 14, 2002.

France, M. "What About the Lawyers?" *Business Week,* December 23, 2002, 58–62.

France, M. "The SEC's Plan Shouldn't Make Lawyers Squawk," *Business Week,* January 27, 2003, 54.

Friedman, T. *The Lexus and the Olive Tree* (New York: Anchor Books, 2000).

Gibson, C. *Financial Reporting and Analysis, Eighth Edition* (Cincinnati: South-Western College Publishing, 2001).

Giroux, G. "Annual Reports of the Minehill and Schuylkill Haven Railroad Company: 1844–1864," *The Accounting Historians Notebook* (April 1998): 9–10, 30–33.

Giroux, G. *Financial Analysis: A User Approach* (Hoboken, NJ: John Wiley & Sons, Inc., 2003).

Giroux, G. *Detecting Earnings Management* (Hoboken, NJ: John Wiley & Sons, Inc., 2004).

General Accounting Office. *Financial Statement Restatements: Trends, Market Impacts, Regulatory Responses, and Remaining Challenges (GAO-03-138)* (Washington, DC: GAO, October 2002).

Healy, P. "The Impact of Bonus Schemes on the Selection of Accounting Principles," *Journal of Accounting and Economics* 7 (1985): 85–107.

Healy, P., and J. Wahlen. "A Review of the Earnings Management Literature and Its Implications for Standard Setting," *Accounting Horizons* (December 1999): 365–383.

Henry, D. "Mergers: Why Most Big Deals Don't Pay Off," *Business Week,* October 14, 2002, 60–70.

Himmelstein, L., and B. Elgin. "Tech's Kickback Culture," *Business Week,* February 10, 2003, 74–77.

Huffington, A., *Pigs at the Trough: How Corporate Greed and Political Corruption Are Undermining America* (New York: Crown Publishers, 2003).

Jensen, M. and K. Murphy, "CEO Incentives: Its Not How Much You Pay, but How," *Harvard Business Review,* May/June 1990, 138–153.

Jones, J. "Earnings Management During Import Relief Investigations," *Journal of Accounting Research* 29 (1991): 193–228.

Kahn, J. "Off Balance Sheet—and Out of Control; SPEs Are Ripe for Abuse, but Few Went as Far as Enron's Fastow," *Fortune* (www.fortune.com), February 18, 2002.

Leonard, D. and P. Elkind, "All I Want Is an Unfair Advantage," *Fortune,* August 8, 2005, 76–88.

Levitt, A., and P. Dwyer. *Take on the Street: What Wall Street and Corporate America Don't Want You to Know* (New York: Pantheon Books, 2002).

Lowenstein, R. *Origins of the Crash: The Great Bubble and Its Undoing* (New York: Penguin Press, 2004).

Mahar, M. *Bull: A History of the Boom and Bust, 1982–2004* (New York: Harper Business, 2004).

Maremont, M. "Tyco Reveals $8 Billion of Acquisitions Made Over Three Years, but Not Disclosed," *Wall Street Journal,* February 4, 2002, A3.

Maremont, M., and R. Brooks. "Report Shows How Krispy Kreme Sweetened Results," *Wall Street Journal,* August 11, 2005, A1, A6.

Mayer, M. *The Fed: The Inside Story of How the World's Most Powerful Financial Institution Drives the Markets* (New York: Penguin Group, 2001).

McCracken, J. "General Motors, Ford Offset Losses by Dipping into Cookie-Jar Funds," *Wall Street Journal,* November 22, 2005.

McNichols, M. "Research Design Issues in Earnings Management Studies," *Journal of Accounting and Public Policy* 19 (2000): 313–345.

Mulford, C., and E. Comisky. *The Financial Numbers Game: Detecting Creative Accounting Practices* (Hoboken, NJ: John Wiley & Sons, Inc., 2002).

Paton, W., and A. Littleton. *An Introduction to Corporate Accounting Standards* (New York: American Accounting Standards, 1940, reprinted 1974).

Penman, S. *Financial Statement Analysis & Security Valuations* (Boston: McGraw-Hill Irwin, 2001).

Revsine, L., D. Collins, and W. Johnson. *Financial Reporting and Analysis, Second Edition* (Upper Saddle River, NJ: Prentice Hall, 2002).

Schilit, H. *Financial Shenanigans: How to Detect Accounting Gimmicks and Fraud in Financial Reports, Second Edition* (New York: McGraw-Hill, 2002).

Schipper, K. "Commentary: Earnings Management," *Accounting Horizons* (December 1989): 91–102.

Securities and Exchange Commission. *Report and Recommendations Pursuant to Section 401(c) of the Sarbanes-Oxley Act of 2002 on Arrangement with Off–balance Sheet Implications, Special Purpose Entities, and Transparency of Filings by Issuers* (Washington, DC: SEC, 2005).

Sengupta, P. "Corporate Disclosure Quality and the Cost of Debt," *Accounting Review* 73 (1998): 459–474.

Surowiecki, J. *The Wisdom of Crowds* (New York: Doubleday, 2004).

Swartz, M., and S. Watkins. *Power Failure: The Inside Story of the Collapse of Enron* (New York: Doubleday, 2003).

Symonds, W. "Behind Tyco's Accounting Alchemy," *Business Week,* February 25, 2002 (www.businessweek.com, 1).

Toffler, B. *Final Accounting: Ambition, Greed, and the Fall of Arthur Andersen* (New York: Broadway Books, 2003).

Watts, R., and J. Zimmerman. *Positive Accounting Theory* (Englewood Cliffs, NJ: Prentice-Hall, 1986).

Weiss, G. "Just a Minute Mr. Donaldson," *Business Week,* February 10, 2003, 66–67.

White, G., A. Sondhi, and D. Fried. *The Analysis and Use of Financial Statements, Second Edition* (Hoboken, NJ: John Wiley & Sons, Inc., 1998; *Third Edition,* 2003).

INDEX